Key Contemporary Buildings

Plans, Sections and Elevations

Rob Gregory

Key Contemporary Buildings

Plans, Sections and Elevations

Rob Gregory

W. W. Norton & Company
New York • London

For information about permission to reproduce
selections from this book, write to Permissions,
W. W. Norton & Company, Inc.
500 Fifth Avenue, New York, NY 10110

For information about special discounts for bulk purchases,
please contact W. W. Norton Special Sales at
specialsales@wwnorton.com or 800-233-4830

Designed by James Branch
Drawings by Gregory Gibbon and Advanced Illustration
Picture research by Claire Gouldstone

Library of Congress Cataloging-in-Publication Data

Gregory, Rob.
Key contemporary buildings : plans,
sections, and elevations / Rob Gregory.
p. cm.
Includes bibliographical references and index.
ISBN 978-0-393-73242-9 (pbk.)
1. Architectural drawing—21st century.
2. Architecture, Modern—21st century—Designs and plans.
I. Title.
NA2705.G745 2008
724'.70222—dc22
                                    2007030398

ISBN 13: 978-0-393-73242-9 (pbk.)

W. W. Norton & Company, Inc.
500 Fifth Avenue, New York, N.Y. 10110
www.wwnorton.com

W. W. Norton & Company Ltd.
Castle House, 75/76 Wells Street
London W1T 3QT

0 9 8 7 6 5 4 3 2 1

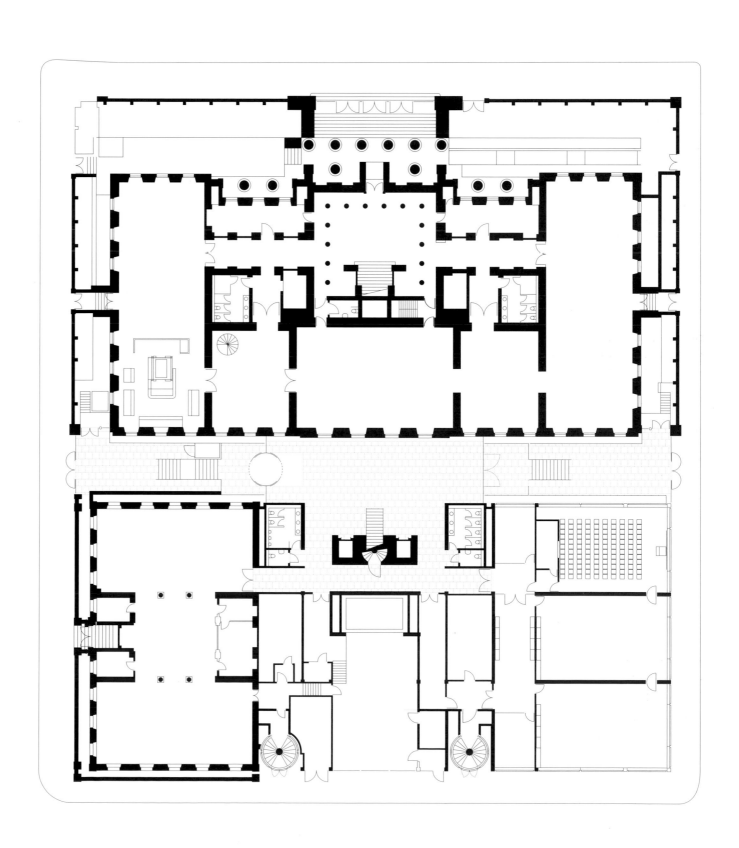

Contents

Introduction

Key Contemporary Buildings:
A Survey of Recent Planning Strategies

'Most people judge architecture by its external appearance, just as books on the subject are usually illustrated with pictures of building exteriors. When an architect judges a building its appearance is only one of several factors which interest him. He studies plans, sections and elevations and maintains that, if it is a good building, these must harmonise with each other.'
Steen Eiler Rasmussen, *Experiencing Architecture*, 1959

As the third volume in the series *Plans, Sections and Elevations*, this book considers a number of key contemporary buildings completed within the first six years of the twenty-first century. When starting out, if the prospect of following on from Richard Weston and Colin Davies was not enough of a challenge, the decision regarding how to structure the book presented further dilemmas. What buildings should be included, and how should they be classified? While Weston's *Key Buildings of the Twentieth Century*, and Davies' *Key Houses of the Twentieth Century* were arranged chronologically to effectively provide a drawn history, representing well-known projects from the well-known canon of twentieth-century architecture, it was not possible to include the same range of projects in this volume.

With more than 90 years of the twenty-first century still to be played out and, correspondingly, with far fewer completed projects to choose from, *Key Contemporary Buildings* makes no attempt to identify a present-day canon of so-called seminal projects. Without the benefit of hindsight, it does not speculate about a building's contribution to an emerging history of architecture by prematurely celebrating unproven merits of so-called iconic buildings. Nor does it attempt to consider the many complicated issues that define the state of contemporary architecture in relation to emerging social, economic, political and environmental issues; issues that deserve to be considered in more detail in books that focus on materials, environmental appropriateness, digital design processes and emerging techniques. Instead, in contrast to the many single-issue titles that prioritize new and emerging attitudes, the format of this book allows us to return to basics to consider the one phenomenon that has remained consistent throughout the known history of architecture, namely, the obligation that architects have to the manipulation of space. As such, this book offers a far more elementary, first principles opportunity to consider the physical anatomy of contemporary buildings by studying the architects' plans, sections and elevations. Through reworked and consistently produced drawings, it allows the reader to consider each project in more detail than is possible in contemporary magazines and monographs. In a sense, there is an element of self-learning that will reward those who spend time reading the drawings, both from the page and on screen by using the accompanying CD-ROM.

The Anatomy of Architecture: Understanding Architecture as the Arrangement of Space

In the most basic terms, an architect shapes space by giving form and substance to boundaries between internal, external and adjacent spaces. On more than one occasion, the history of architecture has been described by commentators as the history of making holes in walls, and through the composition of boundaries – be they solid or transparent, massive or lightweight, hermetic or permeable – architects have created the thresholds that shape our physical world. By encouraging a more elementary understanding of a building's anatomy, as a complete body of solid parts, therefore, secondary notions of trend, tectonic and technique can momentarily be overlooked, allowing a far broader range of buildings that date from antiquity to our current time to be more usefully compared on equal spatial terms.

In what Bruno Zevi refers to as an organic culture, when considering architecture throughout history, it is not right to apply separate standards of judgement; one for historic buildings, another for the Modern, and a third for the emerging avant-garde. Instead, in seeking to apply the same criteria of architectural analysis throughout history, the process of comparing the scale and disposition of space allows us to trade ideas across time, with no loss of worth between generations and cultures. Addressing critics of contemporary architecture, Zevi challenged writers to add new chapters to established historical volumes to bring them up to date in order to ascertain whether fundamental critical concepts were still valid. In his view, the only truly satisfactory history of architecture was one that directly considered space as the chief protagonist of architecture. Directly and quantifiably valuable in terms of real estate, space is a

Sami Parliament – Stein Halvorsen and Christian Sundby

Seifert House – BAU/KULTUR, Michael Shamiyeh

priceless commodity in the production of excellent buildings and will always be architecture's principal unit of currency. As such, plans, sections and elevations are undeniably the best means for us to value the true worth of a space.

The Significance of Plans, Sections and Elevations in the Digital Age

'The plan is the generator. Without a plan you have lack of order, and wilfulness.'
Le Corbusier, *Vers une Architecture*, 1923

As set out in his methodology of how to look at architecture, *Architecture as Space* (1957), Bruno Zevi wrote at length about architectural representation and the significance of the drawn plan. While Le Corbusier had already given the plan a mystique, famously heralding it as the generator of all forms of architecture in his 'Third Reminder', Zevi's explanation was more cautious. In response to the many misinterpretations of Corbusier's theory, Zevi recognized that the promotion of the plan as the generator had gone some way to engender an inappropriate tendency among designers to serve the aesthetic of the plan, in a form of pattern-making that was no less formalistic that the traditions of the Beaux-Arts. In line with Corbusier's more detailed explanations of the 'Illusion of Plans', therefore ('A Plan Proceeds from Within to Without', 'The Exterior Is Always an Interior', and issues of 'Transgression and Arrangement'), Zevi agreed and concluded with the principle that 'a plan is still the sole way we have of evaluating the architectural organism as a whole'. When supported by sections (and to a

lesser extent, elevations), orthogonal scaled projections allow us to analyze buildings in an abstract, but nevertheless measured way.

Against the grain of emerging and increasingly sophisticated digital techniques, therefore, this book returns to the basic technique of constructing plans, sections and elevations. While some may consider this process to be an outmoded and static form of understanding three-dimensional space, in reality few who actively work with space could reasonably say that plans and sections were obsolete forms of representation and measurement. Even the most comprehensive computer models need to be broken down into plans and sections before they can be usefully analyzed and measured. While models have a major role to play in the development and representation of built form, they are most usefully employed to provide an instant likeness of the full proposal in microcosm. At a more advanced level, they can also be used to simulate complex interrelations in structural or environmental performance. Furthermore, when considering the discipline of spatial organization, even if this book were to be accompanied by a CD-ROM of 3-D models, most readers would revert to cutting and carving the assemblage into plans and sections in order to gain a more useful understanding of the nature of its organization. Endlessly navigating a viewer through cyberspace – gracefully flying through space and crashing through insubstantial walls – is no way to give readers a useful measure of a building's true and unique composition. Hence, the reader, particularly one who is just embarking on what will evolve into a lifelong process of architectural education, is

encouraged to take time to read the plans, sections and elevations in detail. With the CD, readers are also encouraged to merge files in order to compare projects more directly, making specific note of circulation, access and the relationship between served and servant spaces.

Plan Types

When considering how to usefully arrange the 96 case studies in this book, it seemed pertinent to group buildings according to the organizational strategy that governed each building's final arrangement. These planning strategies include centralized plans and radial structures, linear structures, terraced houses, stacked plans, courtyards – orthogonal and eccentric – cityscape responses, and infills, additions and extensions. In no particular order these have been set out in chapters, each of which begins with an introduction that ties the planning strategy back to more known examples, referencing case studies that were featured in each of the Weston and Davies selections. This not only serves to link contemporary buildings with more well-known twentieth-century classics, without necessarily having to relate buildings to a particular architectural style or era, but also demonstrates the essential qualities in spatial arrangements that are independent of scale, programme or location.

The book begins with **Centralized Plans**, arrangements that in some respects recall primitive settlements as loose gatherings of space arranged in a concentric order. The chapter features projects that could be described as object buildings, those that are essentially centrally focused and planned

Mercedes-Benz Museum – UNStudio

Art Pavilion – Rene van Zuuk

in the round. Beginning with domestic properties such as **Sou Fujimoto's T House** in Japan and **BAU/KULTUR, Michael Shamiyeh's** Austrian **Seifert House**, and extending to larger-scale cultural institutions like **Stein Halvorsen and Christian Sundby's Sami Parliament** in Norway and **UNStudio's Mercedes-Benz Museum** in Stuttgart, the chapter reveals how architects have orchestrated the relationship between service cores, circulation and accommodation space to establish an essential agent of spatial order. Buildings in this chapter often have to deal with the condition of multisidedness, with perimeters that either exploit specific adjacencies or provide a disengaged foil to further isolate the form of the building from its context.

Linear Structures uncoil centralized strategies to produce buildings that have a strong directional emphasis. Extending traditions established by Peter Behrens' iconic Turbine Factory, Alvar Aalto's Baker House and Louis Kahn's Kimbell Art Museum, the chapter focuses on contemporary examples that either work along the grain, such as **Auer + Weber's** dramatic **ESO hotel** in northern Chile, or across it like **Rene van Zuuk's Art Pavilion** in the Netherlands; both of which exploit the elementary beauty of linear organizations to order space, arrange structure and give form to buildings that have an immediate three-dimensional coherence when broken down into cross-sectional slices.

Terraced Houses continues the study of linear forms in terms of a specific functional type.

In consideration of their party walls, individual units are discussed that combine to assemble elongated urban forms. With a brief look back at one of Britain's archetypes of post-industrial housing, the chapter considers contemporary dwellings, including individual infills within existing terraces, such as the **two houses on Borneo Sporenburg** in the Netherlands by **MVRDV** and **Stanley Saitowitz/ Natoma Architects' 1028 Natoma Street apartment block** in San Francisco, and new collective forms such as the **Sound Wall Homes** by **VHP s+a+l** in the Netherlands and the pioneering **BedZED** development by **Bill Dunster Architects** in England.

Turning plans on their side, the chapter **Stacked Plans** addresses the issue of high-rise buildings, considering a number of recent tall

Sound Wall Homes – VHP s+a+l

BedZED – Bill Dunster Architects

buildings. Recalling some of the world's early high-rises, including SOM's 21-storey Lever House (1950), and Mies van der Rohe's 37-storey Seagram Building (1954), the chapter analyzes recent examples, such as **Foster + Partners' 30 St Mary Axe**, **Ateliers Jean Nouvel's Torre Agbar** in Barcelona, and **Carme Pinós' dramatic Torre Cube** in Mexico. The chapter, however, is not solely interested in matters of size, but instead considers the manner in which stacked plans are arranged and how each floor relates to the next, with innovative forms of circulation, servicing and spatial hierarchy, such as **Steven Holl Architects' Simmons Hall** at MIT, **Toyo Ito's Sendai Mediatheque** in Japan and **David Chipperfield Architects and b720 Arquitectos' America's Cup Building** in Valencia.

When considering **Courtyards – Orthogonal**, a rich and varied array of historical precedents is revealed, from primitive prehistoric settlements and the evolution of simple agricultural farmyards, through to more considered architectural ensembles such as monasteries, university quadrangles and cathedral cloisters. Broadly comprising four ranges of accommodation, interest usually focuses on the organization of circulation around the courtyard, access to the courtyard, and how corners are turned, and throughout the twentieth century the courtyard type developed through the influence of Modernism. New attitudes to space and formal disposition, as epitomized by the Bauhaus Building in Dessau by Walter Gropius [see p. 125], broke up traditional arrangements to juxtapose pavilions

more freely to create multiple external courtyards, while during the same period the seminal Casa del Fascio in Como created one of Modern architecture's most celebrated internal courtyards. Contemporary examples of this planning format include the private **Long Island Residence** by **Tod Williams and Billie Tsien**, **BRT Architekten's** offices for **Swiss Re** in Germany and **John Pawson's** delightfully austere **Novy Dvur Monastery** in the Czech Republic.

Due to the breadth of this planning category, a second chapter, **Courtyards – Eccentric**, is included that extends the study to include buildings where the courtyard is not constrained by orthogonal or axial geometries. Extending the formal eccentricities of Le Corbusier's Monastery

America's Cup Building – David Chipperfield Architects and b720 Arquitectos

Sendai Mediatheque – Toyo Ito

Swiss Re Offices – BRT Architekten

Novy Dvur Monastery – John Pawson

at La Tourette [see p. 151] and Sverre Fehn's Archbishopric Museum of Hamar [see p. 152], this chapter includes buildings where subtle inflections in plan and section have produced uniquely shaped spaces, either in response to the topography of the site, or to the more sculptural preoccupations of its designer, such as **Morphosis' Diamond Ranch High School** in California and **Sauerbruch Hutton's Federal Environmental Agency** in Germany.

The book concludes with two chapters that focus on urban conditions. Firstly, **Cityscape Responses** features relatively conspicuous buildings that respond to urban conditions, such as **Rafael Moneo's** beautifully composed **Town Hall Extension** in Spain, the inventive and tailor-made **Jaume Fuster Library** in Barcelona by **Joseph Llinás**, and

Zaha Hadid Architects' long awaited **Phaeno Science Centre** in Germany.

The final chapter, entitled **Infills, Additions and Extensions**, includes a series of highly bespoke insertions, such as **Jamie Fobert Architects' Anderson House** in London, **Hopkins Architects'** extension to the **Manchester City Art Gallery**, **Renzo Piano's** restrained expansion of New York's **Morgan Library** and **Peter Cook and Spacelab's** 'friendly alien', the **Kunsthaus**, in Graz – buildings that exemplify the sort of infills and additions that are richly and subtly changing the cities around us.

In recognition of the shortcomings of this book, it should be acknowledged that there are a number of inconsistencies and omissions. Not all of the plans and sections have been drawn, and

generally elevations were the first drawings to be edited out if space could more usefully be occupied by an additional plan or section. On occasion, projects have been included that were completed one or two years before the turn of the century when it was felt that these were of such significant merit that to exclude them would have been to the detriment of the overall selection.

It should also be stated that the interpretation of each project has been honed to relate specifically to the particular planning category in which it is listed. Many of the projects could equally and justifiably be related to a number of planning categories; however, repetition would not provide good value to the reader, so ultimately a decision had to be made that related more to the balance

Diamond Ranch High School – Morphosis

Federal Environmental Agency – Sauerbruch Hutton

Town Hall Extension – Rafael Moneo

Jaume Fuster Library – Josep Llinás

of the contents. **Herzog & de Meuron's de Young Museum** in California, for example, is an incredibly sophisticated building that could easily have been assigned to a number of categories. Conceived as a series of buckled strips, it is clearly a variant on a linear organization; the tower that gracefully turns to lock into San Francisco's city grid may equally have warranted analysis as a series of stacked plans; and as a compelling object, it certainly can be read as a sculptural cityscape response – albeit set within a man-made landscape. Finally, however, the courtyards became the focus of the analysis, penetrating and articulating what is essentially a simple orthogonal steel box.

In all cases, it is hoped that by studying these buildings, the categories will pale into insignificance, and that instead each plan, section and elevation is rigorously scrutinized in order to bring the measure of the spaces more clearly into focus. Above all else, this book allows readers to consider each building in elementary terms, serving as an antidote to the emerging tendency in architectural representation that focuses solely on three-dimensional imagery, be it through photographs or digital visualizations – media that fail to present an essential understanding of the anatomy of architectural space.

It should, of course, be remembered that well in advance of the so-called digital revolution Rasmussen reminded us in the quotation below that an architect's drawings are not an end in themselves. Despite our efforts, therefore, in attempting to bring this collection of buildings more clearly into focus, neither art nor architecture exist in the pages of this book, or indeed in the data contained on the accompanying CD-ROM.

'Architecture is not simply produced by adding plans and sections to elevations. It is something else and something more. Its limits are by no means well defined. [Architecture] should not be explained; it must be experienced.'

Morgan Library and Museum – Renzo Piano

Centralized
Plans

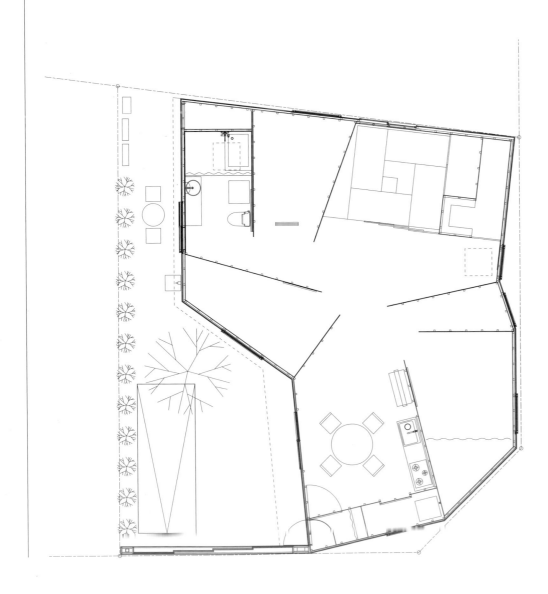

Melnikov House
Façade and Ground Floor Plan

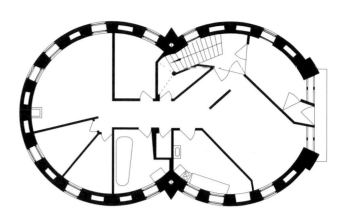

When starting out in architectural education, students are usually set basic tasks in spatial arrangement. In one such elementary task, students are given an inventory of art works to be exhibited within a 9 metre (30 foot) cube, in spaces that have either been carved from a solid or defined by planes inserted into a notional 9 metre (30 foot) void. While this challenge may seem elementary, it certainly is not simple, and no matter how many years experience a designer may have, most would consider this to be an extremely stimulating task. With no context, no real site, and no obvious ordering devices, there could be any number of reasonable starting points in terms of ordering the spaces, connecting them through circulation and setting up relationships between each of the works

of art. To an extent, the same could be said of any building built on a flat, featureless site with no immediate obligations to neighbouring properties. When working with isolated forms, establishing order is of critical importance, serving not only as the most obvious starting point for the rationalization of structure and space, but also in bringing an appropriate hierarchy to elements within the plan.

This chapter features a number of projects that could loosely be described as object buildings; those that are essentially centrally focused and planned in the round. The analysis considers how the form of such buildings has been influenced by the notion of establishing an agent of order. Houses fit well into this category, being detached

and set in low-density areas where the influence of a built context diminishes. Colin Davies' analysis in *Key Houses of the Twentieth Century* includes a number of well-known projects, beginning in 1927 with **Konstantin Melnikov's House** in Moscow which was based on two interlocking cylinders. Other distinctive centralized plans followed, such as Buckminster Fuller's Wichita House in Kansas of 1947, John Lautner's Malin Residence in California of 1960 and **Mario Botta's Casa Rotunda** in Switzerland of 1980, all of which consider the relationship between service cores, circulation and accommodation space.

Today, the contemporary house extends these investigations further still, and a number of recent residences have been included in this chapter.

Casa Rotonda, Mario Botta
Façade and Ground Floor Plan

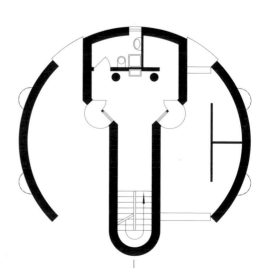

Poli House

LCM/Fernando Romero's Ixtapa House, a luxurious beach house in Guerrero, Mexico, is perhaps the most sculptural in its form, with a curvaceous plan that creates a generous shelter under which a large family can come together to relax. On an even more dramatic site **Pezo von Ellrichshausen Architects** has created the **Poli House** on the Coliumo Peninsula, Chile, a unique home that opens up its heart by effectively eliminating a central service core. Reminiscent in many ways of a medieval fortress, planned within massive rampart walls, stairs, services and storage have been set within the depth of a heavy perimeter wall. This not only frees up space at the centre of the plan for full- and half-height voids, but it also enriches the circulation around the house with two secret staircases, hidden

within the thickness of the walls that oppose one another in location and orientation. By contrast to the mass of this powerful composition, **Sou Fujimoto's T House** in Japan is far less substantial in its material composition. In planning, however, it is an equally significant example of a centralized plan, configured as a single volume and divided by simple stage-set partitions. Recalling primitive housing models where private areas were traditionally arranged around a central core, each of this home's eight principal rooms are ordered in a radial manner with no spatial hierarchy, and no central hall. Built entirely of timber, and set between continuous floor and roof planes, the house has a powerful material and spatial coherence, and suggests an inherent flexibility in its tectonics. By contrast, the layout of

BAU/KULTUR, Michael Shamiyeh's Seifert House in Volkersdorf, Austria, is literally set in stone with two robust concrete cores that set up tense relationships between the interior and exterior. This domestic subcategory is concluded with **Sami Rintala's Element House** in Anyang, South Korea, which as a folly is an exercise in spatial and material exploration.

A number of larger-scale examples have also been featured, including functionally expressive buildings such as **Grimshaw's** awe-inspiring **Eden Project Biomes** in Cornwall, and **Foster + Partners' City Hall** in London, both of which justify their spherical forms in terms of environmental and material efficiency, providing maximum volume with minimum envelope, and thereby vastly reducing

T House

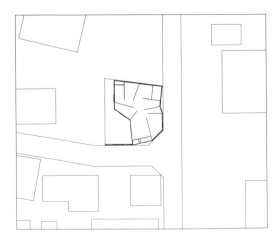

Seifert House

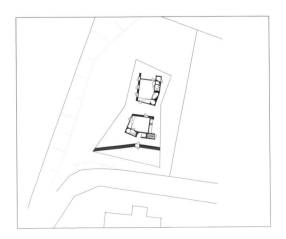

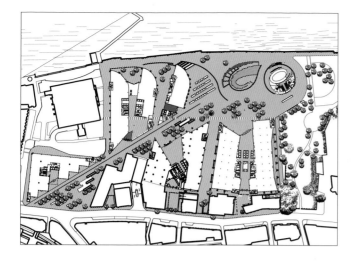

City Hall, London

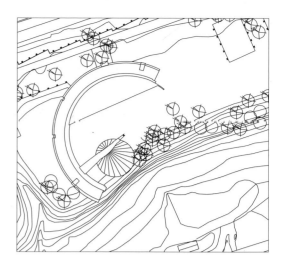

Sami Parliament

exposure to the outside world with 25 per cent less surface area than cubes of equivalent volume. Four significant cultural buildings have also been included, including **O'Donnell + Tuomey's** delightful **Lewis Glucksman Gallery** in Cork, Eire, which uses its autonomy to address two distinct aspects – one more civic, acting as a gatehouse to University College Cork, the other more scenographic, emphasizing the building as a picturesque composition within a landscape setting; **Stein Halvorsen and Christian Sundby's Sami Parliament** in Karasjok, Norway, which utilizes its centrally planned arrangement to make a very particular place in a context that is otherwise dominated by loose scatterings of unremarkable prefabricated buildings; **UNStudio's Mercedes-Benz Museum** in

Stuttgart, Germany, which uses a trefoil configuration to arrange the museum's exhibition on nine spiralling surfaces that ascend from ground to roof in an attempt to dramatically redefine the conventional museum experience; and **Snøhetta's** enormous 170,000 cubic metre (6,003,493 cubic foot) reading room, the **Bibliotheca Alexandrina** in Alexandria, Egypt, which provides space for over 2000 readers within its 160 metre (525 foot) diameter plan.

The chapter concludes with two category oddities, with **Dorte Mandrup Arkitekter's Jægersborg Water Tower** in Gentofte, Denmark, which integrates 40 new apartments and a youth centre within the structure of a water tower; and **Shigeru Ban's Imai Day Care Centre** in Japan,

which is not so much a centralized plan but a centralized section, providing a simple toy-like form in which children can play.

Mercedes-Benz Museum

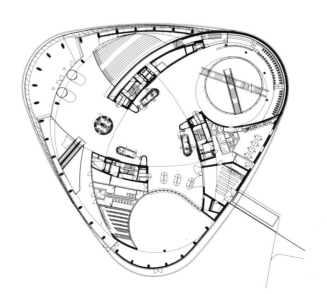

Ixtapa House

LCM/Fernando Romero

Guerrero, Mexico; 2001

Highly sculptural plans can be difficult to categorize. When space has so obviously been moulded – as if shaped by hand in clay – analyzing drawings can seem nonsensical. Nevertheless, this building deserves consideration in plan and section due to its uniqueness, due to the justification of its curvaceous forms, and due to its adaptation of the traditional Mexican beach-house type.

Built on a private beach on the Pacific Ocean, 249 kilometres (155 miles) up the coast from Acapulco, this home was conceived as a place where a large family could gather together to spend time, and to contemplate and enjoy this unique and extraordinary coastal site. Traditionally, Mexican beach houses comprise wooden columns that support a high palapa roof (a form of tropical thatch) that allows the sea breeze to pass through the roof to ventilate the shaded area beneath. The Ixtapa House adapts this model with a large upper storey that shades a spacious open-sided family room.

On the ground level the plan extends into an elliptical form to include an exposed terrace and swimming pool. To the rear of the site, as a privacy barrier, two solid cores contain a kitchen, television room and master bedroom suite, while on the

upper level nine bedrooms are arranged around a sinuous hall to provide adequate accommodation for visitors and family members.

Entering from the northeast, visitors reach the expansive and panoramic sheltered space by passing through a narrow passageway set between the two cores. The eccentricity of the planning provides generous shelter both on arrival and in the main reception area, with the cores composed as extrusions of the form above, sitting within generous overhanging soffits. In section, the smooth lines of the plan are echoed as the cores merge seamlessly with the soffits, as if constructed from one continuous material. The cross-section also describes the building's organizational order, with space divided into two conditions: public and private. A discrete, but equally sculptural stair heightens the sense of privacy; prolonging and extending the threshold between inside and out – public and private – as it curves and rises to follow the concave plan form.

While the main living/reception area had to be spacious enough to accommodate large groups of people, it also had to be intimate in its character. This was mostly achieved through its form, with enveloping curves creating a cave-like enclosure.

Further spatial control was achieved through the integration of fixed furniture, such as the curvaceous double-sided sofa, which provides communal seating on the inside concave aspect, and occasional seating on its outside edge, simultaneously defining a route to the swimming pool beyond. The building's sculptural form was also justified by the architects as a way of reducing the scale of what is essentially a large ten-bedroom house, with softened edges yielding to spectacular views where the landscape remains the dominant quality of the space.

1 Elevation

2 Section A–A

3 First Floor Plan

1 Guest Room

4 Ground Floor Plan

1 Entrance
2 Kitchen
3 Television Room
4 Master Bedroom
5 Bath
6 External Living Room
7 Terrace
8 Pool

19

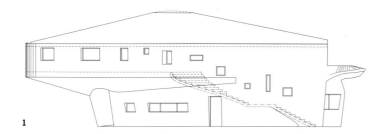

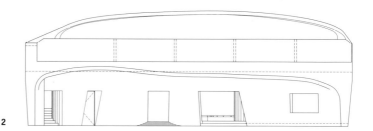

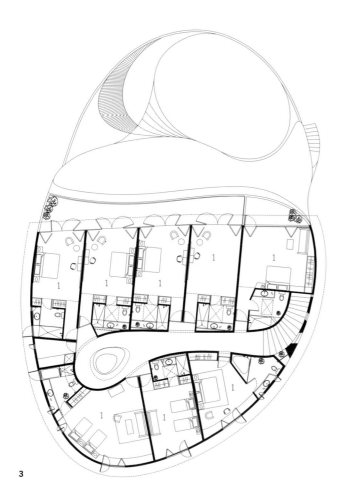

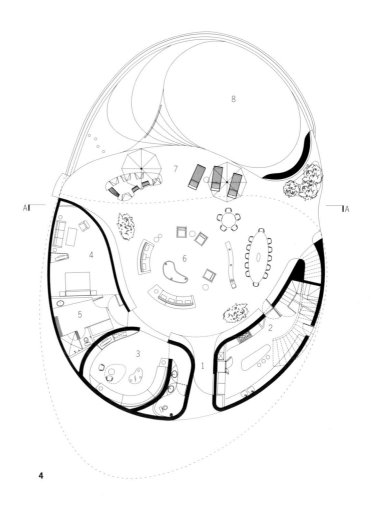

Poli House

Pezo von Ellrichshausen Architects

Coliumo Peninsula, Chile; 2004

When considering centralized plans, the location of cores – for circulation and servicing – often dictates the form of the spaces that surround them. In this distinctive house, however, set high on the Chilean Coliumo Peninsula, the core has effectively been eliminated through the skilful integration of stairs, services and storage into the depth of a heavy perimeter wall; reminiscent in many ways
of medieval fortresses with massive rampart walls.

The house, equivalent in height to a modest two-storey dwelling is, in fact, organized on three principal levels, linked by two voids – one half-height, the other full. The house also has two secret staircases, each set within the thickness of the walls, that oppose one another in location and direction: the first links living, kitchen, dining and bedroom spaces, by turning the southeast corner in an anticlockwise direction; the second leads directly from ground floor to roof terrace by dog-legging clockwise around the northwest corner, providing views both into and out of the house en route.

The ground floor living room sits beneath the two voids and is split-level, with a subtle two-step shift defining two separate zones. From here the full-length single-level dining and kitchen space is

reached via five more steps, giving it an elevated yet connected relationship with the living room. The two bedrooms are appropriately made remote, reached via the southeasterly anticlockwise stair. Each bedroom turns to face opposite directions (west and north respectively), both with en suite shower rooms held within the thickness of the perimeter wall, with views into the inner void, and with a similar split-level to the living room that extends out onto a private balcony set within deep reveals.

Very nearly composed as a perfect cube with a square plan – but falling slightly short in height – the rough-cast concrete perimeter walls are punctuated by a series of deep square openings. These either expose thick concrete reveals, with glazing set flush with the inside skin, to give the illusion of 1 metre (approximately 3 foot) deep walls, or, by contrast, they allude more directly to the wall's secret inner life where, for example, the externalized northwesterly clockwise stair pauses with a half-landing, where a more revealing and honest thin edge frames a simple unfilled opening.

The house, commissioned by a local cultural organization, not only has a secret stair but also a double life, functioning as it does as an informal cultural centre. It is therefore more appropriate that

it is at once domestic and monumental through its composition and use of material. The simplicity and power of its form, however, can also be justified on more than simply aesthetic terms, responding as it does to the practicalities of building with semi-skilled labour and basic materials in an extremely remote location – the Poli House was built by local farmers and fishermen who only had one small concrete mixer and four wheelbarrows between them.

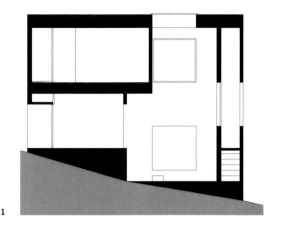

1

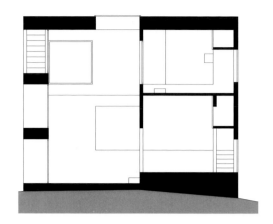

2

3

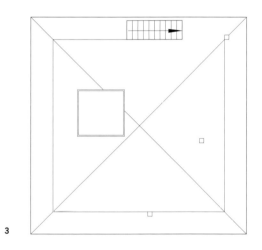

4

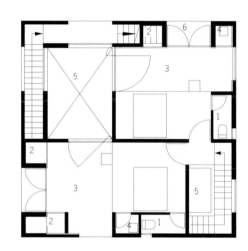

3 Roof Terrace Plan

4 Upper Floor Plan

1 Bathroom
2 Closet
3 Bedroom
4 Sink
5 Void
6 Balcony

B

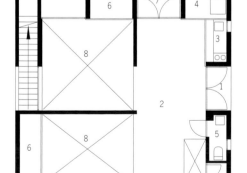

5

6

A   A

B

5 Upper Ground Floor Plan

1 Entrance
2 Dining Room
3 Kitchen
4 Storage
5 Bathroom
6 Closet
7 Balcony
8 Void

6 Lower Ground Floor Plan

1 Living
2 Studio
3 Access to Terrace
4 Balcony
5 Closet

N

0   2.5   5m
    7.5   15ft

T House

Sou Fujimoto

Gunma, Japan; 2005

In the 2005 *Architectural Review* Awards for Emerging Architecture, jury opinion was divided over the merits of the planning of this distinctive house. The T House by Sou Fujimoto is essentially a single-volume space divided by simple stage-set partitions. It provides accommodation for a family of four, and also serves to display the owner's private collection of contemporary art. While some jury members thought the house would be completely unworkable, with no doors and with the building's contorted spaces being impossible to inhabit practically and providing little flexibility, others believed that the configuration of the house represented exactly what the client wanted, that is, a unique, bespoke, albeit unorthodox series of tailor-made spaces.

Recalling primitive housing models where private areas were traditionally arranged around a central core, each of this home's eight principal rooms are ordered in a radial manner. Rather than being organized around a centralized hall, however, each space is effectively a subdivision of the single volume, with no spatial hierarchy, and no central hall. Held between a single-surface floor and ceiling, rooms are simply divided by lightweight timber walls.

The architect describes the plan as an 'intoned open plan', an experiment in the 'architecture of distance'. Being radially intonated (or bent) at several points, the spaces have different depths, and a different extent of relationship with one another; i.e. different relative distances. Through this, a diverse range of spatial qualities has been achieved, with different levels of privacy and containment. As a 'convoluted cavern' – another of the architect's descriptive terms – the space reveals a satisfying degree of complexity to anyone walking through it, with every step taken revealing changing views and new spaces.

Made simply from 12 millimetre (0.5 inch) thick plywood fixed to 45 x 45 millimetre (1.8 x 1.8 inch) vertical studs, the material qualities of the walls add further layers of complexity. With each partition having a finished and an unfinished face, articulated on one side by a smooth, painted surface and on the other by an unpainted surface, regulated by exposed unpainted studs, an alternating arrangement of totally wooden or totally white rooms has been created, changing the nature and perceived scale of each room, while adding a satisfying coherence to the house as a whole.

While the slenderness of the stud walls implies endless flexibility, making it seem as though the walls could be easily removed and reconfigured in any position, the walls are in fact structural. The house is a lightweight timber frame, built with basic skills on site. With a diaphragm roof, however, effectively acting as a stiff plate by spanning in all directions, it is conceivable that a strategy could be proposed which would allow the roof to be propped while the partitions are relocated. This strategy could be developed further by the layout being governed by a number of discrete 45 x 45 millimetre (1.8 x 1.8 inch) structural posts, all easily concealed within the walls.

1 Storage
2 Skylight
3 Child's Room 1
4 Bathroom
5 Japanese Room
6 Slide Door
7 Storage
8 Piano Room
9 Skylight
10 Child's Room 2
11 Study Room
12 Master Bedroom
13 Parking
14 Living/Dining Room
15 Closet
16 Kitchen
17 Storage
18 Entrance

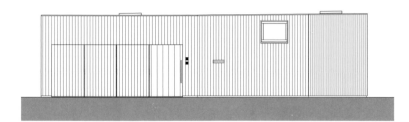

1

2

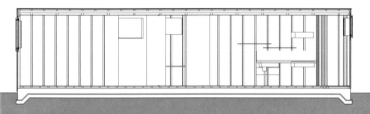

3

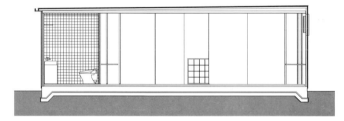

4

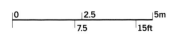

0   2.5   5m
7.5   15ft

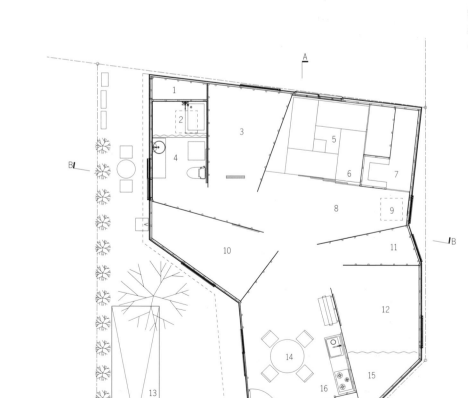

5

Seifert House

BAU/KULTUR, Michael Shamiyeh

Volkersdorf, Austria; 2005

This house was built after 63-year-old Mrs Seifert lost her former property in a fire. Despite her age, she seized the opportunity to turn this apparent disaster into a life-changing opportunity by building a home that was more attuned to her preferred way of life. Unlike her old home, this radical new house was built to connect her daily life more directly with nature, allowing her to experience the changing seasons throughout the year. Essentially designing a glass box, the balance between privacy and openness was one of the architect's principal challenges when considering the arrangement in plan.

As an art dealer, the client had a keen interest in the philosophy of spatial organizations. Through this, and following discussions with the architect, a design process ensued that investigated the relationship between spatial determinism and freedom and flexibility of use. Drawing on two extreme examples from the Modern Movement, the architect and client compared the specific flexible arrangement of Rietveld's Schröder House (controlled by sliding screens and disappearing corner windows), with the static universal attitude to space seen in Mies van der Rohe's Farnsworth House (which set service cores and enclosures

within an otherwise empty glass box). The Seifert House is, to some extent, a hybrid of both formal responses.

The plan as built sets two solid cores within a crystal-like glass envelope. The concrete cores, which are materially consistent with the simple flat soffit that sits above, contain all of the necessary cellular spaces including a home cinema and a bathroom. Around these static solids, the glazed space is seen as the more dynamic, changeable, Rietveldian space (albeit with none of its distinct aesthetic associations) that creates a more direct relationship with the changing landscape beyond. Within these tapering volumes, living and sleeping areas have been arranged, set within an in-between realm around the perimeter that opens up and closes down specific views and aspects.

Compositionally, the relationship between the solid cores and the transparent perimeter sets up strong spatial tensions. With their solid mass, the cores exert a form of gravitational pull on the perimeter spaces, with the crease in the glass screen and the space between almost visibly expressing the force of attraction. This is a unique example of a centralized plan whereby – despite there being no singular central focus – the plan

somehow embodies a curious and inherent sense of complete self-centredness. Solid and void seem to be in imperfect balance to produce a harmonious relationship between the interior, exterior and the all-important spaces in between.

In contrast to the fully glazed skin wall, a concrete wall has also been integrated into the perimeter. This wall not only defines the entrance court and supports a generous canopy above, but also serves to conceal the garden from view until visitors have entered the house.

1 Entrance
2 Wardrobe
3 Living Area
4 Home Cinema
5 Kitchen
6 Library
7 Bathroom
8 Sleeping Area
9 Parking

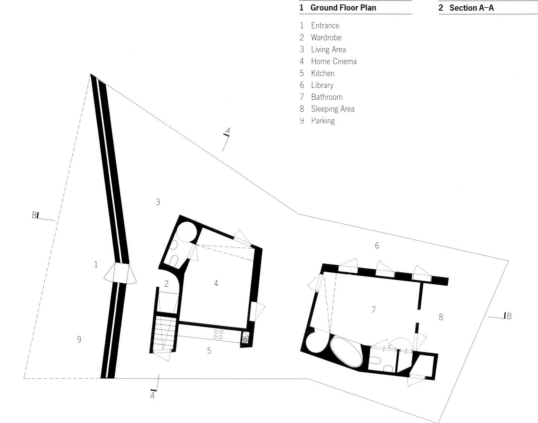

1

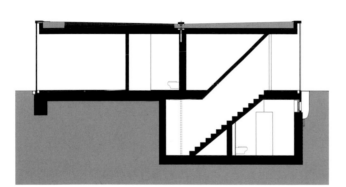

2

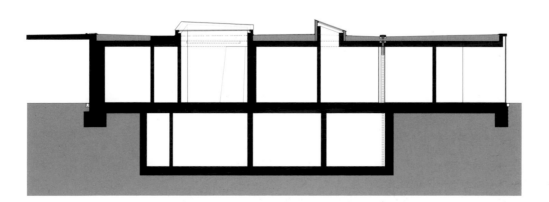

3

0   2.5   5m
7.5   15ft

Element House

Sami Rintala

Anyang, South Korea; 2005

It is rare for architects to be given the opportunity to exercise their spatial virtuosity in such pure isolation. With standard commissions for buildings, the demands of programmes, site and end user inevitably become necessary influences. This house, however, is one such example of pure spatial and material exploration, comprising as it does a home for no one in particular. Built as part of a wider public art project in Anyang, 25 kilometres (15.5 miles) south of the South Korean capital, Seoul, this curious cubic assemblage was described by its client as a 'unique conceptual piece of architecture that symbolizes elements of nature'. As one of 52 unique commissions set within the Anyang resort – a river valley that extends 1.5 kilometres (0.9 miles), Element House comprises five connected cubic volumes. With a distinctive asymmetrical silhouette, the composition centres around one major cube – clad in rusty steel plate – with four smaller cubes that step up and around it at varying heights. The name Element House came from the concept that each of these smaller cubes would be designed to include a possible suggestion for the use and presence of nature's four basic elements: earth, air, fire and water. With one cube below ground, only three of the small cubes are immediately obvious to approaching visitors; however, once inside the principal cube, the disposition and logic of the circulation becomes immediately apparent.

Entered beneath the overhang of the uppermost timber cube and through a narrow timber doorway, the central cube is partially open to the sky and serves as a large gravel-based hallway. Facing the entrance in the opposite corner of the plan is the first element cube which, being built at grade, is devoted to the earth. To the left, accessed via a robust cast-concrete stair, is the basement 'water cube' – presumably referring to the hidden level of the river valley's water table. Above these – accessed via two simple cantilevered steel stairs – are the cubes representing fire and air. The 'fire cube' is on the first upper level, with a simple concrete hearth set in one corner beneath a glazed flue-cum-rooflight. On the second floor is 'air', the uppermost and most precarious of all the cubes, with a large frameless picture window and a strict five-person capacity limit.

Throughout the composition, the scale is heavily governed by the proportion of the principal cube, with each of the smaller element cubes being exactly one-quarter of the volume of the central cube. Hence, each of the timber boxes can notionally be seen to have been pulled out of the central cube, rotated on one edge to enable each to exploit their own specific orientation and outlook. While clearly revealing the aesthetic preoccupations of its Finnish architect, with crisp timber cladding, this home for no one feels perfectly placed in the heart of its Korean forest, and serves as a delightful spatial experiment; compositionally unbalanced, but curiously centred in its disposition.

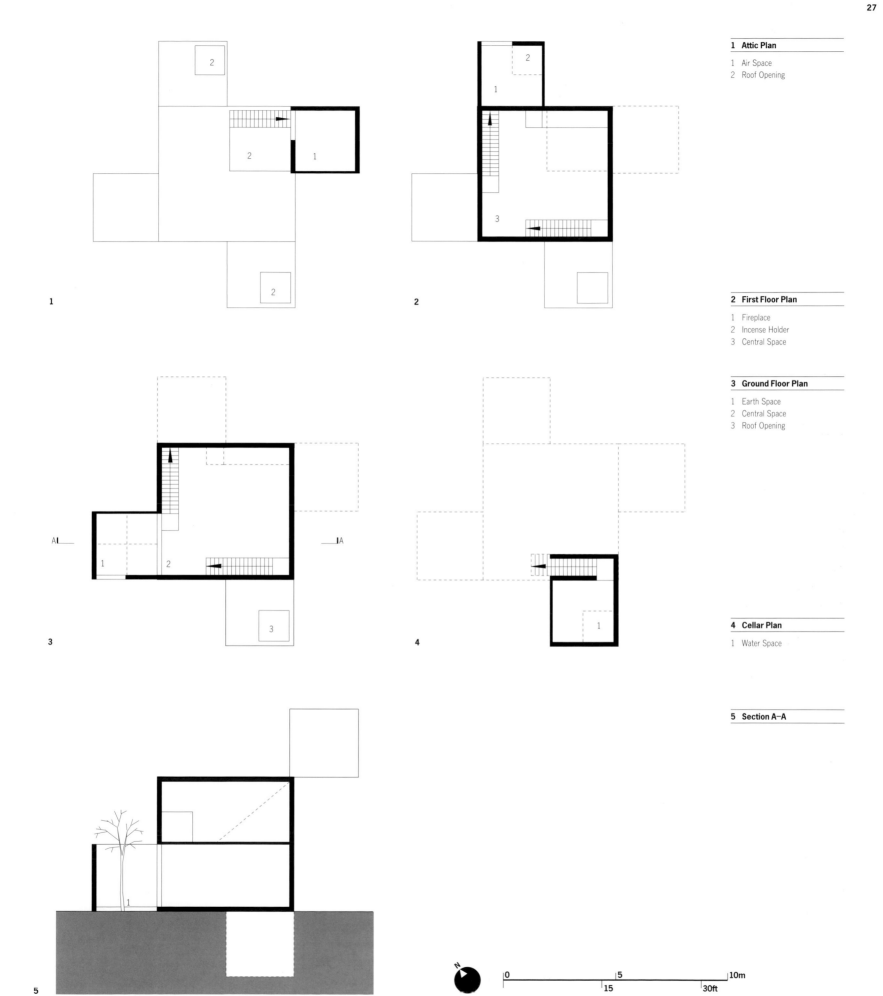

1 Attic Plan

1 Air Space
2 Roof Opening

2 First Floor Plan

1 Fireplace
2 Incense Holder
3 Central Space

3 Ground Floor Plan

1 Earth Space
2 Central Space
3 Roof Opening

4 Cellar Plan

1 Water Space

5 Section A–A

Eden Project Biomes

Grimshaw

Cornwall, UK; 2001

No study of centralized planning systems would be complete without a dome. However, in our relatively secular times, domes are rare in contemporary architectural practice. This building, however, by British architectural practice Grimshaw, is the exception to that rule – a secular building, perhaps, but nevertheless a heaven-sent and truly biblical experience for all who visit Cornwall's own Garden of Eden; a truly inspired millennium project that now gives two million or so pilgrims every year the opportunity to experience the climate and landscape of regions that they may never have the opportunity to visit themselves.

As a fitting homage to the pioneering American designer Buckminster Fuller – who inspired many of the leading protagonists of the so-called 'British High-tech' – the Eden Project includes eight interconnected geodesic domes. It also continues the very British tradition, established by Decimus Burton and others, who pioneered the development of innovative tropical glasshouses, of delicate structures where skeleton and skin combine with efficiency and finesse to create lightweight intricate and transparent enclosures.

The Eden Project was built to showcase global biodiversity and, as it is the largest plant

enclosure in the world, one of the principal self-imposed challenges set by the design team was to create maximum volume with the lightest and most economical enclosure possible. Spheres are known to be the most efficient form of enclosure, containing the maximum volume with the minimum surface area. However, they are also known to be one of the most complicated forms to construct. Clearly then, there was little point in reinventing the dome and, as such, Fuller's pioneering study into geodesic geometries was the inspiration for this project (having already proven that it is possible to create a structure that weighs less than the air it contains).

Covering 2.2 hectares (5.4 acres), and clinging to the exposed face of a redundant china clay pit, the eight conjoined Bucky balls (as they were affectionately named) range in radius from 18 metres (59 feet) to 65 metres (213 feet), with each being sized according to the plants they were to contain. Creating a combined volume of almost half-a-million cubic metres (17.7 million cubic feet), each individual Biome (to use the official name) is subdivided into hexagonal modules that range in diameter from 5 metres (16 feet) to 11 metres (36 feet). Each of the icosahedral geodesic frameworks

is then braced by a secondary structure of diagonal, circular hollow-sections that combine to create a rigid shell between primary and secondary layers. ETFE foil is then used in inflated pillow sections to clad each of the outermost hexagonal frames, and flowering air vents at the top help to control air distribution.

At the centre of the necklace of Biomes is a low-lying link building that separates the Humid Tropics from the Warm Temperate zones, and which also contains all the essential utilities associated with any busy visitor centre. Since 2001, as with any truly sustainable story of creation, the Eden Project has continued to grow and flourish, with new facilities added in 2003 and 2005. Plans are under way for a fifth phase, The Edge, containing plant life from the Dry Tropics alongside a series of temporary and permanent exhibits on climate change and other environmental issues.

1   Humid Tropics Biome
2   Biome Link Building
3   Warm Temperate Biome

1

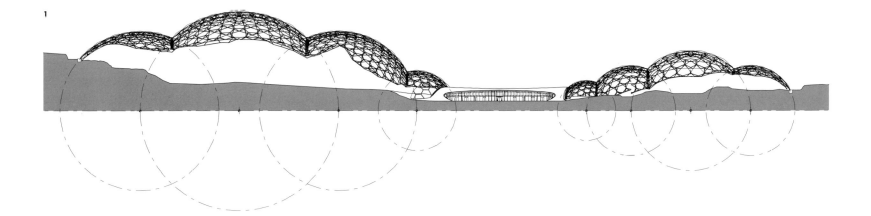

2

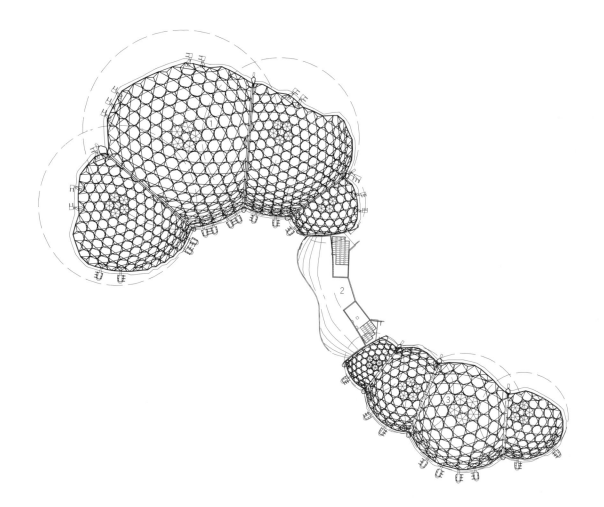

N

0	25	50m
	75	150ft

City Hall

Foster + Partners

London, UK; 2002

There have been numerous examples of architects using transparency and concentric planning as a metaphor for democracy, and Foster + Partners' building for the Greater London Authority is one of the most recent. Whether or not the all-seeing eye was part of Foster + Partners' original concept, the building's spherical form is strongly justified on environmental grounds. Providing maximum volume within the minimum envelope has helped reduce exposure to solar gain, with 25 per cent less surface area than a cube of equivalent volume. This early concept, however, has raised many complex issues with the building's detailed resolution.

When each floor plan is considered in isolation, the building remains relatively simple with nine diminishing circular floor plans stacked one above the other. In section, however, the building as a whole adopts its eccentric character, as each floor plate is offset along the principal bisecting axis that runs north–south from front to back. With this, the resultant form leans back, further reducing its exposure to solar gain with self-shading to the south and maximizing daylight penetration to the north by presenting a full-height window with the largest possible surface area. Internally, situated behind this window, the building is dominated by

a large vase-shaped assembly hall, with a spiralling ramp that leads to a publicly accessible common room and roof terrace, providing spectacular views across to the City.

While in planning terms this may all seem reasonably straightforward and logical, the principal challenge of this building is how the resulting form has been clad, and how it impacts on the building's crooked structure and radial dividing walls. Instead of resolving the sphere in the manner pioneered by Buckminster Fuller, this building has been cut into nine slices, each with its own unique geometry that resolves eccentricities in plan and section. Clad effectively level by level, no two cladding cassettes are the same, as the pitch and skew of each level reaches its maximum value to the north. Defined by four unique corner co-ordinates, sophisticated manufacturing techniques made the procurement of the façade viable, and despite the building's twisted logic it has been remarkably well built, with tolerances of less than 5 millimetres (0.2 inches) between adjacent units.

Pioneering in terms of design procurement, site surveying, fabrication and construction, City Hall was also innovative in terms of acoustic design, with Arup Acoustics developing a new form

of acoustic modelling, effectively visualizing sound waves in dynamic computer animations. This very much influenced the shape and size of the vase-like assembly chamber, and identified the opportunity to place acoustic absorption within the underside of the delicate ribbon-like ramp.

City Hall has many critics, not least because of the controversial profile of its principal occupant, the mayor of London, but also due to its curious form. Despite the high level of technical resolution, the building has won little praise for its pug-like proportions. However, it shouldn't be forgotten that some people like pugs, and this building has certainly produced some extremely well-resolved new techniques.

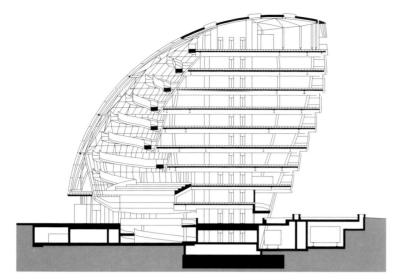

1

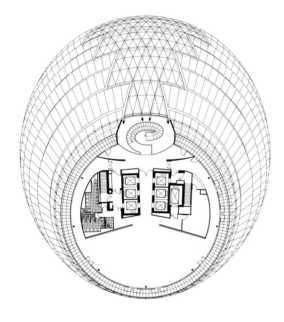

2

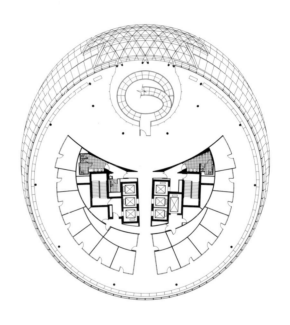

3

2 Ninth Floor Plan

3 Sixth Floor Plan

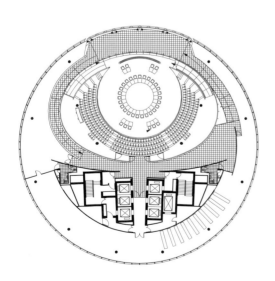

4

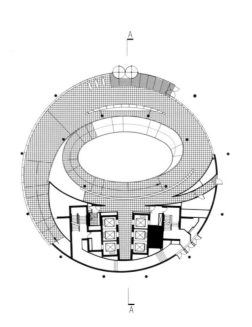

5

4 Second Floor Plan

5 Ground Floor Plan

0	5	10m
15	30ft

Lewis Glucksman Gallery

O'Donnell + Tuomey

Cork, Eire; 2004

While not easy to categorize, the Lewis Glucksman Gallery, situated close to the entrance of University College Cork, is an extremely significant building of its time. Some even herald it as the alternative winner of the 2005 Stirling Prize – it somewhat predictably lost out to the host city's Scottish Parliament Building [see pp. 202–3]. Regardless of such conjecture, however, it remains one of the most accomplished works to date by the Dublin-based practice O'Donnell + Tuomey, and deserves close scrutiny in order to unpick hidden delights held in both plan and section.

Through its location, set somewhere between city and park, the building performs two simultaneous roles: to the north and west it performs a civic role, addressing the relative formality of university and townscape, and acting to some extent as a gatehouse to the campus; to the east and south, it is seen more clearly in picturesque isolation, elevated high above a neatly kept lawn and set against a backdrop of trees. Locked into the site's northwest corner, therefore, the building sits on a solid and formally assertive stone podium that contains two levels of accommodation. Built partially into a slope, the stone monolith contains toilets and stores at the

lowest plinth level, and a loading bay, function room and café on the upper level. Above this, the principal gallery spaces are elevated in a curvaceous timber box, and linking the two, with vertically modulated glazing that cuts up into the timber, a glazed lobby steps back to create a public route. This route, articulated at high level by an axial window that provides a preview of a gallery, encourages all who pass by to enter, led by the light via the principal stair.

With a twist in plan that effectively turns the principal axis of the galleries east by 45 degrees, the largest double-height galleries are cantilevered out in two triangulated L-shape spaces. These run east and south around the orthogonal gallery core. The core, which extends the geometry of the podium, contains three floors, with two smaller black box galleries (suitable for projections and light-sensitive work), stairs, lift and a roof terrace to the north.

While apparently whimsical when seen in plan, the soft curves and angular window boxes of the galleries help to locate the spaces within their context, providing opposing views – first to the east on the second floor, and then to the west on the fourth. Through its curves, views and subtle

shifts in geometry, the plan implicitly encourages movement through its spaces, giving a level of sophistication and intricacy that belies this building's relatively small scale.

This is a fine example of how to conceive a building that is planned completely in the round. With no discernible front or back, it is both a compelling object in its own right and a highly contextual and well-anchored addition, placed within a delightful setting.

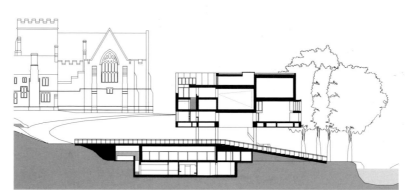

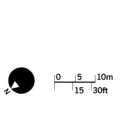

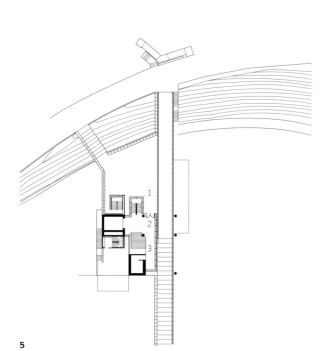

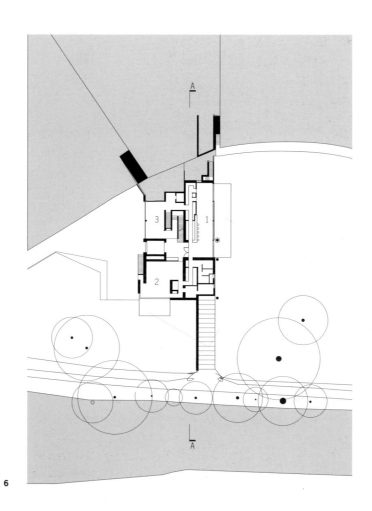

1 Third Floor Plan

1 Terrace
2 Reading Desk
3 Gallery 2

2 Second Floor Plan

1 Close Control Gallery
2 Void over Gallery 1

3 Section A–A

4 First Floor Plan

1 Office
2 Book Shop
3 Void over Showcase
4 Gallery 1

5 Upper Ground Floor Plan

1 Forecourt
2 Entrance Hall
3 Showcase

6 Lower Ground Floor Plan

1 Café
2 The River Room
3 Service Yard

0 5 10m
15 30ft

Sami Parliament

Stein Halvorsen and Christian Sundby

Karasjok, Norway; 2000

This building has received much admiration for its ability to satisfy two apparently contradictory objectives, exhibiting as it does qualities of temporary lightness and robust permanence. Situated on the northeastern tip of Norway, in a region that drifts east to meet Russia, the building forms an administrative base for the partially settled community of Sami, the Lapps, many of whom still pursue a nomadic way of life across the borders of Scandinavia and Russia. While formally determined in plan, setting out accommodation in a suitably monumental (albeit asymmetrical pattern), the building's material expression responds to the spirit of the place, being more fragile and almost self-built in its articulation.

As a whole ensemble, the new Parliament makes a very particular place in a context that is otherwise dominated by loose scatterings of unremarkable prefabricated buildings. With little urban coherence, the building provides a welcome focus within a challenging and at times harsh environment, set in a region that receives no light at all for two months during the winter, and experiences temperatures that can plummet to an inhospitable 40°C below zero. Understanding the realities of such a harsh environment, Halvorsen

and Sundby devised a plan that made a powerful gesture, not only for purely formal reasons but also for practical ones, with a semicircular range of accommodation that shields occupants from the biting northerly winds.

Eccentrically located to one side of the settlement's centralized plan, a conical debating chamber has been positioned, linked to the crescent with a glazed shard and bearing an unmistakable likeness to a traditional nomad's tepee. To the north, the crescent is thickened with a linear infill block that strikes a chord across the arc to contain a library and cafeteria. Within this arrangement, the building exhibits many subtleties in plan and section that add richness to what may otherwise be read as an overtly diagrammatic arrangement. The debating chamber is one such element that could have become little more than an overblown caricature of a flimsy tent. In its execution, however, it has been scaled up and abstracted with finesse to provide a sculptural and functional focus for the Parliament. With space for 39 members, the form is severed by a glass shard. This bridging element not only links the chamber to the Parliament's principal circulation spine which runs around the inner edge of the crescent, but

also divides the main chamber from a triple-height anteroom which gives access to the gallery above. In section, the conical form also helps to unite elected members with their people, with the public gallery sitting concentrically above it, reaching forward to the centre of the cone, instead of being remote and relegated to the back of the space.

Other delightful subtleties include the point of emergence, where the curved circulation spine re-emerges from behind the cafeteria, and the battered outer edge of the curved walls that serve to further emphasize the building's grounded and robust stance and form.

1

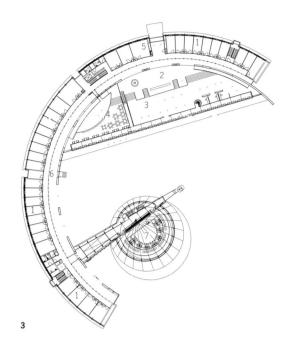

3

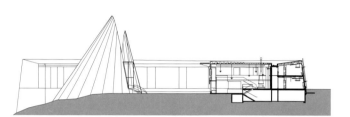

2

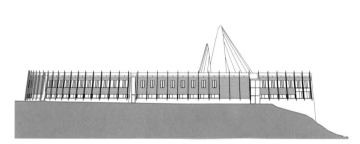

5

4

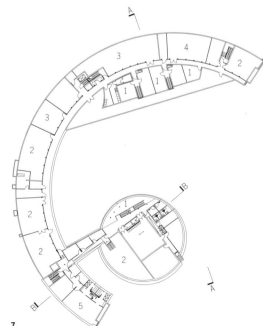

7

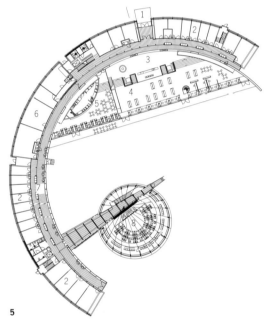

6

N

0 5 10m
15 30ft

1 East Elevation

2 Section A–A

3 First Floor Plan

1 Offices
2 Library Upper Level
3 Library Lower Level
4 Café
5 Committee Rooms
6 Gallery
7 Chamber

4 North Elevation

5 Ground Floor Plan

1 Main Entrance
2 Offices
3 Library Upper Level
4 Library Lower Level
5 Café
6 Committee Rooms
7 Gallery
8 Chamber

6 Section B–B

7 Basement Plan

1 Library
2 Technical Room
3 Archive
4 Storage
5 Gym

Mercedes-Benz Museum

UNStudio

Stuttgart, Germany; 2006

Since the early 1990s, UNStudio has produced many intellectually stimulating and formally intriguing buildings. The Mobius House, completed in 1998, is one of their most celebrated works: a contemporary home that expresses the looping 24-hour cycles of family life in spaces that are organized along a double-locked torus, or Mobius strip. The Mercedes-Benz Museum, while built at an entirely different scale, takes these ideas further, with a sophisticated geometry that synthesizes the structural and programmatic organizations of a contemporary museum to create a new landmark building on the eastern fringe of Stuttgart; a building that dramatically redefines the conventional museum experience.

Based on a trefoil organization – a single-stemmed three-leafed clover – the museum's content is set out on nine spiralling surfaces that ascend from ground to roof around the central hollow-stem atrium. Having travelled up the middle of the 42 metre (138 foot) high atrium in one of three vertiginous lifts, visitors begin their experience at the top of the building, from where they can wind down two intertwined ramping routes. The two trajectories lead them on sinuous paths, one leading through five Collection rooms, the other

through a succession of seven so-called Legend rooms. At the intersection of the two routes, visitors can switch at crossover points to experience both journeys, which combine to lead them seamlessly through the 120-year history of Mercedes-Benz. En route, visitors see over 150 vehicles (in collections of voyagers, carriers, helpers, celebrities and heroes), and are taken back through time, from the birth of the car in 1886 to the present day.

In diagrammatic terms, the complexity of the route is unravelled as the UNStudio architect, Ben van Berkel, describes the plan by tracing two routes around the trefoil plan. When traced by the finger, the two routes become one and are revealed as a single continuous circuit. Recalling the perpetual navigation of the Mobius strip, the routes merge by alternating between the centre and perimeter of each of the three trefoil 'leaves' in a six-stage looping sequence that crosses six times where the leaf meets the stem; complicated to explain in words, perhaps, but remarkably simple when traced by the hand of its creator, and far more intuitive to follow when visiting the building oneself. The museum curator worked closely with the architect to ensure that the visitor experience would be easily absorbed. Alternating between the Collection and

Legend rooms, the building expresses the museum's dual function to deposit and to expose. The visitor passes through the more passive naturally lit vehicle depots before experiencing the theatrically orchestrated displays contained within the Legend rooms, in a series of more heavily serviced spaces that are filled with the sound and motion of multimedia presentations.

Constrained within a soft triangular envelope, the building's curious form is derived from its unique centrally planned organization. Externally, therefore, a series of glazed strips expresses the spiralling route, held between the more enclosed Legend rooms that are clad in opaque panels, predictably sprayed in Mercedes' distinctive metallic silver paint.

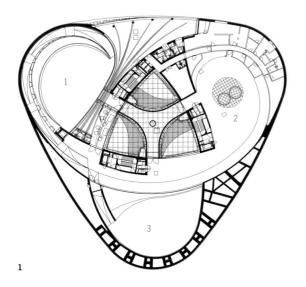

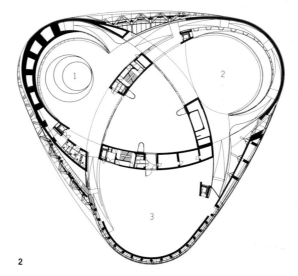

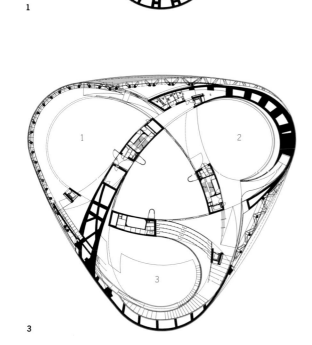

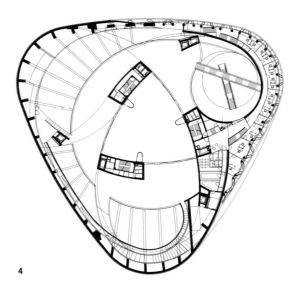

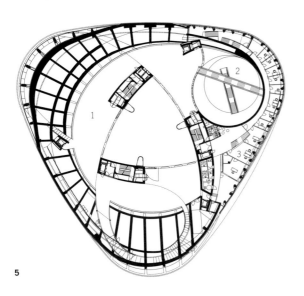

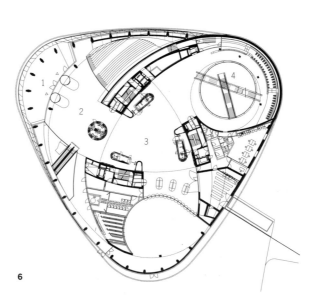

1 Level 8

1 Void above Legend Rooms
2 Legend Rooms
3 Roof Terrace

2 Level 7

1 Legend Rooms
2 Void above Legend Rooms
3 Collections

3 Level 3

1 Collections
2 Legend Rooms
3 Void above Legend Rooms

4 Level 2 Mezzanine

5 Level 2

1 Legend Rooms and Races and Records
2 Fascination of Technology
3 Offices

6 Level 1

1 Main Entrance
2 Lobby
3 Atrium
4 Fascination of Technology

Bibliotheca Alexandrina

Snøhetta

Alexandria, Egypt; 2002

The Great Library in Alexandria follows a long-standing tradition of impressive circular reading rooms, extending the lineage that includes Smirke's British Museum and Asplund's Stockholm City Library. More broadly, however, this huge monument to knowledge re-creates the ancient repository for history and literature founded by Alexander the Great in 331 BC. Its re-emergence at the turn of the third millennium is considered by many as one of the new wonders of the contemporary world.

In 1989 a competition was launched to design the new library, attracting phenomenal interest with 524 entries from over 52 countries. The astonishing decision was made to select Snøhetta, a virtually unknown practice from Norway. Thirteen years later, however, the young team had matured and had produced one of the world's few truly ground-breaking landmark buildings, prompting universal acclaim and catapulting Snøhetta to international prominence.

The basic competition-winning design was deceptively simple for such a large and complicated programme, comprising a large, inclined silver disc rising up over the sea. With a diameter of 160 metres (525 feet), and spread over an internal landscape of 14 terraces, in its completed form this distinctive building accommodates up to 2000 readers in a single space. At over 170,000 cubic metres (6,003,493 cubic feet), it is by far the largest reading room in the world. At this scale, unpicking the details of the plan demands close and focused scrutiny. It is, however, possible – to a limited extent at least – to describe the underlying principles behind the arrangement of the centralized reading room; a space that occupies approximately half the library's volume.

In section, the building's angular form rises from one to 11 storeys in height, and is set four storeys below the ground. With up to six levels of book storage, the vast reading room remains consistent at between four and five storeys in height but gives the impression of being more expansive and monumental through the uninterrupted sight lines that extend across the entire plan, from bottom to top, allowing occupants to overlook all 11 storeys in a single glance.

In plan, the geometry of the circular reading room is governed by a regularized grid of slender concrete piers that create an impressive man-made grove. This grove is set out on a grid of 9.6 x 14.4 metres (31.5 x 47.2 feet), relating to a standardized system of book storage, and at roof level the trunk-like columns divide the building's sloping soffit into triangulated rooflights. Entering at level five – 7 metres (23 feet) above the datum – visitors pass through a secure reception, along the building's central axis, to arrive almost at the centre of both the circular plan and the section, with extensive views both above and below.

To some extent, the formal clarity of the competition-winning design was contaminated by the client's decision to retain a neighbouring 1960s conference centre, resulting in an uncomfortable relationship with the shared entrance piazza that sits between the two. Despite this, however, the building has its own powerful identity which, while serving as a catalyst for future developments, also successfully integrates a hugely complicated functional programme of its own.

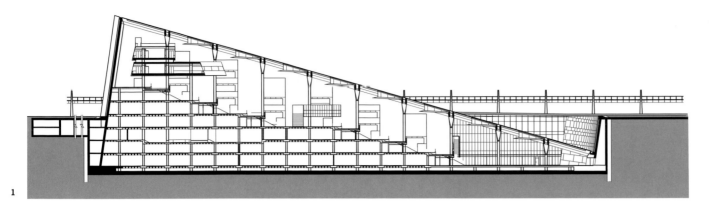

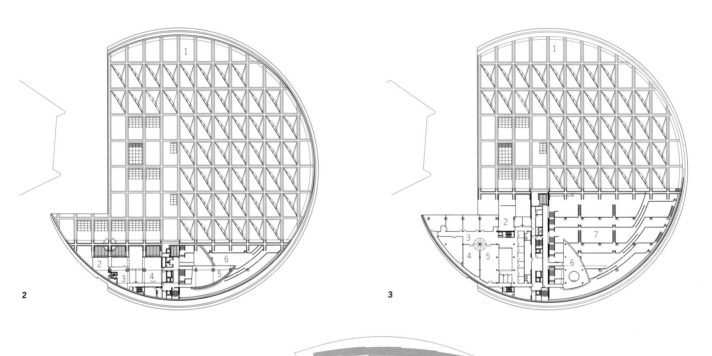

2 Fifth Floor Plan

1 Roof
2 Director General
3 Administration
4 VIP Area
5 Balcony
6 Void

3 Third Floor Plan

1 Roof
2 Workshop
3 Laboratories
4 Lecture Rooms
5 Library
6 Study Room
7 Void

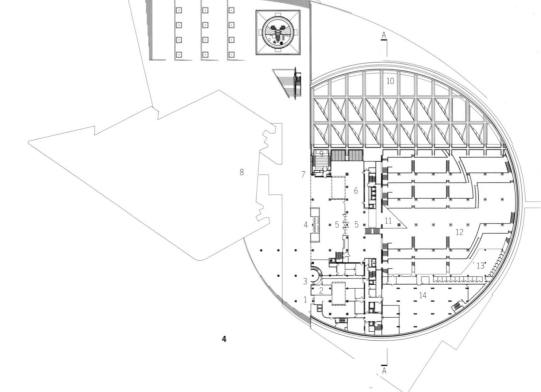

4 Entrance Floor Plan

1 VIP Entrance
2 Security
3 Staff Entrance
4 Main Entrance
5 Lobby
6 Information
7 Plaza
8 Existing Conference Centre
9 Auditorium
10 Roof
11 Balcony
12 Open to below
13 Section IV Books
14 Closed Access Book Storage

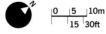

0 5 10m
15 30ft

Jægersborg Water Tower

Dorte Mandrup Arkitekter Aps

Gentofte, Denmark; 2006

Modern water towers are curious structures. Occasionally they can be impressive, when seen as sculptural objects of beauty designed by talented engineers encouraged to produce refined and elegant solutions for prominent landscape situations. In post-industrial urban settings, however, many water towers have lacked the same degree of consideration, often having been governed by far more utilitarian parameters that gave them a considerably overengineered and underrefined appearance, with a bulky concrete structure and ungainly top-heavy proportions. While some remain in use, many are now obsolete, and apart from those who hold a nostalgic appreciation for a bygone era, most people would prefer to have them removed from sight. Those that cannot be removed, however, have to be lived with, and what better way to tackle the issue of living with the visual impact of a water tower than to live directly beneath it? When considered thus, many similar towers can suddenly be seen as profitable development opportunities for those ambitious developers who are happy to risk operating at the more quirky end of the housing market. Instead of being viewed as unfortunate eyesores, therefore, many towers can provide architects with an ultimate

challenge, as was the case with the Jægersborg Water Tower, situated in the Gentofte suburb of Copenhagen.

Historically, water towers – like windmills (with which they were often combined) – included internalized accommodation. Hence, conversions of this type represent a logical return to form. With a central structural core, water towers offer ideal opportunities for adaptation with valuable space between the tank and the street providing prime and accessible airspace ripe for occupation.

Unlike Jo Crepain's conversion of a relatively small water tower into a private home [see pp. 120–21], this intervention is more interesting as an investigation into centralized planning, demonstrating how eight apartments can be placed within a predetermined hexagonal grid.

In this instance, the architects worked within the existing structure, which comprised six hexagonal columns at the core and 12 circular columns at the perimeter. With a stair and lift core occupying one of the 12 segments, and the central core being used for additional assigned storage, the other 11 segments were occupied by two plan types: a simple orthogonal unit that sits between two old and two new columns; and a triangulated

unit which, when paired up, shares the diamond-shaped space defined by two old and four new columns.

With the lower four levels being given over to a youth centre and other community purposes, the upper five levels were converted into flats, providing up to 40 new one-bedroom studio apartments, each with its own protruding bay window that offers unobstructed views of the surrounding landscape, adding a new layer of articulation to the dramatically reinvented tower.

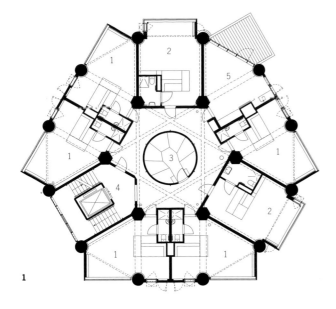

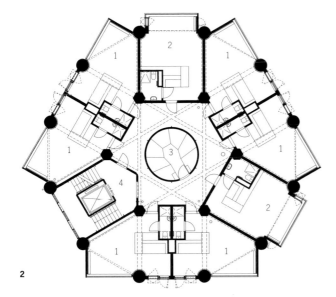

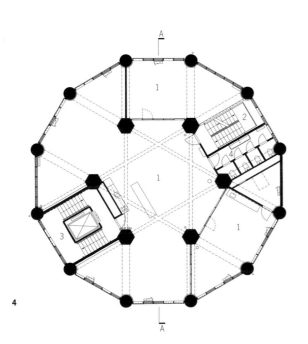

1

2

4

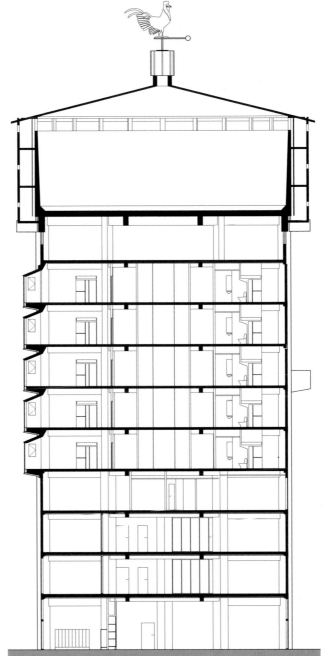

3

1   Seventh Floor Plan

1   Apartment Type A
2   Apartment Type B
3   Storage
4   Communal Stair
5   Community Room

2   Fourth Floor Plan

1   Apartment Type A
2   Apartment Type B
3   Storage
4   Communal Stair

3   Section A–A

4   Second Floor Plan

1   Community Room
2   Stair
3   Communal Stair
4   Lavatories

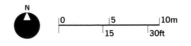

N

0   5   10m
     15   30ft

Imai Daycare Centre

Shigeru Ban

Odate, Japan; 2001

This is not so much a centralized plan as a centralized section. It could also, quite legitimately, be studied as a linear organization. In this instance, however, the building's distinctive cross-section is of particular interest, relating as it does not only to Shigeru Ban's ongoing technical quest to explore the possibilities offered by basic materials, but also to the typology of simple toy-like forms; an entirely appropriate metaphor considering its function as a daycare centre for young children. Although not a proven theory, cavernous womb-like spaces are clearly popular with children; crawling into a gift box rather than being distracted by the gift itself is the prerogative of any inquisitive child. As such, in that it has been created as a simple box within which to play, the parents of children attending this daycare centre may not struggle – as some do elsewhere – to leave their children while they go to work.

The building is 27 metres (88 feet) long and 10 metres (32 feet) high, and is composed as a tube held within a box that has been rotated through 45 degrees. As an inversion, perhaps, of fitting a square peg into a round hole, the extruded timber form helps to reduce the scale of the internal space and to create a simplified and less imposing volume, easily identifiable by young

children. As a simple lattice, the timber tube is formed like a trellis, with equal widths of plywood lapped and bolted in a simple grid. When bent into an arch, this two-way structure combines to create a rigid shell-like form which is firmly anchored beneath the timber floor.

To maintain the simplicity of the space, a freestanding low-level box has been inserted, which contains the kitchen, toilets and washing spaces. The proportions of this box have also been controlled to mimic the elevation of the main entrance doors which are set within a glazed screen mounted inside the timber tube.

Externally, the roof form is designed to withstand the crushing effect of the winter snow with alternating strips of ribbed steel and polycarbonate sheeting. Propped and held away from the timber tube – which in effect acts as a compression ring – the pitched roof creates a generous void, which becomes a large filter for diffused light. This light passes through the open weave of the timber skin, animating the space within. The void also contains background artificial lighting which creates a similar effect in the early morning and late afternoon.

Combining traditional Japanese

preoccupations with a delicate lightness of touch, beautifully detailed timber joinery, paperthin translucent screens, and an inherent sensitivity to the transmission of light, this apparently childlike building has much to teach, playful but richly layered as it is.

1 Section A–A

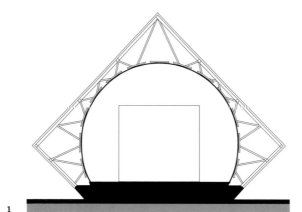

1

2 Section B–B

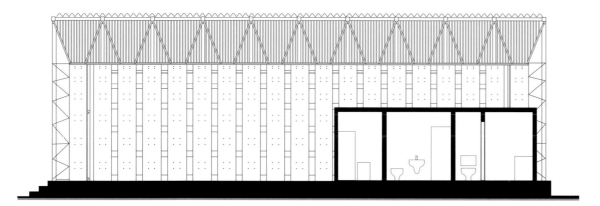

2

3 Ground Floor Plan

1 Play Space
2 Staff Room
3 Lavatories
4 Kitchen

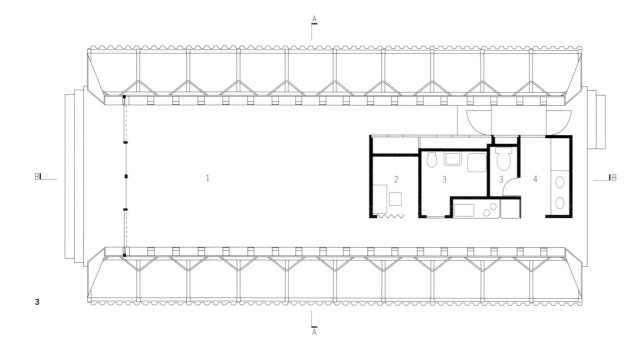

3

0   5   10m

15   30ft

Linear Structures

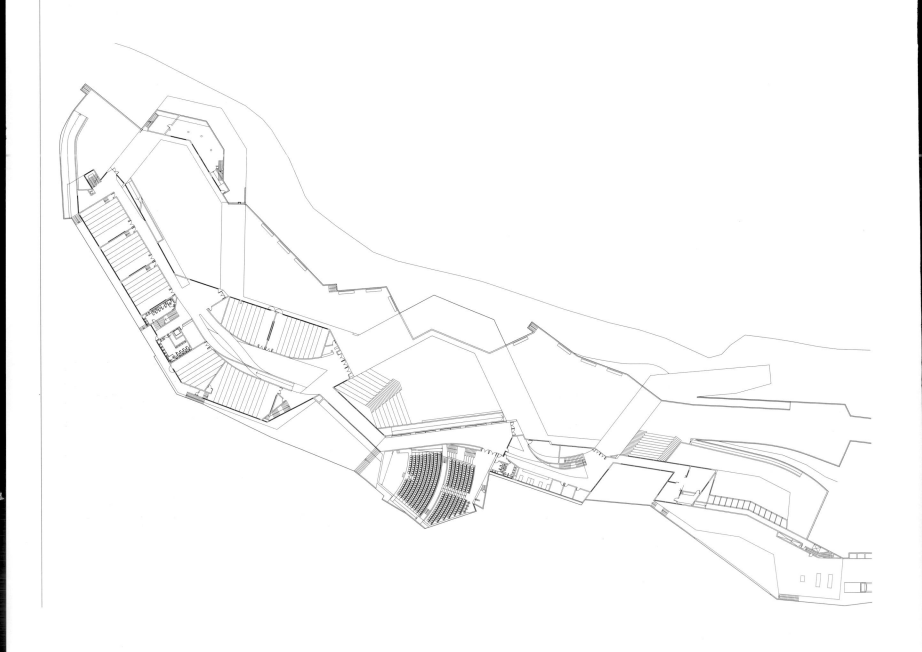

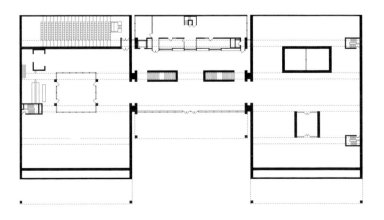

Turbine Factory, Peter Behrens
Façade and Section

Repetitious, ordered and well proportioned, linear structures can be appealing on many levels. In Richard Weston's *Key Buildings of the Twentieth Century*, a number of seminal projects were identified that had linear organizations. The first of these was **Peter Behrens'** iconic **Turbine Factory** in Berlin, completed in the first decade of the century. At over 200 metres (656 feet) long and divided into 21 expressed bays, the building was extremely significant, cited as the first truly industrial building that brought the machine aesthetic into the domain of architectural tradition, and was noted for the classical undertones of its structural organization. In 1937 Alvar Aalto's Baker House in Cambridge, Massachusetts was one of the earliest examples of linear planning in a sinuous form, taking a simple

structure and making it relate more specifically to its site. Later still, **Louis Kahn's Kimbell Art Museum** (1967–72), in Fort Worth, Texas, remains unrivalled in the clarity of its plan, setting major and minor bays of served and servant space in an alternating linear configuration. In ordering space, arranging structure and giving form to buildings, linear structures have an elementary beauty. When broken down into cross-sectional slices, they also have more immediate three-dimensional coherence, and the examples given in this chapter attempt to extend many of these themes.

As an example of an exaggerated linear form, **Auer + Weber's** dramatic **ESO Hotel and Information Centre** in northern Chile is perhaps the most extreme, producing a building that is more

than 150 metres (490 feet) long. Built in response to a brief to provide over 100 bedrooms, each with an uninterrupted view, the composition was also built as a response to its exceptional landscape setting, presenting a beautifully and highly composed repetitive façade within an expansive and apparently endlessly shifting desert landscape. Similar in scale and also built in response to an equally sublime context, the form of **The Peñalolén Campus** (also in Chile) by **José Cruz Ovalle Architects** resonates with its mountainous backdrop, forming a series of craggy blocks of accommodation arranged on either side of a linear route. Here, the route also makes a space, likened to a street, which broadens to create internal and external communal spaces.

Kimbell Art Museum, Louis Kahn
Façade and Ground Floor Plan

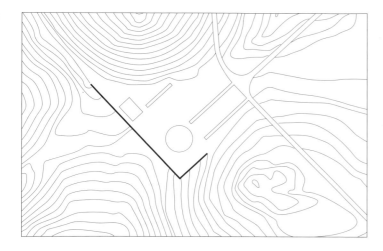

ESO Hotel and Information Centre

At the other extreme of scale, two single houses have been selected for consideration, each of which works in opposing orientations. While the **Agosta House** on San Juan Island, Washington, by **Patkau Architects**, is experienced as three zones that work across its linear grain, acting as a three-stage filter between the enclosed arrivals courtyard and the expansive views seen from within, the spaces within **Sean Godsell Architects' St Andrew's Beach House** in Victoria, Australia – an elevated cage – are arranged along the length of its linear form, with a staggered route that shifts across the plan in a living room that forms a fulcrum at the heart of the home.

The repeated bay quality of linear structures is also discussed, both in terms of how this helps to rationalize the structure and how it helps to modify the external form of the building by incremental shifts in cross-sectional geometry. Four examples demonstrate this notion, starting with the simplest, the **Peregrine Winery** in Gibbston Valley, New Zealand, by **Architecture Workshop**, which sets out an array of props with increasing pitches to create a dramatic double-curved canopy. Following a similar tactic, **VJAArchitects' Rowing Club** in Minneapolis, Minnesota, maximizes a sculptural effect with the minimum means by producing a double-curved roof from 45 identical straight trusses that are simply propped on two triangular clerestories set in opposing directions. In the third example, **Rene van Zuuk** uses standardized off-the-shelf components from an agricultural 'three hinge'

portal frame kit of parts to create a unique enclosure for the **Art Pavilion** at Zeewolde in the Netherlands. And, on the island of Hirvensalo in southwest Finland, **Sanaksenaho Architects** have created the gently tapering **St Henry's Ecumenical Art Chapel** by using 19 variants of the same laminated timber A-frame.

Seen in contrast to these more structural assemblages, **Sou Fujimoto's Care Centre** in Hokkaido, Japan, presents a truly unique configuration. As a linear arrangement of cubic volumes, it is also based on repetition. In this instance, however, the units of repetition relate more haphazardly to the landscape, by collectively forming a sinuous linear cluster, comprising 11 identically proportioned square units linked by ten

Care Centre, Hokkaido

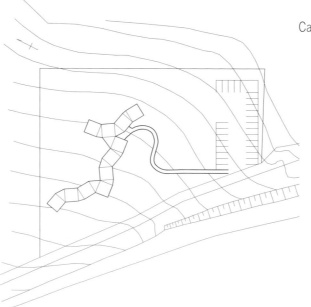

Echigo-Matsunoyama Museum
of Natural Science

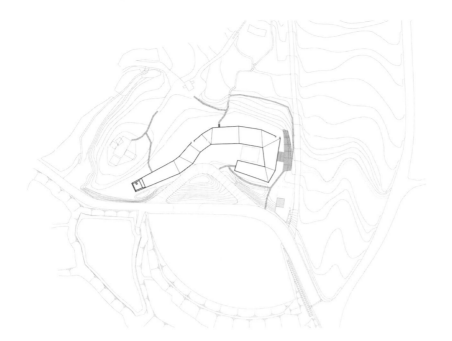

interstitial triangular spaces. With this arrangement, the building creates a wide variety of spaces of all sizes, providing a city-like diversity.

Four final examples have been included that fit less easily into any single subcategory, other than the fact that they all exploit elongation in their form. These are **Edouard François' Social Housing** in Louviers, France, which builds thin strips of accommodation around a collection of ancient pear trees; the **Echigo-Matsunoyama Museum of Natural Science** by **Takaharu + Yui Tezuka**, which ignores efficiencies, structural or otherwise, to simply produce a unified and singular form with an extruded cross-section that snakes its way across the landscape as a single continuum; the **Dutch Embassy** by **Dick van Gameren and Bjarne**

Mastenbroek in Addis Ababa, Ethiopia, which sits within an existing wooded eucalyptus grove, maintaining the gradient of the existing landscape along its length; and, finally, a delightful oddity in the form of **Atelier Tekuto and Masahiro Ikeda's Lucky Drops House**, a house-cum-aircraft wing that is agonizingly skinny, tapering from a slim 3.2 metres (10.5 feet) to less than a metre (3 feet) along its 17 metre (56 foot) length.

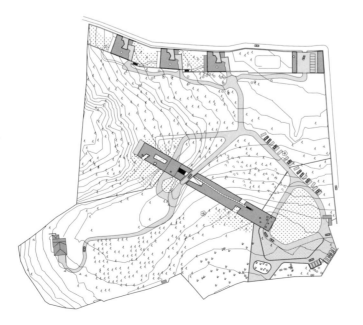

Dutch Embassy, Addis Ababa

ESO Hotel and Information Centre

Auer + Weber Architekten

Cerro Paranal, Chile; 2002

The ESO Hotel is an accommodation building for the European Organisation for Astronomical Research in the Southern Hemisphere. Lying low in the Atacama Desert in northern Chile, it is located in one of the world's hottest and driest places – and is consequentially beneath some of the world's clearest skies.

In seeking to accommodate over 100 bedrooms for astronomers from around the world, Auer + Weber not only had to contend with the practical difficulties of building in such a remote and extreme environment, but they also faced the challenge, architecturally, of how to make an appropriate response within such a distinctive and dominant lunar landscape. In this respect, the iron-oxide-impregnated concrete matches the colour of the natural terrain, while the building's principal limb, which contains the bedrooms, appears to grow out of the ground, as if it were an extension of the relentless stretch of the dry, bleak landscape.

In simple terms, the building comprises two conjoined blocks of accommodation with the linear bedroom block meeting at right angles with a more compact cluster of communal facilities to the north. At the corner an 11-bay terrace is served by a large dining room, while the internal corner pivots around

a circular courtyard that contains a large internal garden; a covered oasis-like space containing a sheltered artificial landscape where residents can relax by the swimming pool.

Compositionally, the architects have exploited the opportunities that arise from designing a repetitive façade with each bedroom articulated by a deeply incised concrete wall. Arranged over four floors, the linear monolith is thereby broken down into a recognizable scale, with each room set behind a concrete panel, and set apart from the next with an L-shaped window. While minimizing manageable levels of sunlight penetration, each bedroom makes the most of the southerly views with a full-height window at which to stand, and a high-level clerestory that provides spectacular views of the sky when viewed from the bed.

In contrast to the cellular bedrooms, double-height communal areas are set back within the depth of the plan to provide sheltered external balconies. These continue the running order of the building, but subtly change the fenestration by omitting concrete panels at the lower level; the upper panels remain to provide shade to the double-height inset glazed screens behind. Apparently flat when seen in drawn form, when set

within its spectacular environment the repetitive nature of the building's façade is constantly animated by an ever-changing array of sharply defined shadows.

While the passing sun breaks up the potential monotony of the southerly façade, in terms of circulation the plan also responds well, avoiding the plight of the endless corridor with a series of terraced ramps set within a dimly lit and cavernous triple-height void. In plan, section and elevation, therefore, Auer + Weber have created a well-grounded and well-mannered hulk of a building from which to marvel at the heavens above.

1 Section A–A	2 Section B–B	3 Section C–C	4 Ground Floor Plan	5 Lower Ground Floor Plan

4 Ground Floor Plan

1 Ramp
2 Entrance
3 Courtyard
4 Offices
5 Dining Room
6 Terrace
7 Bedrooms

5 Lower Ground Floor Plan

1 Foyer
2 Swimming Pool
3 Bedrooms

1

2

3

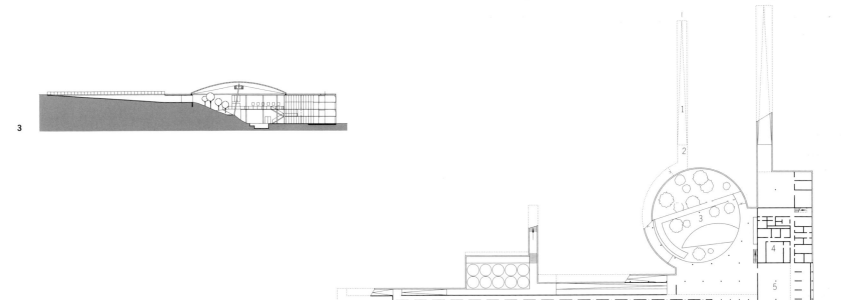

4

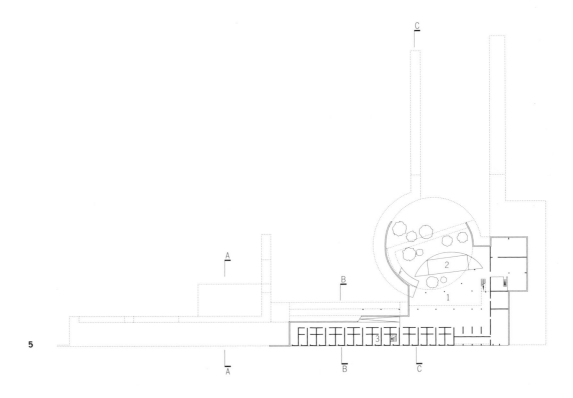

5

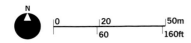

Agosta House

Patkau Architects

San Juan Island, Washington, USA; 2000

Situated on San Juan Island, a rural island off the Pacific coast in Washington state, USA, this house was designed for a couple who had made the bold decision to relocate from New York City. Curiously, their retreat to a rural idyll brought a new series of security issues. Within a brief that included many conventional landscape responses, such as those to views, orientation and topography, this house also called for a 3.5 metre (12 foot) garden enclosure; not, it should be noted, to keep out thieves and robbers, but to protect residents from the wild deer that may stray from the extensive Douglas fir forests that surround it. While this may or may not have directly informed the architect's planning strategy, the series of courtyards that have been created gives the plan an order and identity that is worth investigating. As with many architects, analogies often serve to clarify less tangible intentions, and with this house the architects' analogy sets up three zones of spatial experience, defined by reservoir, dam and sea.

The house sits along a ridge and forms what the architects describe as a 'spatial dam'. Against the dam to the south is the protected courtyard or 'spatial reservoir', and to the north the 'spatial sea' – an ocean of views to Haro Strait and the islands

of British Columbia beyond. The three elements combine, with the first being the reservoir, a small but significant piece of defensible external space that forms the forecourt; the second being the house itself, or rather the dam, which controls the flow of the occupants' experience of the external environment; and the third being the landscape beyond, the spatial sea, where the viewer's experiences are ultimately discharged.

The house plan comprises two conjoined and parallel ranges of accommodation. The first from the south is the service core and contains lavatories, kitchen and utility spaces, while the second contains three principal living areas for work, rest and play. The service range differs in composition to the living range, and sits under a simple flat roof. The living range, by contrast, rises up within a skewed box structure that brings light in from both sides. Echoing the angles of the raised box roof, the walls of both ranges are battered in section to emphasize their dam-like quality.

The spatial organization of the house is the result of extruding the cross-section and manipulating it either by erosion, to create exterior in-between spaces that subdivide the house, or by the insertion of non-structural bulkheads that

organize the interior into finely scaled spaces. Through this the plan not only separates served and servant spaces, but also gives privacy to the bedrooms, with each being positioned at opposite ends of the north range, with the guest bedroom made more remote by access via a narrow passageway held within the service range.

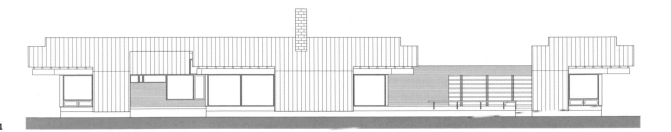

1 Elevation

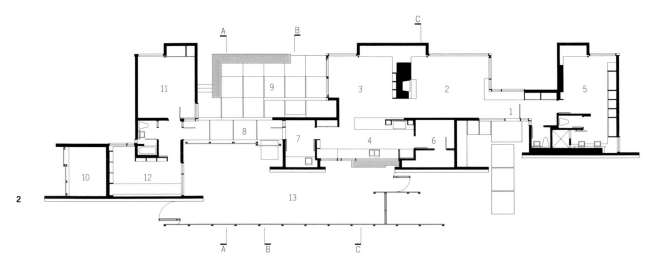

2 Floor Plan

1 Entry
2 Living Room
3 Dining Room
4 Kitchen
5 Master Bedroom
6 Storage/Mechanical
7 Mud Room
8 Covered Walkway
9 Terrace
10 Garden Shed
11 Guest Room
12 Studio
13 Fenced Garden

3 Section A–A

4 Section B–B

5 Section C–C

St Andrew's Beach House

Sean Godsell Architects

Victoria, Australia; 2006

It is well known that linear plans exist in the domestic sector, derived both from adapted so-called loft living where spaces are carved up into a number of connected cells set within a larger volume, and (as in the case of this example) from beautifully composed freestanding pavilions. Sean Godsell has produced a number of houses that arrange internal functions within light- and heat-diffusing layers. With his latest house, built on St Andrew's Beach on Victoria's Mornington Peninsula, he triumphs again, ordering space, structure and the ritual of life with a homely precision.

The linear organization rationalizes the structure into a simple diagram, whereby the long axis of the house defines two full-depth full-length trusses. Each of these cross-braced trusses is then hung from two square-section columns and linked across the short axis by elements that complete the structure as a rigid box. Elevated above the ground, to exploit even better views and to leave space below for cars and storage, the house is entered via a single-flight steel stair. From here all spaces are connected by a staggered route that takes the form of two half-length passageways on opposite sides and at opposite ends of the plan. The crossover for the route takes occupants through the heart of the

principal living room which, acting as the fulcrum, is situated towards the west end.

The plan, as you would expect, is decidedly rational with rooms arranged one against the other along the long axis. From the arrival point – in the centre of the living room, between the dining and seating area – spaces are disposed with an increasing level of privacy as the northern passageway leads away from the living room, past a separate study, to three equally sized bedrooms, each isolated from the next by shared bathrooms. At both ends of the house the route is terminated by a sheltered terrace that further serves to accentuate the principal axis and to anchor the occupant to the stunning long view.

Clad in standardized industrial metal grating (oxidized to produce a rich reddish-brown), the skin of the house not only acts as a climatic moderator, providing both shade and ventilation, but also expresses the order of construction, clearly showing the layers by articulating each room as an isolated object set within a breathable membrane. With two skins separated by the expressed structure, in extreme weather conditions all rooms can be double buffered, with the corridors remaining effectively external zones. In more moderate

conditions, the stunning full-width swing door at the westernmost end of the living room, and the screens and doors in both skins, can be held open to let air and light filter through. Externally, the triple layering of the envelope is fully expressed on the end portals, with an inset metal frame articulating the structure set between the internal (glass) and external (metal) skins.

1 Elevation

2 Roof Plan

3 First Floor Plan

1 Deck
2 Living Area
3 Kitchen
4 Study
5 Laundry/Bathroom
6 Bedroom
7 Bathroom

4 Ground Floor Plan

1 Entrance Deck
2 Storage
3 Carport

1

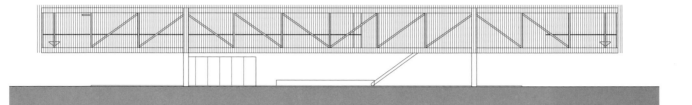

2

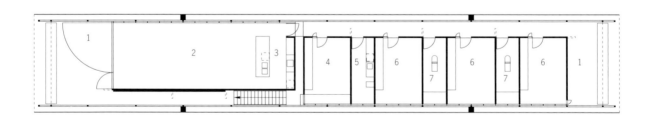

3

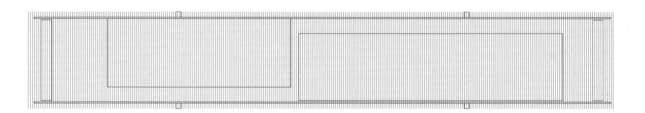

4

N

0   5   10m
  15   30ft

Peregrine Winery

Architecture Workshop

Gibbston Valley, New Zealand; 2004

This distinctive structure is situated in the most southerly wine-producing region of the world, and usefully combines the component efficiencies of a repetitive cross-section with the potential for a linear organization, to produce a distinctive landscape response. In the midst of the Southern Alps, the building's sweeping roof line sits beneath the dramatic mountain ridge lines to shelter and unify a series of agro-industrial process spaces. Lying low on the terraced floor of the Gibbston Valley, the Peregrine Winery processes 650 tonnes of grapes per year, producing, among other wines, a wonderful Pinot Noir. The new facility was designed not only in response to utilitarian demands, but also to help establish a strong brand for the emerging wine label. As such, when describing its graceful curve, the architects draw on a number of thematic references, seeing it both as a description of a metamorphosis (similar to the process of wine-making itself), and more literally as a frozen image of the rotation of a wing in flight, with the peregrine falcon being the winemaker's mark. Whatever rationale you choose to adopt, the result is extremely satisfying.

The wine-making process usefully conforms to a linear organization, literally with grapes in at one end and bottles (or in this case, barrels) out at the other. Here, that process is largely readable, with the visiting public invited in at the southerly end to enjoying tasting sessions in a subterranean space dominated by row upon row of barrels, laid out in the Barrel Room. In plan, the only deviation from the linear organization is to the northeast, where an external fermentation area is set into the terraced landscape.

At 140 metres (459 feet) in length, the roof is the most dominant feature, sitting independently above the bunker-like concrete substructure. Clad in a translucent skin (employing Durolite GC), the wing-like roof form is simply propped on a galvanized structure, narrowing in width as it rises in height towards the visitors' entrance, twisting along its way up to a 25 degree slope. The lightness of the structure is further exaggerated by the specification of perforated beams, in contrast with the bunker beneath.

The area directly beneath the canopy is accessible as an external concrete plinth, on which visitors can walk to gain access to the conference suite served by its own sunken court. En route, spectacular views are offered of the Kawerau Gorge to the east.

The canopy was built to help maintain a necessarily stable environment for the process spaces below, closing down to the direct sun at one end and opening up above the less sensitive visitor centre to the south. It is also, despite its apparent fragility, engineered to keep snow from settling on the concrete podium, and is without question an extremely useful device in terms of moderating the complex's impact on the landscape, acting as a foil to the otherwise bulky bunkers. With grace and elegance, the winery has a delightfully ephemeral presence in the landscape.

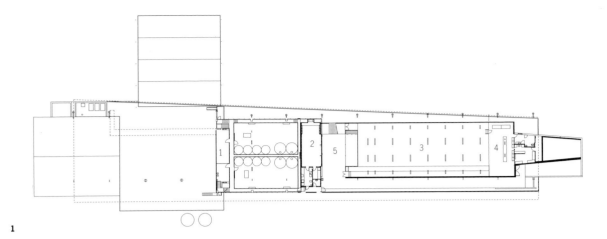

1

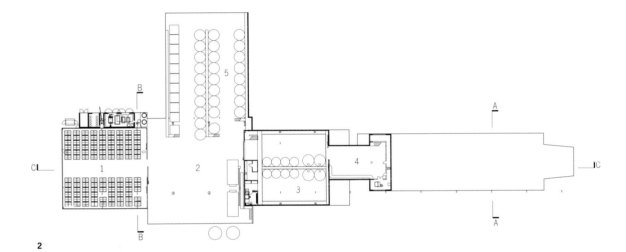

2

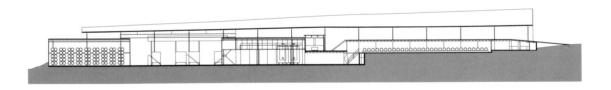

3

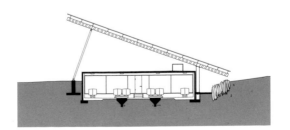

4

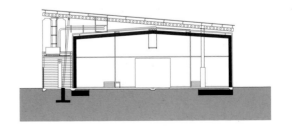

5

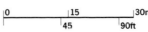

0 15 30m
45 90ft

Rowing Club

VJAArchitects

Minneapolis, Minnesota, USA; 1999

Rowing is a sport in which a balance of poise, posture and power is essential. As such, this delightful riverside pavilion is a fitting response, designed by VJAArchitects on the bank of the Mississippi, in Minneapolis, Minnesota.

While modest in scale, it is a clear demonstration that simple ideas are often the most effective. Built in solitary isolation in a sensitive and picturesque riverside setting, the pavilion has a well-balanced presence, being both necessarily understated and sufficiently well mannered, giving the club members a building that serves them well and makes them proud. Taking the twist of an oar blade as its inspiration – the twist that helps rowers optimize their stroke – the twin-peaked roof form lends the pavilion a graceful and elegant style.

Built to replace an old club house that was burnt down by vandals, the simple, elegant timber frame building rises from the ground with noble dignity. Clad in horizontal cementitious boards, the 600 millimetre (24 inch) module established by the timber frame is expressed externally in the high-level clerestory windows. Set at an incremental gradient, these windows and the vertical framing rise up towards opposing corners to help generate the roof's twisted profile. Spanning the width of the

building, between each of the long triangular clerestories, 45 identical and straight trusses complete the beautiful double curve; this is a structure where maximum effect is achieved through minimum means.

Due to the building's orthogonal floor plan, combined with the regular gradient of the clerestory, the height of the mid span of each truss is concurrent with the next. Internally, this produces a level datum along the length of the building, forming a spine around which each of the trusses rotates. The linear emphasis that this produces – an emphasis that is visually amplified by the alignment of the triangular truss struts – is further reinforced by two stair cores that flank the mezzanines. These not only split the plan to provide small enclosures for changing areas, toilets or storage, but also provide direct access from the outside to the mezzanines above; a pair of simple raised platforms, principally used as training decks and meeting areas.

Despite being orthogonal, a subtle rotation also occurs in plan through the positioning of two double-height voids at opposing corners beneath the low point of the roof. The effect of these, together with the twist of the roof, enables this

single volume to produce a remarkably varied series of spatial effects, with perspective and depth being distorted as the roof twists.

Externally, the building's linear symmetry is further reinforced by the composition of two large sliding doors at either end, which being clad in copper give the building a quiet articulation. The final twist occurs on the riverside façade in the form of a high-level sliding screen, also clad in copper. Accessed from the riverside mezzanine, this screen slides to expose the building's skeletal timber frame, through which onlookers can enjoy excellent views of the Mississippi River beyond.

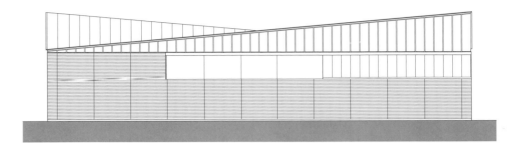

1 East Elevation

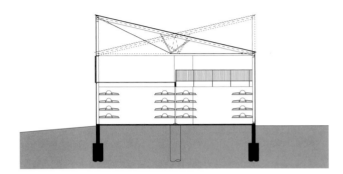

1

2 Section A–A

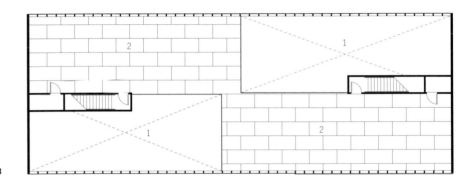

2

3 First Floor Plan

1 Void
2 Mezzanine

3

4 Ground Floor Plan

1 Entrance
2 Scull Storage

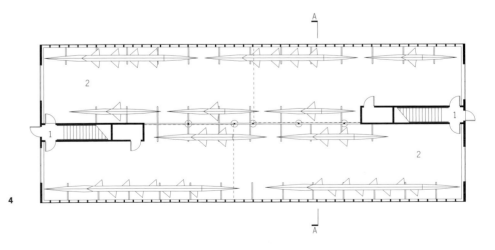

4

0   5   10m
15   30ft

Art Pavilion

Rene van Zuuk

Zeewolde, The Netherlands; 2000

One of the few common denominators in the work of Rene van Zuuk is the desire held by client and architect to create something special. Throughout his work, Zuuk seeks out the particular by employing methodologies of the commonplace. With an understanding of building technology, he has repeatedly produced eye-catching buildings by using known technologies, a principle that exploits minimum means to maximum effect. More often than not his work is laden with sculptural intent, and the Art Pavilion at Zeewolde is the latest in a growing lineage of distinguished projects.

Positioned at the end of Art-track Zeewolde – a 7 kilometre (4 mile) art trail in the Netherlands – this gently twisting pavilion is another good example of how apparently repetitive cross-sections can be adapted to sculptural effect. Inspired by the work of Richard Serra, the building makes direct reference to Sea Level, Serra's long black concrete wall which features as part of the Zeewolde trail; both are seen as man-made objects set in harmonious contrast to the stratified Dutch landscape.

Due to budget limitations, a cheap standardized system was sought that could be used to create an appropriately distinctive structure. By adapting components from a standardized 'three

hinge' portal frame – a construction system more commonly used to create cheap agricultural barn structures well known in the surrounding agricultural polder landscape – this non-standard building has been given a unique and distinctive shape; a shape that is optimized when viewed in the landscape, set against the calm waters of the adjacent lake.

The cranked timber frames are leant one against another, with two joints at the base and a shared central joint at the ridge line; this application exploits subtle shifts in setting out, both in plan and section, to fracture the ridge line and misalign the building's footings. When seen in section, the timber frames are set out in a spiralling array that produces a gentle fanning silhouette; a twisted gradient, one against the next. Then, to further exaggerate this vertical twist, a lateral twist occurs in plan as the building's enclosure tapers to create shifting overlaps, most obviously expressed at the ridge level where a large crack exists; a feature that is likened by the architect to a tectonic fault line. To articulate the juxtaposition of each opposing lean-to structure this rooftop fault line is glazed; a detail that is repeated at the structure's base, where the hem of the building's cladding is lifted to reveal its

slender ankle joints.

Sheathed in profile metal sheeting, the building's exterior is clad with corrugated aluminium, which seamlessly envelops the curved profiles. Internally the profile sheeting is perforated and/or lined with plasterboard to help improve the building's acoustic character, while providing a shifting surface for dancing water reflections. Timber pods provide additional internal enclosure, in a space that otherwise focuses on the glazed end wall from where magnificent views are gained over the pond towards the artists' work.

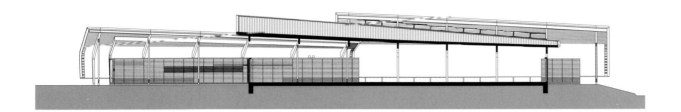

1 Long Section

1

2 Northwest Elevation

2

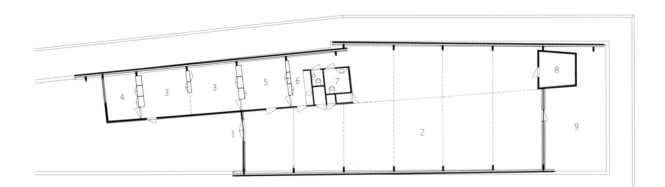

3

3 Ground Floor Plan

1 Entrance
2 Exhibition
3 Office
4 Director
5 Library
6 Pantry
7 Restrooms
8 Storage
9 Terrace

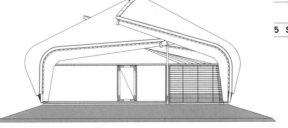

4

5

4 North Façade

5 South Façade

0   5   10m
  15   30ft

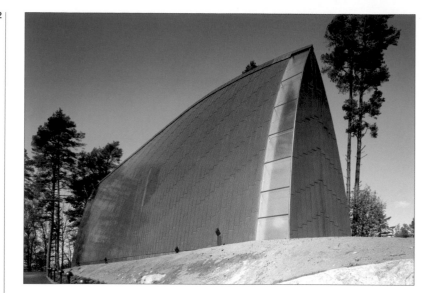

St Henry's Ecumenical Art Chapel

Sanaksenaho Architects

Hirvensalo, Finland; 2005

Linear planning strategies often exploit the benefits of repetition. Whether structurally or spatially repetitive, repeated bays bring order, logic and the benefit of economies of scale. By contrast to issues of pure rationality, however, this delightful chapel, located on the island of Hirvensalo in southwest Finland, demonstrates how a relatively basic linear system can also be used to create a more sculptural effect, exploiting incremental changes in plan and section to produce an apparently complicated form and silhouette.

The chapel's distinctive pointed section is formed by 19 laminated pine frames, set at 2 metre (6.5 foot) intervals. Having the same cross-sectional profiles, but varying in height, when arranged in linear array, any shifts in plan result in corresponding shifts in the profile of the ridge. Therefore, at its narrowest point in plan the ridge sits at its lowest level, and conversely, at its widest point the chapel reaches its maximum height. The rate of incremental change is also a significant factor when controlling the effect on the overall form. When the space tapers at a uniform rate, for example, as it does between bays one and 12 – producing a straight line in plan – simple rules of geometry dictate that a uniform incline will also be produced in section. Accordingly, therefore, applying the same geometric logic when the plan is allowed to bow (as it does between bays 14 and 20 – approaching and passing its widest point), the gentle curve in plan produces a curve of similar amplitude at the ridge. At each end of the chapel one final subtle geometric shift occurs as each end wall inclines to terminate the 40 metre (131 foot) long interior. And, with the structure in place, the surface between each frame is clad with 100 millimetre (4 inch) planks of untreated pine that complete the chapel's internal skin. With pine floorboards and common alder benches, the material continuity has a resonant coherence which allows the spatial effect to be appreciated in unadorned isolation. Glass is the only other material introduced to the space; in bays one and 20 full-height and high-level glass introduces light to dramatic effect.

Externally, the chapel is clad in vertical copper sheets that make it resemble a rusty upturned hull, with its razor-sharp copper keel clearly visible on approaching the site. With time, however, the cladding will soften, oxidizing and turning green to help this curious and somewhat alien form to more sympathetically complement its wooded context.

1 Section A–A

2 Ground Floor Plan

1   Entrance
2   Toilet
3   Stair to Basement

1

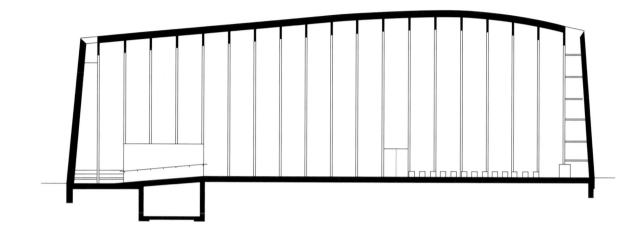

2

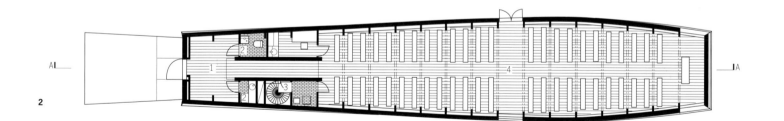

A

A

Care Centre

Sou Fujimoto

Hokkaido, Japan; 2004

Reminiscent of Charles Moore's celebrated 1960s Californian cliff-top settlement, this recent hillside care centre is an example of ordered informality in linear form. Through an ingenious manipulation of modular plans and elevated forms, Sou Fujimoto has created a settlement with its own striking identity, with distinct landscape and place-making qualities. Adopting the contemporary interest in applying a single cladding material to both walls and roof, the buildings are simply articulated in black profiled cladding, producing an overtly contemporary composition that sits on a south-westerly slope overlooking the sea in Hokkaido, in the northernmost part of mainland Japan. Providing accommodation for up to 20 mental health patients, the campus consists of a sinuous linear cluster of buildings, comprising 11 identically proportioned square units linked by ten interstitial triangular spaces. Three roof types – flat, mono-pitch and ridge – and three storey heights further articulate each unit's form, adding complexity to the building's silhouette as it descends the subtle gradient of the site. The 5.4 x 5.4 metre (17.7 x 17.7 foot) units contain cellular accommodation – bedrooms, living rooms and offices – separated by triangular alcoves, entrances and circulation zones.

The form of the building was specifically ordered in response to the sensitive brief. Seeking to create a comfortable home for 20 residents, the designers wanted to create a context that, in a controlled, secure and sensitively handled way, would mimic the diversity and sense of unpredictability of city life. The form brings about a wide variety of spaces, of shapes and sizes, gaps, dead-ends, nooks and crannies, creating a series of in-between places where people are naturally inclined to find refuge. Likened to a city, this arrangement seeks to create alleyways and tiny squares on every corner, instead of spaces, corridors and communal areas that recall the anonymous and potentially intimidating effect of wide roads and large public squares. Domestic dimensions and city-like diversity are therefore combined into a new series of internal spaces, from where views across the coastal conurbation of Hokkaido also give the residents a controlled link to their wider context. The building also creates a number of loosely defined external garden spaces.

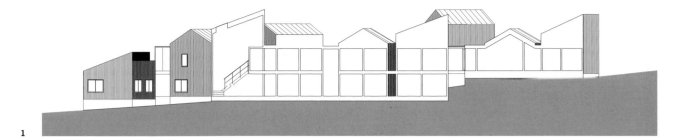

2 Section B–B

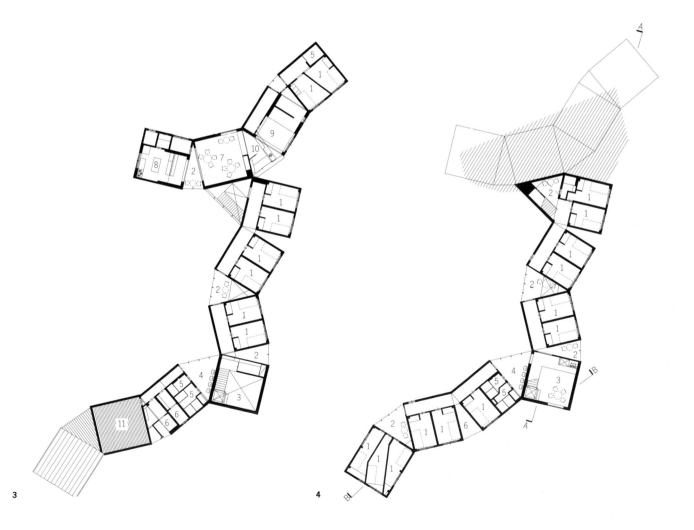

3 Upper Ground Floor Plan

1 Bedroom
2 Alcove
3 Void
4 Washing Room
5 Toilet
6 Bath
7 Dining Room
8 Kitchen
9 Office
10 Entrance
11 Roof Terrace

4 Lower Ground Floor Plan

1 Bedroom
2 Alcove
3 Living Room
4 Washing Room
5 Toilet
6 Terrace

Social Housing

Edouard François

Louviers, France; 2006

Edouard François is better known for his flamboyant experiments with integrated planting solutions, such as the seeded gabion walls in Montpellier in 2000 and the distinctive Flower Tower of 2004 that incorporated supersized plant pots filled with mature bamboo on the balconies of a Parisian apartment block. François' playful reputation may lead some of those considering the merits of his social housing scheme in Louviers to limit their investigation to the few hundred millimetres that define the building's distinctive rough-cut timber skins. This would, of course, be an unfortunate oversight, as beyond the light-hearted inventiveness, François is an architect whose interests lie far beyond the façade. His buildings also serve deeper social, economic and environmental priorities.

Situated in the small Normandy town of Louviers, 100 kilometres (62 miles) north of Paris, this 18-apartment scheme sets three narrow fingers of accommodation in a casual and apparently haphazard linear arrangement. Closer inspection, however, reveals that the site is peppered with a number of ancient pear trees that could not be removed. In placing the slim fingers between the trees, the apartments are accessed via two even

thinner blocks, each of which contains a shared staircase which provides access to three apartments on each of the development's three levels. This configuration not only accentuates the relative slenderness of each element by separating circulation and accommodation, but also gives each apartment a greater sense of autonomy. Either accessed directly from the ground, or across one of 12 access bridges, each apartment has its own front door. Furthermore, most of the apartments – except for those at the northern end of the ground floor – also benefit from additional space with ante-rooms being located within the ends of the tapering circulation cores. These spaces, despite being un-tempered and largely open to the elements, provide an extra threshold for the occupants and effectively privatize the access bridges from where residents can enjoy canopy level views of the grounds.

By contrast to the tapering circulation cores, the apartments themselves are set out in simple rectangular blocks. These blocks differ in size, with two of them divided on each level into two two-bedroom units. The larger unit situated in the middle of the site provides more space for six three-bed configurations. Organized in a similar layout, the entrances lead directly into the open

plan living areas. In the smaller blocks, the kitchen, bathroom and bedrooms are contained in a neat cellular arrangement at the southern end of each plan, while in the bigger three-bedroom apartments the kitchen is separated and moved to the other end of the living room.

All five blocks are clad in rough-hewn chestnut palings, suspended horizontally by a simple system of twisted galvanized wire. With this natural skin, the continuity of the surface serves to unify the blocks into a more coherent whole, veiling five very basic blocks.

1   Section A–A

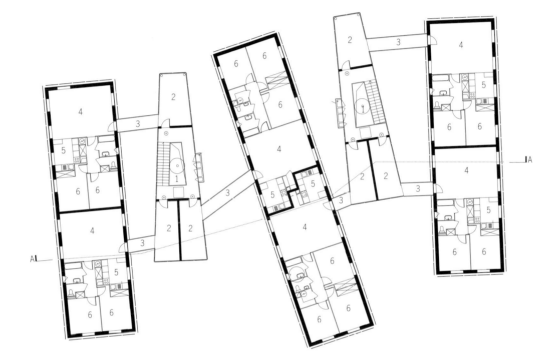

2   Second Floor Plan

1   Communal Stair
2   Private Entrance Room
3   Link Bridge
4   Living
5   Kitchen
6   Bedroom

3   First Floor Plan

1   Communal Stair
2   Private Entrance Room
3   Link Bridge
4   Living
5   Kitchen
6   Bedroom

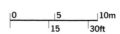

Echigo-Matsunoyama Museum of Natural Science

Takaharu + Yui Tezuka

Niigata, Japan; 2003

Unlike other examples in this chapter, the Echigo-Matsunoyama Museum of Natural Science in the Niigata prefecture of Honshu does not optimize the efficiencies, structural or otherwise, of repetitive or extruded cross-sections organized in a linear plan. Instead, the building exemplifies the spatial and sculptural effect of a form that literally snakes its way across a landscape: a form that is at once unified and singular, while also being complex, multifaceted and surprising. Sitting on the edge of a forest in eastern Honshu, Japan's largest island, the building overlooks mountains and meadows, winding its way around a sheltered garden, and terminating in a tail-like observation tower.

While the centre has no explicit structural order, it is built employing basic known technologies, comprising a simple steel frame, insulated and clad in site-welded, Cor-ten steel panels backed with an insulating urethane foam. The structure is very much like that of a submarine. The hard metallic finish of the rusty skin is set in stark contrast with the crisp white walls that line the interiors, punctuated as the plan changes direction with huge frameless picture windows.

The internal spaces are organized as a single continuum that runs from the refectory at one end,

to the base of the observation tower at the other. Between these, internal cellular space is set against one wall, freeing up the other to stand in isolation as a continuous gently faceting surface. Extending these facets, the internal ceilings are also articulated as irregular-shaped polygons, crisply folded one against the next.

Throughout the year the region is exposed to 30 metres (98 feet) of falling snow, with drifts of up to 7 metres (23 feet) in depth, resulting in the building being almost completely buried during the winter. While the external skin is reinforced to withstand the pressure of the snow loads, the windows had to be specially fabricated in composite acrylic panes, up to 75 millimetres (3 inches) thick, to withstand the huge drifts. The snow becomes a spectacular exhibit in its own right when viewed through the windows from within. Seen against the crisp white walls, shades of white merge as the compacted snow presses hard against the window panes, while externally the building's contorted form creates a drift-free sheltered arrival court.

Offices, laboratories and administration spaces are set within a two-storey range of accommodation organized around the knuckle of the plan. And, perhaps most surreally, while

surrounded by supersized windows onto the outside world, the internal spaces include an intimate gallery that contains the most exquisite collection of butterflies.

With no lift, only the most eager and physically able visitors can climb the 34 metre (112 foot) high observation tower to the west, from where they can escape the suffocating snow drifts to see above and beyond the snow-capped tree canopy; a truly elevating experience. Likened to a lighthouse, a cave, a shelter and an abandoned industrial shed, this magical building has many phenomenological readings, and spatially its internal planning exploits perspective and views with maximum effect.

1 North Elevation

2 Section A–A

3 Mezzanine Level Plan

1 Restroom
2 Japanese Room

4 Ground Floor Plan

1 Entrance
2 Usuke Shiga Collection
3 Exhibition Space
4 Viewing Tower
5 Reception
6 Office
7 Meeting Room
8 Laboratory
9 Kyororo Hall
10 Culinary Arts Experience

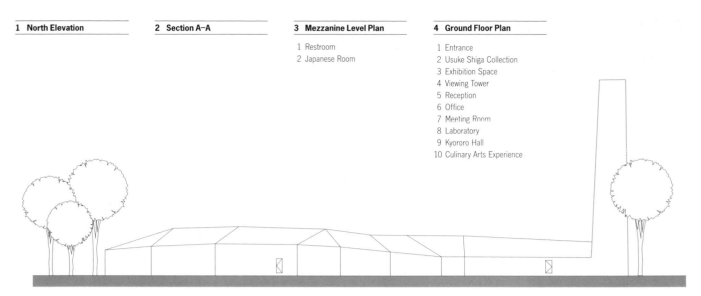

1

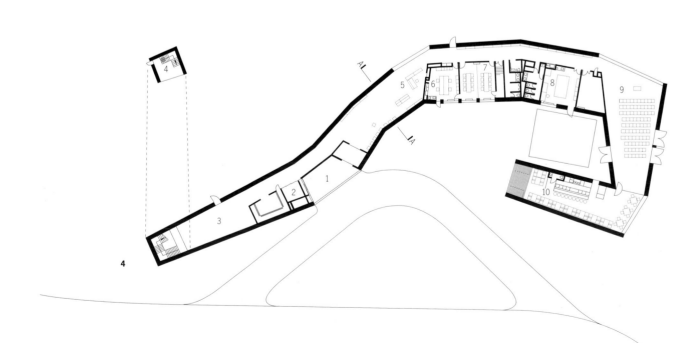

2

3

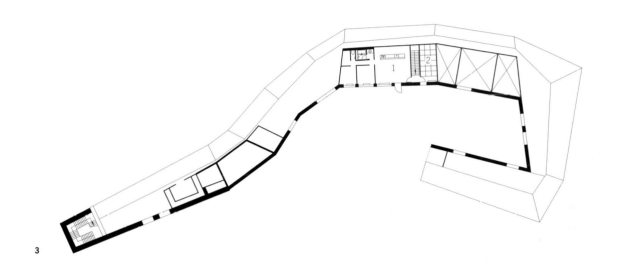

4

0 5 10m
15 30ft

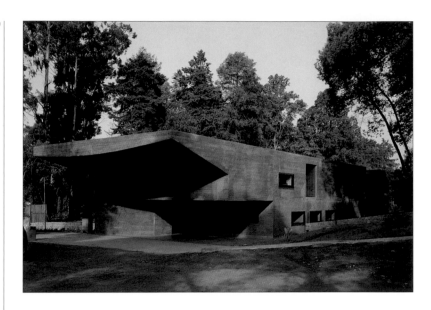

Dutch Embassy

Dick van Gameren and Bjarne Mastenbroek

Addis Ababa, Ethiopia; 2006

Linear arrangements are not necessarily generic non-specific responses, led by efficiency and ordered by abstract organizational logic; they can also be responsive, bespoke and specifically shaped in response to programme and context. The chancellery building at the Dutch Embassy in Addis Ababa, Ethiopia, is a fine example of such a condition, where a simple, formally direct and monolithic – apparently alien – form can be set within a sensitive landscape with an unforced sense of equilibrium. Recalling the solidity and permanence of Ethiopia's remarkable Coptic rock churches, ambitiously carved into the earth – this rough-cast pigmented concrete could as easily be an ancient ruin. It is, in fact, the latest in a series of contemporary, secure, purpose-built embassies to be constructed in the developing world by Western diplomatic departments, and it is a suitably fine example of how sensitive contextual design can prevail over alternative approaches that may seek more nationalistic showmanship.

As part of a wider complex of embassy buildings, the chancellery sits in the middle of an undulating wooded eucalyptus grove. The two-storey slab-like form, 140 metres (459 feet) long, is carved into the ground, with the landscape rising and falling along its length. Where the land reaches its highest point, a road cuts through the upper floor to effectively split the building in two, with the westernmost end housing the ambassador's residence, and the easternmost end the main body of the chancellery. With an incised roof, temporarily flooded during occasional downpours, the building is in the ground and of the ground with the deepest of incisions giving access to, and letting light deeper into, the cavernous spaces beneath. Circulation (as well as form) also conspires to anchor this new building to its terrain, with the main public corridor following the lie of the land, rising in gradient and cranking in plan as it extends from its generously sheltered east entrance. This circulation spine has the quality of an external alley, not only due to the polished concrete floor unifying the materials as if carved from the same block, but also due to its apparently haphazard layout. Furthermore, with each room along its length rising with the gradient and reducing in height, these spaces could not be further removed in their nature from a standard institutional bank of cellular offices. Instead, each space is unique, allowing programmatic necessity and context to merge so that larger public functions comfortably exist near the entrance, while more intimate private offices can withdraw deeper into the plan while still being illuminated by deeply cut crevasse-like patios.

The sculptural malleability of this form also exploits another quality of linear arrangement in that it creates a strong sense of front and back – head and tail – with the brow-like canopy to the east that sits above the chancellery's main entrance balancing the more discreet stumpy tail that gives shelter and enclosure to the ambassador's private residence to the west.

1 Section A–A	2 Section B–B	3 Roof Plan	4 Upper Level Plan	5 Lower Level Plan
			1 Central Hall	1 Main Entrance
			2 Ambassador's Office	2 Central Hall
			3 Bridge	3 Reception
			4 Administration	4 Library
			5 Patio	5 Ambassador's Private Quarters
			6 Salon	

1

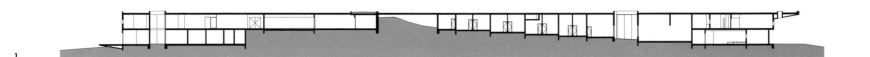

2

3

4

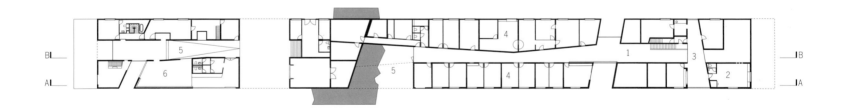

5

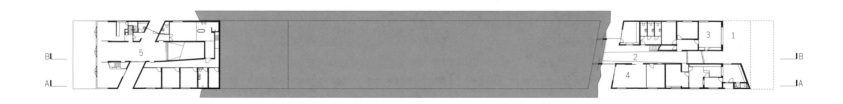

Lucky Drops House

Yasuhiro Yamashita (Atelier Tekuto) with Masahiro Ikeda (Masahiro Ikeda Co., Ltd)

Tokyo, Japan; 2005

Similar in form to St Henry's Ecumenical Art Chapel in Finland by Sanaksenaho Architects (see pp. 62–3), this miniature house in Japan extends and domesticates the principals of linear repetition. Tiny, even by Japanese housing standards, this single-volume home may be over 17 metres (56 feet) long, but it is extremely thin, tapering as it does from a slim 3.2 metres (10.5 feet) at the front to less than a metre (3 feet) in width at the rear.

Even on this apparently unusable sliver of land, the Japanese earthquake regulation that sets any walls 500 millimetres (20 inches) from boundaries and neighbouring properties still had to be enforced, clearly establishing a challenge for the architects who are rapidly acquiring a reputation for designing highly inventive – if at times unorthodox – 'micro-homes'.

Likened to an aircraft wing – sliced along its length and set on end – this structure is decidedly more expressive than the aforementioned ecumenical example. With a lightweight tubular frame clad in a thin skin of translucent polycarbonate, the aviation metaphors continue, as does life inside the wing, sharing the same spatial restrictions as one might expect to encounter on any lifelong long-haul flight.

The structural cross-section uses a similar profile to that adopted by Sanaksenaho Architects. However, in this instance the taper in plan (and therefore in section) is regularized (that is, straight) to produce straight lines in both diminishing orientations. The curved cross-section, however, does serve to further articulate the form, with a subtle crease forming where the vertical walls begin to bend towards the ridge. In this example, the complexity comes internally through the necessary integration of domestic utilities and services required to provide a suitable environment for two people.

A long section taken through the house reveals the truth behind the façade that enables this house to function at all, with a full-length sunken pit, approximately 1 metre (3 feet) deep, giving sufficient height at the rear to divide the house into two usable levels. Entering from the street – through a more formalized glass façade – the additional height makes space for an interstitial mezzanine landing that gives visitors a full-length view of the interior. From here, stairs lead down to the principal living areas contained in the pit, and up to the open-mesh metal sleeping deck, which extends the full length of the house and leads to

the tiny garden at the rear.

The sunken pit contains the principal living spaces – or zones – with a living area located beneath the entrance mezzanine. A kitchen is neatly built within the depth of the structural frame at the centre of the plan, and an enclosed bathroom is squeezed into the apex at the rear, complete with a typically oversized Japanese toilet and tapering bath. Here the volume reaches its maximum compression – both in plan and section – as the underside of the sloping platform falls to the rear, giving access to a small postage stamp-sized plot of land, which provides just enough space for a single tree, making it perhaps a contender for Tokyo's smallest garden award.

1 Section A–A

2 Second Floor Plan

1 Bed Loft

3 First Floor Plan

1 Void
2 Entrance Deck

4 Ground Floor Plan

1 Bathroom
2 Kitchen
3 Living Room

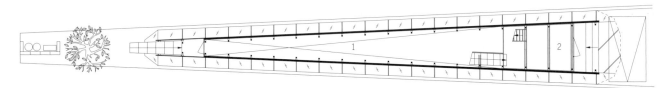

1

2

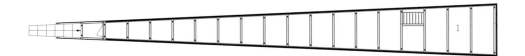

3

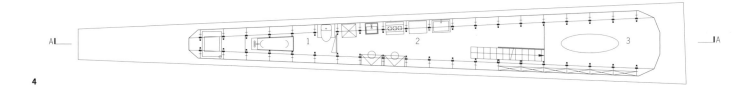

4

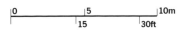

0   5   10m

15   30ft

Terraced Houses

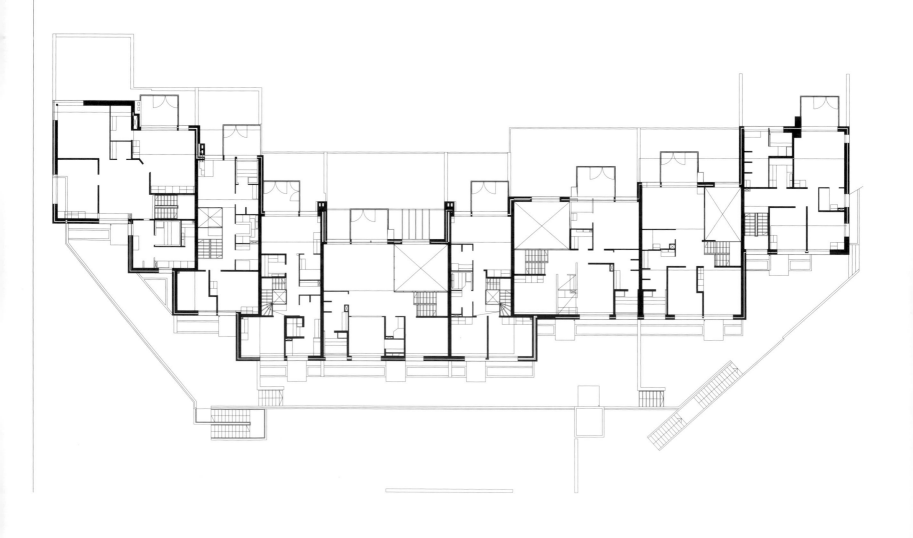

Chimney Pot Park, Shed KM for Urban Splash
Section Model

Of all categories in this book, the terrace arrangement is most directly linked to a specific functional type: the terraced house. As such, the examples in this chapter are all domestic. Unlike linear organizations, terraced arrangements comprise a series of conjoined units that are essentially separate and self-contained, divided by cross-axial party walls. As such, terraced houses unify two modes of planning, being individually planned to optimize space contained between two blank walls, and collectively planned as urban figures that make streets that express the compound effect of each unit.

The origins of large-scale terraced developments date back to the mid-nineteenth century when Britain's speculative housing market first addressed the provision of affordable mass housing in urban areas. Through its widespread application the terrace house endures as one of Britain's most significant contributions to the problem of mass housing. By studying historical plans it is possible to trace advances in their basic spatial configuration, with shifts in the disposition of stairs, services and principal accommodation spaces in relation to the all-important party walls; the essential part of any terrace.

Historically the terrace emerged as one of the most cost-effective and spatially efficient modes of housing. Densely arranged the houses were economic in terms of land and material use, were quick to build, and with relatively low external wall ratios, were easy to keep warm. In comparison with other forms, such as tenements, they were also more desirable, giving even the poorest families an identifiable home, each with its own front door.

The back-to-back house was one of the most basic terraced inventions offering a radical alternative to tenements, and generating a strong sense of community cohesion by being arranged around shared courtyards with a privy at one end and a pump at the other. A more sophisticated solution came with the 'through terrace', which improved the quality of the internal spaces by providing light and access at both front and back. As the most enduring type, the through terrace allowed adaptation and ultimately evolved into the form we are familiar with today. While minimizing the area of exposed wall, maintaining a single-room

Gallaratese Housing Block, Aldo Rossi
Northeast Elevation and Second Floor Plan

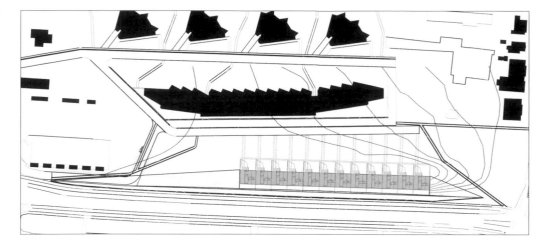

Sound Wall Homes

frontage, the through terraced house exploited the length of the party wall. Two rooms deep, each included a small backyard, an outdoor privy and a back alley, promoting the now commonplace social ritual of having neighbourly exchanges over backyard walls. In a series of staged adaptations, single storey scullery annexes containing a basic sink and a boiler were built across half of the rear wall. These ultimately grew to incorporate the privy (still accessed from outside), and to include more sophisticated kitchens and bathrooms. Third bedrooms could also be added on the upper level, and a final development came with the widening of the floor plans, which provided additional width for a front-to-back passageway and a separate stair; elements that combined to allow the four or five principal rooms to function independently.

For over 150 years, therefore, collective forms of terraces have helped shape our cities, define our streets and provide much-cherished homes. Unsurprisingly they remain an extremely popular housing type. Set within well-proportioned streets, symmetrically scaled and ordered with a pleasing rhythm, the Victorian terraced house continues to provide contemporary solutions, either being adapted within its original form or dramatically remodelled, as exemplified by **Aldo Rossi's Gallaratese Housing Block** in Milan (1969–76) which epitomized his interest in promoting a return to time-honoured urban patterns, and **Shed KM's** recent proposals for Urban Splash in **Chimney Pot Park**, Salford, northern England.

When considering contemporary forms, the practical, economic and social advantages still remain. Often built in more limited numbers on smaller more specific sites, they can be shaped into almost any formal configurations to suit topographical conditions, to turn corners and to contain and shape public spaces. Be they straight, gently graded, staggered or dramatically curvaceous, the best terraced houses continue to provide architects, developers and urban planners with exemplary design solutions, such as those featured in this chapter.

As derivative forms of the archetypal terraced house, variants of the straight terrace still respond to new conditions. The short terrace of single-bedroom houses by **CASA Arkitekter**, for example,

EOS Housing

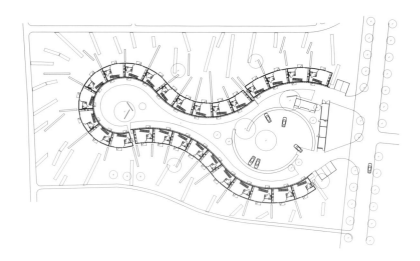

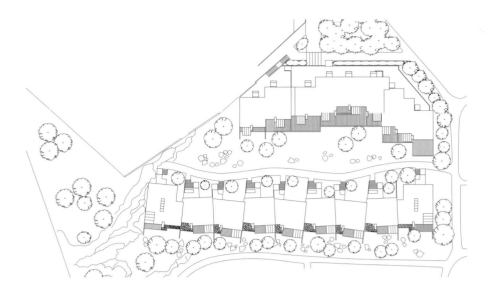

give couples or single occupants an alternative to apartments or studio flats, providing relatively small units with the big-house benefits of front and rear gardens and two floors. **The Sound Wall Homes** by **VHP s+a+l** in Hilversum, the Netherlands, recall the single aspect arrangement of the traditional back-to-back, and demonstrate how a terrace can respond to a found urban condition on a troublesome roadside plot, with a repeated array set with their backs against a wall. **The exhibition houses** by **Architectural Office Marlies Rohmer** apply the notion of the served and servant spaces, by articulating standard cores and flexible living spaces, to produce a distinctive form and staggered streetscape. In contrast to these, three other examples focus on the place-making opportunities

offered by terraces. These are the sinuous **EOS Housing** development in Helsingborg, Sweden by **Anders Wilhelmson**, which demonstrates how terraces with oblique party walls can be planned to create distinctive and unique shared spaces; **DOK architecten's Bastion Island waterside homes** which show how the duality of a terrace can be used to define two contrasting environments; and **Marja-Ritta Norri's** terraces in Finland, which offer a more suburban example on the edge of Helsinki.

Single infill solutions that respond to an increasingly prevalent tendency to redensify the city have also been featured. These are **two houses** by **MVRDV** that demonstrate how ambitious spatial configurations can challenge the apparent constraints of party wall plots; and **Stanley**

Saitowitz's 1028 Natoma Street apartment block in San Francisco, which recalls the format of the so-called 'Tyneside Flat', by neatly inserting four units, one above the next, into a narrow plot that may otherwise have been occupied by a more traditional large town house.

Finally, this chapter also includes **BedZED**, a new type of mixed-use medium-density development by **Bill Dunster Architects**, which demonstrates a new interpretation of the terrace, with a distinctive spatial organization that integrates three units into one cross-sectional arrangement, creating streets and alleyways of its own.

Bastion Island Waterside Homes

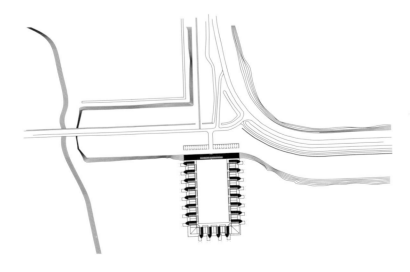

BedZED

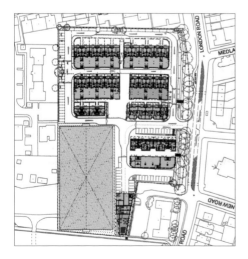

Amtmandsstien

CASA Arkitekter

Naestved, Denmark; 2001

Single-bedroom apartments are commonplace. Single-bedroom houses are less so. In response to this, and to recent shifts in the housing market that reflect an increasing demand for single-bedroom units, this terrace of eight houses in Denmark provides an alternative to the more common flat or studio plan formats. They are by no means small, however. At approximately 125 square metres (1345 square feet), they each provide a spacious alternative for single people or couples looking for something other than gritty open-plan lofts or chic city centre apartments. By creating spacious single-bedroom houses, these homes optimize the utility benefits of small houses, each with front and rear gardens, integrated garages and the big-house feel of two floors.

The form of the terrace is articulated at the front and rear by protrusions. To the front, along the easterly elevation, a series of stair towers gives privacy to the inset sheltered entrances, while to the rear, single-storey pavilions contain living spaces to define more private westerly garden courtyards.

On the ground floor the plan is split in two, front to back, with service and living zones being defined by the length of the integral garage. With this, the lobby, lavatory, stair and garage are neatly contained, leaving a clearly defined L-shaped space for kitchen, dining and living purposes. The fall across the site is also resolved within this division, with a split level being introduced at the base of the stair, further separating the arrival and circulation spaces from the more internal living spaces that sit four steps lower at garden level. A simple kitchen bench extends the service zone on the southerly party wall, and full-height glazing turns the corner of the courtyard, unifying the dining and living spaces and reorienting the internal spaces around more private aspects of the courtyard. The continuation of this glazing around the second more exposed corner offers wider views beyond.

Without the intrusion of the garage, the upper levels are more generously proportioned, with the added benefit of a higher sloping ceiling and a dual aspect arrangement. Two roof terraces are provided: one above the garage which shelters beneath the eaves; the other on the roof of the garden pavilion, providing an excellent vantage point from where to enjoy expansive city views across Naestved.

The benefit of two floors is further exploited by a series of cut-outs in the upper floor. A small light-well at the top of the stair brings light to the stair lobby, and helps resolve the geometry of the bedroom which, by necessity, is deeper and steps out from the adjacent bathroom. A second larger void above the dining room separates the upper living room from the roof terrace, which is then accessed via a simple narrow bridge.

Despite having been built for a very specific market, as with all good homes the units within this terrace are adaptable to changing needs. It is not inconceivable, for example, to imagine a second bedroom being provided directly above the garage, without the loss of the dining room gallery or access to the roof terrace.

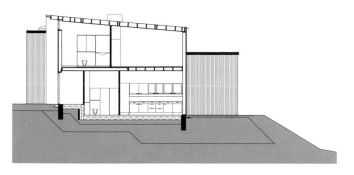

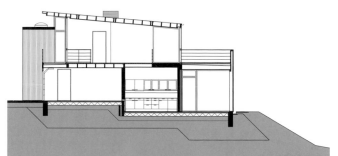

1   Section A–A

2   Section B–B

1

2

3   Northeast Elevation

3

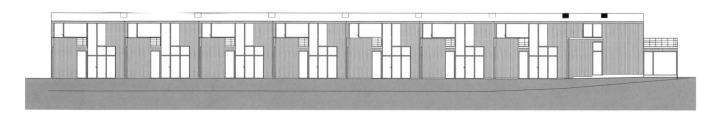

4   Southwest Elevation

4

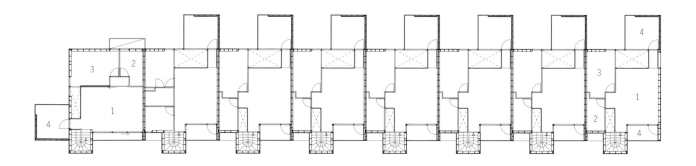

5   First Floor Plan

1   Mezzanine
2   Bathroom
3   Bedroom
4   Roof Terrace

5

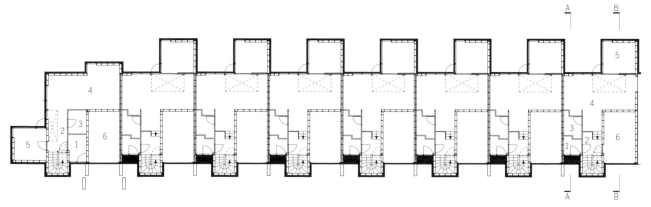

6   Ground Floor Plan

1   Lobby
2   Hall
3   Utility Room/Toilet
4   Kitchen/Living Room
5   Garden Room
6   Garage

6

Sound Wall Homes

VHP s+a+l

Hilversum, The Netherlands; 2001

In today's complex urban environment, it is not uncommon for architects to be asked to produce solutions for unorthodox places. This site in Hilversum is one such case, almost invisible to passing vehicles and effectively buried into the embankment of a busy road. In such instances, the terrace is a useful and adaptable plan form, not only due to its ability to twist, turn and conform to almost any large-scale urban geometry, but also through the philosophy that there is security in numbers. A group of single houses in this location could easily have been dwarfed, being built in such close proximity to a main road, with the knock-on effect of making the residents feel more than a little conspicuous in their homes. In this terrace, however, the units create a very effective united front, joining forces to provide a far more considerable combined physical presence. Through the repetition of elements – bays, structural grids, doors, windows and other motifs – a terrace, even a relatively low terrace like this one, can pack a pretty powerful urban punch. Set against the potentially dominant form of the road, this terrace forms a new wall that is so striking to the eye that you could be forgiven for not noticing the road behind it.

This development has become known as the Sound Wall Homes. Set against two staggered retaining walls, and with solid and inclined roofs, the buildings have been designed to form their own acoustic barriers. The two-storey houses comprise two primary forms: at the lower level a continuous and relatively muted brick plinth is set back to leave as much of the ground as possible untouched; and above there is a more articulate array of trapezoidal cantilevers. The internal functions remain consistent to this formal division, with the plinth containing a deep double garage, two equally sized bedrooms, and a series of utility rooms-cum-bathrooms. In the protruding pavilions above, the principal living spaces are set in front of the master bedroom, en suite bathroom and kitchen.

While the dramatic form of the living spaces may appear somewhat arbitrary and wilful, the introduction of an oblique angle does have its advantages – not only does it visually lighten the cantilevered mass and give each inset terrace as broad a view as possible, but it also gives the windows along the re-entrant façades a valuable, albeit slight, view beyond the terrace and neighbouring properties. The cantilever itself also provides sheltered parking spaces for visitors, and

brings an appropriately dynamic rhythm to the overall composition, with each bay poised like a racing car in the pits.

The playful geometric composition of the terrace extends beyond the limits of the sheltered forecourts, with inlaid tracks providing a vehicular route to each garage across the neat lawn.

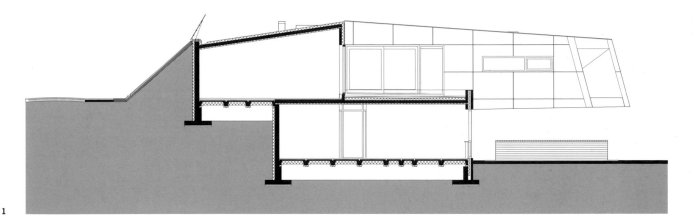

1

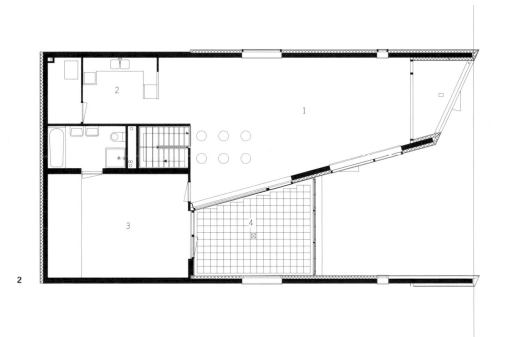

2 **First Floor Plan**

1   Living/Dining Room
2   Kitchen
3   Master Bedroom
4   Terrace

2

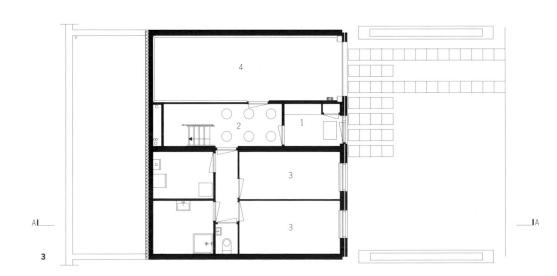

3 **Ground Floor Plan**

1   Lobby
2   Hall
3   Bedroom
4   Garage

A

3

Exhibition Houses

Architectural Office Marlies Rohmer, Amsterdam NL

Almere, The Netherlands; 2001

Expositions have long served as the laboratory of architectural ideas. In 1851, as part of the Great Exhibition, the British architect Henry Roberts produced designs for model homes that were displayed as workable and affordable housing solutions suitable for widespread application in the mass housing market. Seventy-four years later, in 1925, Le Corbusier revealed his Modernist machine for living, which in itself became a design icon. And another 76 years on, at the so-called 'Wild Living' expo in Almere, this terrace of 18 houses by Architectural Office Marlies Rohmer extended this tradition, demonstrating how core and module plans can be used to produce a number of varying sized units set within the coherence and discipline of the terrace form.

The houses are aimed at a market that is increasingly dominated by first-time buyers who cannot easily afford to buy a new home. The concept therefore provides a standardized core for the fixed elements, leaving the majority of the space free to allow each occupant to customize the living spaces to their own needs and within their own means. Each house is divided into two blocks: a solid core contains essential components of the contemporary home; and a double-height volume

provides more flexible space (a concept that was originally envisaged by the architects as a solid chimney stack and plug-in camper van). In reality, the two blocks maintain their individuality. However, they are articulated in a more conventional manner, with the notional permanence of the cores being formally exaggerated in solid masonry blocks, made to look even more ancient with Egyptianesque battered walls. By contrast, and reflecting the notion of flexibility, the living modules take the form of crisp Modernist boxes, sharply detailed with an aluminium glazing system. This arrangement is clearly readable from the outside, with the servant spaces being enclosed with small windows, and the served living spaces being fully glazed and, by contrast, brightly lit and more spacious.

The slate-clad cores are all the same size and appear as an array of towers arranged in a straight line. Between these, the container-like modules vary in width and depth depending on the accommodation required, and extend beyond the face of the cores. Collectively, the shifting modules give the terrace an irregular profile as they step in and out – an informality that is amplified when the hinged shutters are opened in a random and haphazard manner.

Internally, the cores contain a stair, bathroom, toilet, provision for storage and kitchen. They also provide a more conventional lobbied entrance. The modules are then essentially left as open voids, to be fitted out as required by the occupants. These can contain two separate floors, or a mezzanine accessed via the core. With the cores extending to three storeys, roof terraces could easily be incorporated to provide a more private area of external space at a high level.

1 Section A–A   2 Elevation   3 Elevation   4 Second Floor Plan   5 First Floor Plan   6 Ground Floor Plan   83

                                                             1 Bathroom   1 Mezzanine Level   1 Entrance Lobby
  2 Void   2 Hall
  3 Rear Entrance
  4 Kitchen/Living Area

1

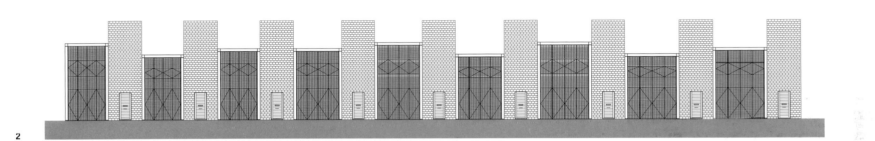

2

3

4

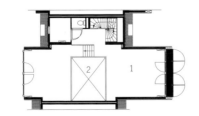

5

6

0   5   10m
         15   30ft

EOS Housing

Anders Wilhelmson

Helsingborg, Sweden; 2002

Terraces don't have to be straight. The graceful terraces of Bristol and Bath demonstrate this fact with an assured elegance with which we are all familiar, and more recently modern masters such as Alvar Aalto and Oscar Niemeyer have developed striking plastic forms. Here is a more modest, but nevertheless equally distinctive, contemporary version; a snaking multiple-curved terrace of 27 houses in Helsingborg, southern Sweden. With just two narrow breaks in plan to provide useful access to the rear gardens, the apparently continuous chain of two-storey units uses its sinuous form to create a number of varied public and private realms. To the front, a communal entrance courtyard provides common ground for co-operative residents and visitors, with two teardrop-shaped spaces linked by a compressed and elongated pinch point; a space that will in time be dominated by three large chestnut trees. To the rear, alternating subterraces use their fully glazed concave and convex façades to give each dwelling its own unique aspect, with each home having a private rear garden. The garden walls shown in plan reflect the radial geometry of the party walls, and closer inspection reveals that each unit is in turn subdivided into three facets that equally dissect the

splayed plans; within this geometric framework a number of variant plan types exist according to the number of bedroom options provided.

Each house uses circulation as a buffer zone set against the more public front wall, within a full-height light-well which contains a simple, straight flight of stairs that helps to geometrically exaggerate the faceted curve of the wall (a geometric relationship of straight against curve that seems better resolved using facets). At the point of entry, the stair landing above sits at its furthest distance from the front elevation, helping in part to define a lobby space between itself and a small lavatory that is set within an otherwise open-plan living area. A kitchen runs along the opposite party wall, adjacent to the base of the stair. Rising upstairs, against the sloping wall that spatially adds to the front/back emphasis as it gently leans towards the garden, the upper floor contains the sleeping areas which can be subdivided as needed. Full-width balconies give views over the gardens.

Ingeniously, plan, section and elevation combine to help create very clear and distinct characteristics of front and back, despite some slightly awkward geometries. This is further optimized by the choice of façades, with the rear

elevations being fully glazed, in contrast to the front elevations which are clad in corrugated Rheinzink®.

1

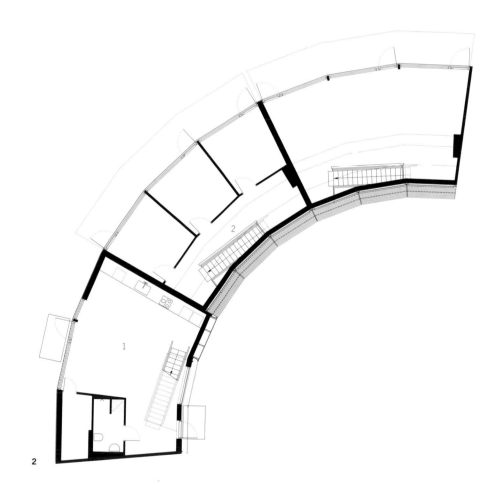

2

Helsinki Terrace

Marja-Ritta Norri

Helsinki, Finland; 2001

These two terraces were built on a partially developed site on the edge of suburban Helsinki. A number of years after work ceased on a large subterranean concrete car park, architect Marja-Ritta Norri was commissioned to design a medium-density housing scheme, with the complication of having to use the bunker-like structure that remained from the previous scheme.

The two terraces are distinct in form, with the northern terrace adhering to the orthogonal geometry of the partially completed car park. In contrast, the southernmost terrace responds more softly to the landscape with a series of cranked plans and splayed party walls. Set apart, the two terraces create a common semiprivate garden that rises gently from east to west. From its constrained entrance at the bottom of the slope, the garden widens to create an informal and unforced sense of place. Both terraces are entered from the north, allowing each of the 17 houses to benefit from private south-facing gardens.

Focusing on the southernmost terrace, the plans are juxtaposed one against the next with a geometric shift that is accommodated within a generous circulation and service core. While the principal accommodation is held within a tightly

planned orthogonal arrangement which is basically square in plan, the entrance, lobby, stair, storage and utility spaces are set within these triangular spaces. The orthogonal accommodation zones are divided into four quarters, allowing each house to be individually planned with either the inclusion of double-height voids or additional bedrooms. A series of simple glazed conservatories then break out from the master bedroom at first-floor level, spanning between the single-storey garden and a single corner column.

The eccentricity in plan is particularly successful, not only in breaking down the formal bulk of the nine-house south terrace but also in helping to define specific external spaces at the front. To the north, low-level garden walls, canopies and small sheds draw out the splayed geometries of the party walls to create a series of contained and defensible forecourts that bring privacy to the sheltered entrances and form a buffer to the shared gardens.

While distinct in layout, the two terraces are unified by a series of common formal motifs. Set upon the plinth of the existing structure (which was retained to provide space for resident parking), the northern terrace creates a series of elevated

gardens, defined by the same language of low-level brick dividing walls, in this case orthogonally oriented. The terraces' distinctive roof lines also share common traits, each being articulated by brick chimneys, rendered brick parapet walls and glazed sun spaces. The net result of this care and rigorous attention to detail has been that the architect has successfully created a unified mid-density housing scheme that, while being geometrically and formally varied in response to site and landscape, offers a wide range of units with 17 unique houses that vary from 136 to 245 square metres (1464 to 2637 square feet).

1 North Elevation

2 South Elevation

3 South Terrace First Floor Plan

4 South Terrace Ground Floor Plan

5 North Terrace First Floor Plan

6 North Terrace Ground Floor Plan

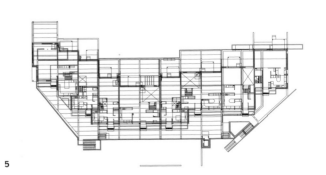

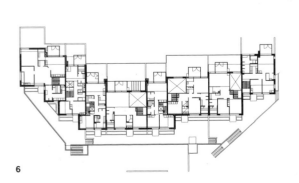

1

2

3

4

5

6

N

0 5 10m
15 30ft

Two houses on Borneo Sporenburg

MVRDV

Amsterdam, The Netherlands; 2000

Traditionally, the terrace house optimizes space by building unit against unit between a series of shared party walls. Private external space is then commonly included to the rear, with street access from the front, and on-street car parking provided where available. On this site, however, these traditional components did not exist.

The site, in the Borneo Sporenburg area of Amsterdam, was recently master-planned by Dutch architects West 8. Each plot is 5 metres (16 feet) wide, 18 metres (59 feet) deep and 12 metres (39 feet) high. By backing each plot directly onto a canal, and by adding the requirement for on-plot parking, the master plan has inspired some highly imaginative modes of reinvention for the traditional terrace typology. These two houses by MVRDV are especially noteworthy in terms of their ingenious manipulation of plan section and elevation, with each providing two distinctive strategic approaches.

Plot 12 is perhaps the most daring, effectively dividing the already narrow plot into two even thinner, equal slivers of accommodation. With the one side of the plot fully occupied over four levels, the other side is left as a void. The four-storey block is bound by two solid end walls that face street and canal, and a fully glazed mid-party wall that bisects

the plot. Within the void, held between the glazed mid-party wall and the adjacent property are two double-height 'bridge blocks'. In plan, the bridging blocks break out from the principal spaces, while in section they are staggered to create a complex arrangement of internal cellular spaces and external terraces. The internal elevations are also extremely well considered, with the length of the four-storey block fully glazed between each of its blind bookend walls, with all internal spaces overlooking the void, addressing the party wall. The four main spaces within the bridging blocks are then each given their own private aspects, with three alternating windows and a skylight. Two external terraces are also provided – one at level four on the roof of the canal-side bridge block, the other semi-sheltered at the level of the canal.

By contrast, plot number 18 conforms to the more traditional orientation for terraced houses, with the accommodation reaching from party wall to party wall. The spatial interest here centres on how voids are cut into the long section, both internally to create double-height spaces, and externally where the canal elevation staggers to create both rooftop and sheltered canal-level external terraces.

Together these ingenious canalside houses are exemplary demonstrations in high-density house planning.

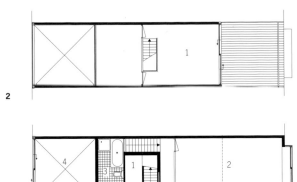

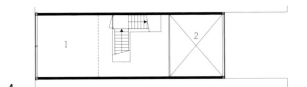

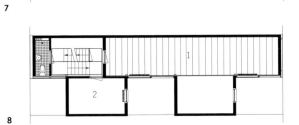

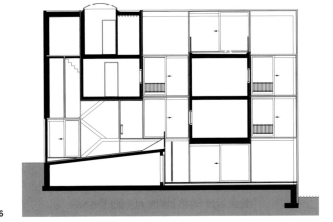

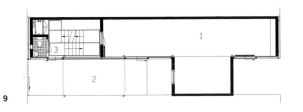

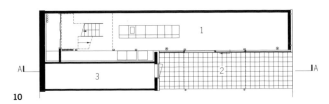

Plot 18

1 Section A–A

2 Third Floor Plan

1   Studio

3 Second Floor Plan

1   Storage
2   Bedroom
3   Bathroom
4   Void

4 First Floor Plan

1   Living Room
2   Void

5 Ground Floor Plan

1   Garage
2   Storage
3   Kitchen
4   Dining Room
5   Sunken Garden
6   Entrance

Plot 12

6 Section A–A

7 Third Floor Plan

1   Living Room/Bedroom
2   Terrace
3   Bathroom

8 Second Floor Plan

1   Studio 2
2   Guest Room

9 Upper Ground Floor Plan

1   Studio 1
2   Car Park
3   Entrance

10 Lower Ground Floor Plan

1   Kitchen/Dining Room
2   Terrace
3   Storage

1028 Natoma Street

Stanley Saitowitz/Natoma Architects

San Francisco, California, USA; 2006

In 1988, Stanley Saitowitz published a number of city portraits in the February issue of the *Architectural Review*. In these paintings he included San Francisco, where he continues to work today in offices that are located in his own purpose-built building at 1022 Natoma Street. Describing San Francisco as a receptive feminine city, his portrait emphasized the manner in which the streets run down the hills, likening them to waterfalls, flowing between the city's street-walls, that step in and out in echelon as a series of slim, vertical façades. Almost 20 years on, Saitowitz continues to work in this context, adding to the distinctive city grain. Over recent years he has produced many ingenious housing developments and this four-unit apartment block is his latest example, rather conveniently situated next door to his office.

1028 Natoma Street gives little away when seen from the street. Comprising two interlocked metallic volumes, it simplifies the form of the traditional San Francisco town house façade with a bay-like protrusion that sits above the street, echoing the offices next door.

The plot is typically narrow and deep measuring 7.6 metres (25 feet) wide by 24.3 metres (79.7 feet) deep. Within this, the plan is divided into even narrower strips, one of which contains shared elements, the other private storage and utilities. The building is served by two staircases that provide access and escape for all levels; one from the street via a lobby, the other directly from the ground-floor parking space. A special lift has also been included, which makes the first-floor apartment wheelchair accessible. Between the stairs is a three-storey light -well that brings light and air deeper into the heart of the plan. Hence, each of the three upper-level apartments has windows on three sides, with views across the city and into the private light-well. In a city where most properties maximize floor areas by extending from party wall to party wall, this is a rare spatial treat. And, while the first-floor apartment does not have a light-well, with the space being used to accommodate the lift and a larger accessible toilet, it does benefit from its proximity to an elevated courtyard to the rear.

Along the length of the other party wall, within a slice that is barely 1 metre (3 feet) wide, are the mechanisms of day-to-day life, including a bathroom (accessed side-on from the sleeping quarters), a toilet and a linear kitchen. The living-wall also includes ample storage space and a fireplace in the living room. With glass sliding screens, all storage areas can be left open or closed, animating the pure form of the single-volume apartment. Above the wall, running along its full length, is a concealed lighting strip that illuminates an uncluttered soffit and, within the space, a single freestanding screen separates areas for living and sleeping.

From the street, the bay window is veiled by a meshed screen of horizontal aluminium rods. While this appears to be opaque in daylight, at dawn and dusk light from inside reveals the proportions of the windows behind. On the ground floor, the entire plot is allocated to parking.

1 Fourth Floor Apartment Plan	2 Elevation	3 First Floor Apartment Plan	4 Section A–A	5 Ground Floor Plan	6 Section B–B
1 Living		1 Bedroom		1 Car Park	
2 Dining		2 Dining		2 Accessible Lift	
3 Bedroom		3 Living			
4 Fireplace		4 Bathroom			
5 Kitchen		5 Toilet			
6 Toilet		6 Kitchen			
7 Bath		7 FIreplace			
8 Shower		8 Accessible Lift			
9 Light-well		9 Rear Garden			

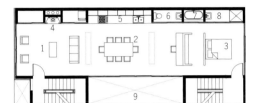

1

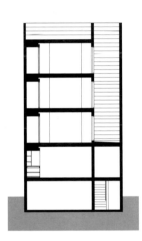

2

3

4

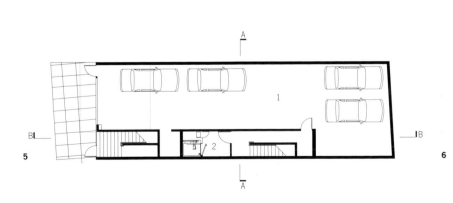

5

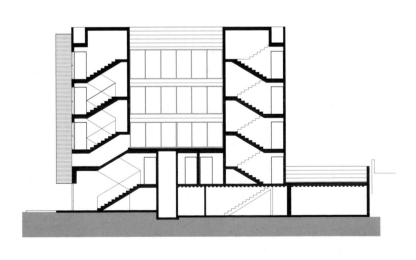

6

BedZED

Bill Dunster Architects

Sutton, UK; 2002

BedZED is the shorthand nickname for the Beddington Zero Energy Development, a medium-density mixed-use live/work development, with communal health, nursery and activity spaces, as well as a site-wide combined heat and power plant. As an exemplary prototype for successful suburban urbanization, the development was built for the Peabody Trust (one of the UK's largest housing associations), and was designed to set new standards in density and energy consumption. In a hostile market, the design team was keen to beat the commercial developers at their own game by adopting their language and currency – the outcome being the creation of an award-winning sustainable community district that provides the same dwelling density as adjacent speculative developments, but with a 35 per cent increase in space provision.

In the simplest of terms the success of this development comes from the ingenious and inventive use of the cross-section. Defined by solar access criteria, a few simple ground rules dictate that dwellings face south and workshops face north. Four variant terraces were developed across the site, with each unit having its own entrance and external garden, and within this the two principal

terraces at the southernmost end of the site deserve closer scrutiny.

In order to maintain solar access to the adjacent properties, each terrace rises north to south from one to three storeys. This accounts for the wedge-shaped form that rises with a slope before culminating in a gently curved roof at its highest point. Within this curious silhouette are three self-contained units. To the north is a split-level live/work workshop, accessed via a mews, which is kept as narrow as possible within the limits of solar access criteria. To the south of the terrace are two dwellings – a two-storey three-bedroom maisonette, which is accessed via a south-facing garden, and a one-bedroom loft apartment accessed via a so-called 'sky garden' which is reached by climbing an external stair from the mews. As an ingenious formal twist, the lower sky garden is linked to the adjacent terrace by a bridge, maintaining the garden-for-all-units rule for the properties accessed directly from the mews. Needless to say, the cross-section is also articulated by a number of distinctive passive environmental devices, including fully glazed solar buffer zones to the south, super-insulated walls and roofs, and the distinctive chimney cowls that assist

passive wind-driven ventilation for all three units.

The development has been extremely well received, and there have been calls for it to be replicated on other suburban sites. It is not only architecturally and spatially innovative, but also represents what the architect describes as the process of using planning gain to facilitate carbon trading; in other words, not only enjoying the social and environmental benefits of a 24-hour diverse live/work community, but also increasing the development potential and revenue necessary to offset the front-loaded costs associated with constructing carbon neutral buildings.

BedZED provides approximately 100 homes, 400 rooms and 100 jobs per hectare.

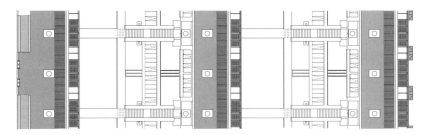

1

1 Section A–A

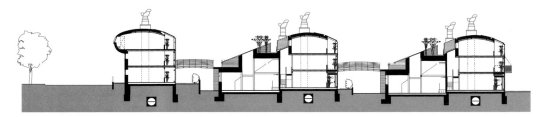

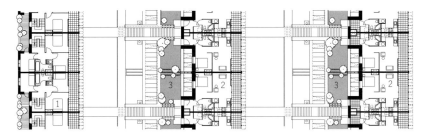

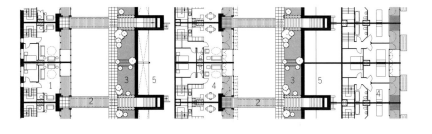

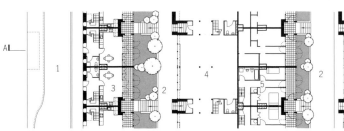

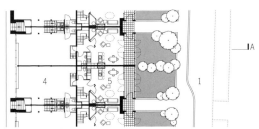

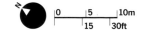

2

2 Roof Plan

3

3 Second Floor Plan

1 Town House
2 1 Bedroom Flat
3 Sky Garden

4

4 First Floor Plan

1 Town House
2 Bridge to Sky Garden
3 Sky Garden
4 3 Bedroom Maisonette
5 Void over Workspace

5

5 Ground Floor Plan

1 Street
2 Access Mews
3 Town House
4 Workspace
5 3 Bedroom Maisonette

0   5   10m
15   30ft

Stacked Plans

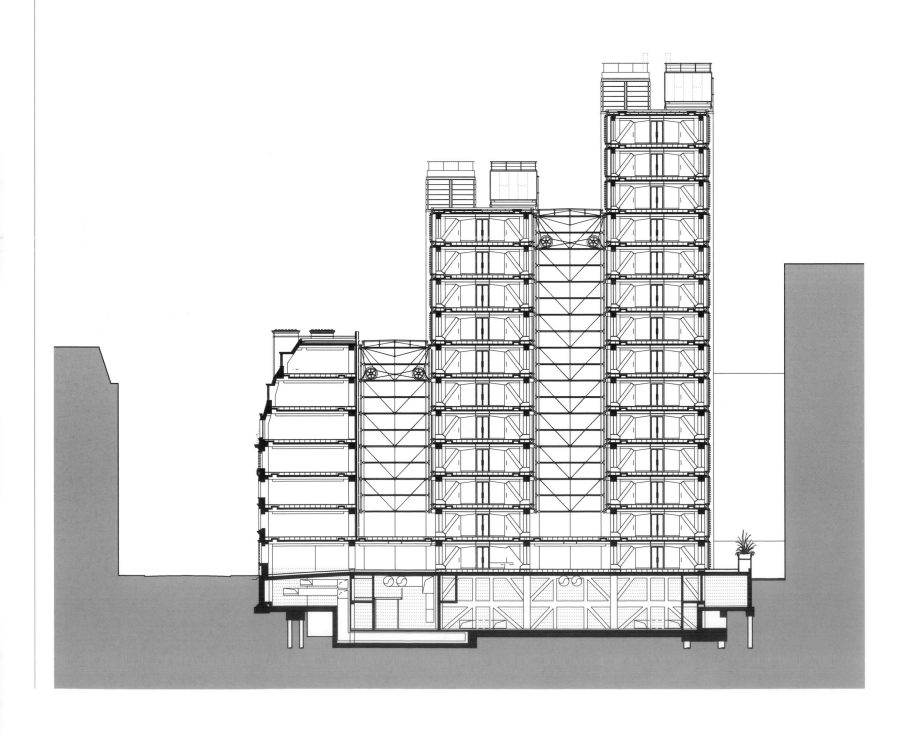

Hong Kong and Shanghai Bank,
Foster + Partners
Façade and East–West Section

Set within the ancient history of architecture, tall buildings are a relatively new phenomenon. Following the Chicago Fire of 1871, when the City's Common Council banned the building of wooden structures within the city limits, the first steel-framed skyscraper rose in technological defiance in 1885, when Major William Le Baron Jenney built the now demolished nine-storey Home Insurance Building. (A building that subsequently rose to 11 storeys in 1891.) Over the past century high-rise buildings have spread further across the world, and the race to build ever higher still continues to occupy the minds of ambitious developers architects and engineers. At the time of writing the tallest building is Taipei 101, with 101 storeys that reach to an astonishing 508 metres (1666 feet).

This, however, is soon to be dwarfed by the building set to be the world's next tallest structure, the Burj Dubai which, while the official details have not been confirmed and will remain secret, is anticipated to reach at least 800 metres (2625 feet). With the built-in potential to increase this height, in order to see off any competitors who may try to seize the imaginary prize, unofficial estimates predict that the final height could rise as high as 940 metres (3084 feet), which is likely to take the building well beyond its proposed completion date of 2008.

Size, of course, is not the most important issue in great buildings, and in the middle of the twentieth century a number of distinguished architects and developers turned their attention to mid-rise towers. Based on the now ubiquitous

podium and tower model, these included buildings such as SOM's 21-storey Lever House of 1950, and Mies van der Rohe's 37-storey Seagram Building completed four years later (both in New York). With less need for the significant reinforcement that gave traditional skyscrapers their staggered silhouettes, with at times fussy clustered forms that braced the tallest skyscraping elements, the podium and tower format was simpler in form and produced refined and elegant buildings that were more sympathetic to the principles of the Modern Movement. Such buildings also made more of an impact on the city's public realm, with podia addressing, defining and serving street-level activity. More recently, in 1979, **Foster + Partners** began work on the **Hong Kong and Shanghai Bank**, which

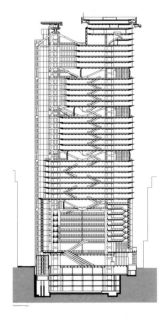

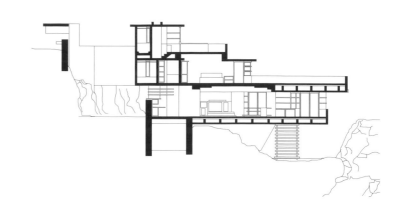

Fallingwater, Frank Lloyd Wright
Façade and Section

was considered by many to be a reinvention of the high-rise, eliminating central core configurations in favour of externalized service risers that gave the building a vertical order, complemented by a new horizontal order governed by atria and intermediate sky gardens.

In response to the sophistication of this later generation of mid- to high-rise buildings, therefore, avoiding the lure of brash and overblown structures that join other contenders for the world's tallest, the high-rise buildings in this chapter are those that respond more specifically to contemporary architectural and urban obligations. These include **Foster + Partners' 30 St Mary Axe**, a revolutionary 41-storey office building with a distinctive diagrid structure that gives form to the building's ambitious

passive ventilation strategy; **Ateliers Jean Nouvel's Torre Agbar**, an equally expressive, but fundamentally different landmark building in Barcelona; and **Carme Pinós'** dramatic **Torre Cube** in Guadalajara, Mexico, which mixes angular and curvaceous forms to create a series of interconnected internal and external environments.

Apart from these, however, the category of stacked plans does not only relate to tall buildings. The category also considers buildings in which the interrelationship between a series of stacked plans is the significant factor, and as such could be applied to buildings that are as few as five, four or even three storeys high. In Le Corbusier's Unité d'Habitation in Marseilles, for example, the relationship between three stacked plans unlocks

the spatial and operational potential for the whole mid-rise housing block, with six central circulation corridors each of which serves two interlocked duplex units that sit together in an elongated yin/yang configuration. Similarly **Frank Lloyd Wright's Fallingwater**, built in 1937 on the edge of a waterfall in Pennsylvania's Allegheny Mountains, also demonstrates the spatial and formal potential of manipulating horizontal planes one above the other. In this chapter therefore, projects have been sought that employ a similar level of spatial ingenuity in section as well as in plan.

Steven Holl Architects' Simmons Hall in Massachusetts, for example, is a not dissimilar proposition to Le Corbusier's Unité, providing 350 units of accommodation in a mid-rise linear block.

30 St Mary Axe

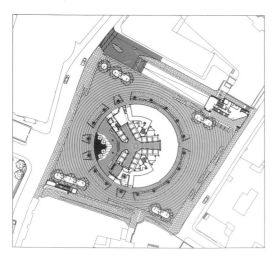

Simmons Hall

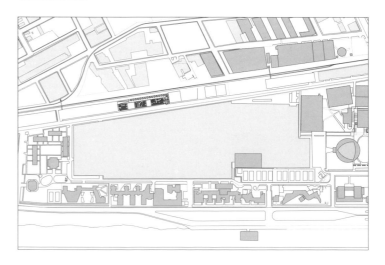

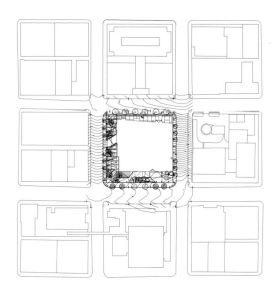

In organization, however, Holl employs a completely different tactic, imaginatively enlivening and reinventing the traditional slab block circulation. Likewise, **Toyo Ito's Sendai Mediatheque** in Japan links a series of stacked plans with a number of fully expressed forms that ingeniously and efficiently service the structure and connect all levels. Within this subcategory, **David Chipperfield Architects and b720 Arquitectos'** hospitality building for the **America's Cup** in Valencia is perhaps the most overt expression of stacked (and staggered) plans, with four platforms connected by stairs and ramps that create a building that is the epitome of simplicity in plan, section, elevation and detail, and which in composition recalls the preoccupations of Le Corbusier.

Working within sensitive contexts also impacts on how stacked plans are arranged, as was the case with **Richard Rogers Partnership's Lloyd's Register of Shipping**, where three narrow towers of accommodation step down in response to rights to light and building conservation constraints, while maintaining the practice's trademark formation of clustered towers of office and service space with interstitial atria.

The chapter concludes with four unique projects that make the most of their vertical arrangement of space, with **OMA's Seattle Library**, which derives its eccentric form by transforming a bar chart into a cross-sectional diagram of a building; **Atelier Bow-Wow's** own home/office, which neatly arranges multiple levels on a tight Tokyo site; **Jo Crepain's**

creative reuse of a redundant water tower in Belgium; and most oddly of all, perhaps, **Zechner & Zechner's Air Traffic Control Tower** at Vienna Airport, which is also part podium office building and part landmark light sculpture.

Lloyd's Register of Shipping

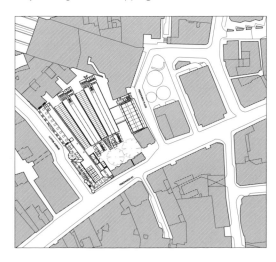

House & Atelier Bow-Wow

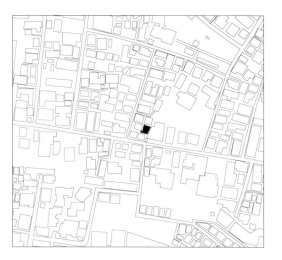

30 St Mary Axe

Foster + Partners

London, UK; 2004

With big buildings come big statistics, and Foster + Partners' Swiss Re headquarters at 30 St Mary Axe is no exception. Ten thousand tonnes of steel support 41 floors that reach to a height of 180 metres (591 feet), clad in 24,000 square metres (258,334 square feet) of glass in more than 5000 pieces, enclosing approximately 46,500 square metres (half a million square feet) of office space – and all this within a relatively small 0.57 hectare (1.4 acre) site. As a new City icon it also has an extremely large presence – as the first high-rise to be built in the City since 1979, it was quickly adopted as the City's number one landmark, frequently featuring in advertisements, music videos and even Hollywood blockbusters.

As an example of stacked planning, the building should also rank highly due to its use of concentrically stacked circular floor plans and spiralling segmental light-wells. It has much in common with Foster + Partners' earlier City Hall [see pp. 30–31] with the geometry of every level differing from the next, and with its distinctive form being justified on environmental grounds. Unlike City Hall, however, where the integration of structure, skin and fit-out was less successfully resolved, at 30 St Mary Axe there is an order and

logic that exhibits none of the former's discomfort and forced formal tensions.

30 St Mary Axe is defined by a distinctive diagrid structure of 36 steel columns that spiral to form an independent self-bracing lattice. This in turn establishes a framework for the environmental and operational strategy of the building, and also rather neatly provides a clear order for the resolution of the complex multicurved façade. Each floor is broken down into 72 five-degree modules, with alternate bays clad with one of two diamond-shaped glazing units: the first being a flat single diamond that spans from floor to floor; the second being split and folded into two triangles to help shape the building's gentle entasis.

In section, incremental variations in the diameter of the floor plates give the building its cigar-like profile, increasing from 50 metres (164 feet) wide on the first floor, to the 57 metre (187 foot) wide 'waist' on level 17, before diminishing to the 25 metre (82 foot) wide private dining room on the 40th floor. And, internally, floors are organized in groups of two and six, linked by the internal light-wells that are integral to the building's ambitious natural ventilation strategy.

While, for commercial reasons, the building

had to offer a base condition of mechanical ventilation, it was designed to exploit pressure-assisted natural ventilation. Optimizing the pressure differential created as wind accelerates around its curved form, spiralling atria were designed to effectively cut across high and low pressure zones to create an internal pressure gradient. This would in turn increase the stack effect within six-pack light-wells, and promote cross-ventilation within the more compressed two-pack zones.

While in terms of pure floor area 30 St Mary Axe may not be the most efficient in terms of space-planning for commercial office space, the internal environment is unique and distinctive, with six orthogonal office domains laid out on a 1.5 metre (5 foot) planning grid between each of the six light-wells.

1

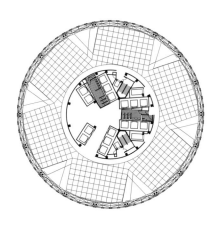

2

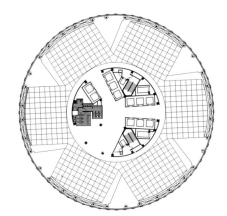

3

4

1   Fortieth Floor Plan

2   Twenty-First Floor Plan

3   Sixth Floor Plan

4   Section
    (core omitted for clarity)

N

0   5   10m
  15   30ft

Torre Agbar

Ateliers Jean Nouvel

Barcelona, Spain; 2005

Despite its apparent similarity to Foster + Partners' 30 St Mary Axe in London, Ateliers Jean Nouvel's Torre Agbar is a very different building. Direct comparisons are, of course, unavoidable, as both buildings are conspicuous icons for their cities, attracting both criticism and praise. If fully explored, comparisons can also serve as a useful framework for analysis.

Unlike Foster's highly articulated extraskeletal diagrid structure, Nouvel's Torre Agbar is initially a 25-storey high cast-concrete shell. With parallel sides, the floor plans are of a regular shape and size, with the building only changing shape when the plan diminishes above level 25. Here the building changes from concrete to steel, with a six-storey asymmetrical cap that hints at the building's inherent and subtle eccentricity. Unlike the Foster building which stacks a series of differently sized circular plans concentrically, one above the other, to create its distinctive cigar-like silhouette, the Nouvel building is eccentric in plan as well as in vertical section. Externally, this eccentricity gives the building a subtle directionality that responds well to its specific position in the cityscape, located as it is on a prominent site at the intersection of Barcelona's Diagonal and Plaça de les Glòries.

Internally, with an offset core, it also divides the floor plates asymmetrically, creating different domains and offering scope for alternative workspace configurations.

With 31 floors (plus three technical plant rooms), the Torre Agbar is 142 metres (472 feet) high, 36 metres (118 feet) lower than Foster's London tower. The most surprising statistic, however (and such buildings are often defined by statistics), relates to its relative slenderness, with the Spanish tower being four-fifths the height of its British rival, but containing only half its volume. Where the so-called 'erotic gherkin' broadens from 50 metres (164 feet) on the first floor, to 57 metres (187 feet) on level 17, before diminishing to 25 metres (82 feet) wide private dining room on the 40th floor, the Torre Agbar is 39 metres (128 feet) at its widest point. This has a significant impact on the environmental qualities of its internal spaces which are ventilated and lit in an entirely different manner to the Foster building, facilitated by its relatively shallow plan depth. Unlike 30 St Mary Axe which makes ambitious and, as yet, unsubstantiated claims to exemplary environmental performance, Torre Agbar is a far less sophisticated building. Heat gains and glare are eliminated by

dramatically reducing the amount of glazing in the façade, and cross-ventilation is simply enabled through 4400 opening windows that pepper its concrete skin. Furthermore, with the concrete remaining exposed within the offices, it also serves as an excellent thermal moderator.

The disposition of the windows gives the tower its unique visual identity, setting single and clustered square openings within a brightly coloured pixelated composition. With the concrete sheathed in a ribbed aluminium skin which is, in turn, cloaked by a layer of glass louvres, the building has been described by Nouvel as 'a fluid mass that has perforated the ground – a geyser under a permanent calculated pressure'. In reality, however, this vision only really occurs in certain lighting conditions when the building does appear to fade into a mist-like apparition.

1 Level 31 Director's Office Plan

1 Entrance
2 Directors' Dining Room
3 Dining Room
4 Office

2 Level 25 VIP Club Plan

1 Entrance
2 Lounge
3 Storage
4 Bar

3 Typical Office Plan

1 Vestibule
2 Waiting Area
3 Meeting Room
4 Coffee Corner
5 Toilets

4 Section A–A

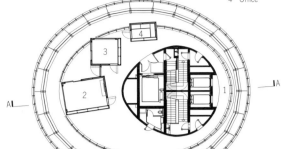

1

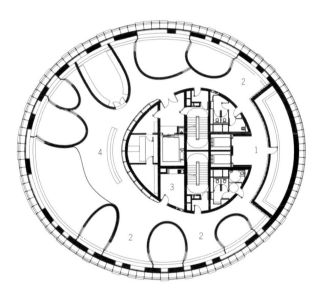

2

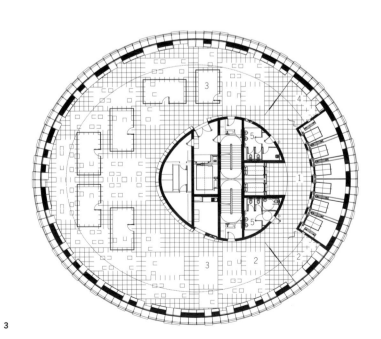

3

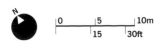

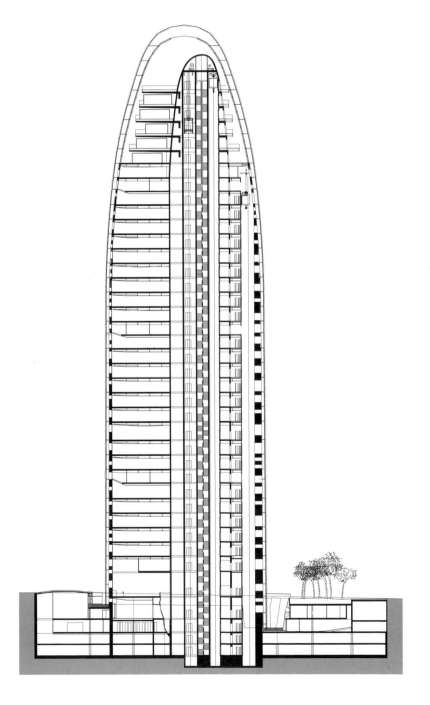

4

Torre Cube

Carme Pinós

Guadalajara, Mexico; 2006

Breaking with planning conventions and standardized types is not easily justified when designing mid- to high-rise office buildings. Where each square metre converts into valuable currency, there are very good reasons why standardized office towers are composed in the manner they are, as issues of efficiency – material, structural and organizational – dictate floor plates, the position and capacity of cores, and the all-important net-to-gross ratios. This distinctive new office tower in Mexico, however, by Spanish architect Carme Pinós, is by no means conventional. Situated within a newly urbanized district to the north of Guadalajara (Mexico's second largest city), the building is at once audaciously iconic, with its striking stature and silhouette, and sensitively subtle in how it is planned and through the attention to details, with delicate timber screens and crisp poured-in-place concrete.

With three massive cores that serve and support the chamfered wedges of accommodation, the tower rises to 16 storeys and is organized around a vertiginous central open-air void. Daringly expressed as timber-clad volumes, each cantilevered segment provides three different floor plate sizes (106, 127 and 200 square metres/1141, 1367 and 2153 square feet), with the smallest two being split in the vertical to form triple-height roof terraces at levels two and five. Within this structure, the architect has been able to create two distinct environments, transforming the notion of the workplace and adding further potency to this unique office building.

Full-height glazing at the perimeter maximizes daylight penetration and creates specific directional views. This glazing is in turn cloaked by delicate timber screens that not only bring warmth to the composition, to complement the otherwise robust quality of the concrete, but also give each occupant the ability to control their own environment by operating sliding screens from a series of precarious interstitial balconies. Through both the disposition of materials and the geometry of tapering floor plates, the open and expansive nature of the perimeter sits in stark contrast to the sheltered core at the centre of the plan, thereby creating two distinct environments for the occupants to overlook. In composition, too, a further tension exists between the fluidity of the concrete and the sharp formality of the timber, as the gently radiused cores (that never quite meet on axis) create a cavernous interior seen in contrast to

the formal directness of the tower's angular exterior.

Through the disposition of its parts, the building is inherently flexible, suiting a wide variety of tenants and allowing multiple users to occupy single segments or entire blocks. Either by remaining autonomous and self-contained within a single floor plate, or by occupying multiple segments and levels, the cores bring both autonomy and unity. Likened to huge tree trunks, the cores also heighten the tension between interior and exterior with only limited views being offered through slot windows that articulate the junction between concrete and timber.

1 Section A–A	2 Section B–B	3 Typical Floor Plan	4 Foyer/Upper Ground Floor Plan	5 Ground Floor Plan
		1 Office Space	1 Entrance Stair	1 Office Space
		2 Light-well	2 Foyer	
			3 Office Space	

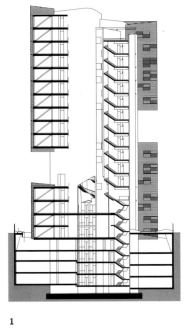

1

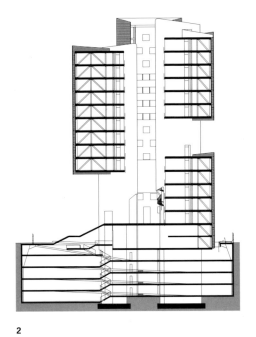

2

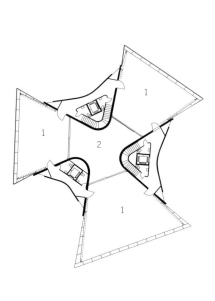

3

4

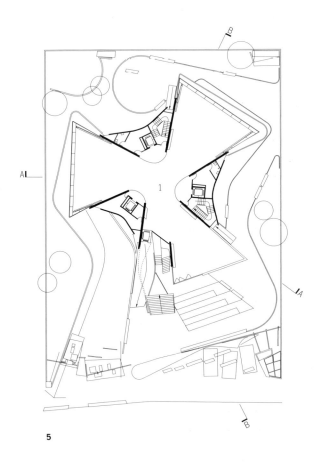

5

0 5 10m
15 30ft

Simmons Hall

Steven Holl Architects

Cambridge, Massachusetts, USA; 2002

Slab blocks have traditionally received a bad press, externally for their repetitive and bland formal dominance, and internally for their apparently endless and poorly lit internal corridors. At more than 100 metres (328 feet) long and 10 storeys high, this building could have suffered the same gloomy syndrome. Steven Holl Architects, however, have succeeded in designing a radical alternative; firstly through the distinctive composition of the building's exterior and, secondly, by imaginatively enlivening and reinventing the traditional slab-block pattern of circulation.

Simmons Hall provides accommodation for 350 students at the Massachusetts Institute of Technology (MIT). It also contains a number of communal spaces, such as a large performance space, dining areas (both inside and outside), computer and photo labs, and music, games and study rooms. Set towards the western edge of the MIT campus – which boasts buildings by Eero Saarinen, Alvar Aalto, Frank Gehry and Charles Correa – Holl's potentially imposing slab block has been given its distinctive shape by two techniques of formal erosion. Externally, these erosions are orthogonal, removing vast chunks of the waffle-like façade to produce deep insets, entrance porches

and two generous open-air roof terraces. Internally, by contrast, the erosions are more fluid, with a series of vertical crevasses that link up to five levels at a time and that bring light deep into the plan from high-level rooflights.

In contrast to the building's crisp exterior, which is clad in aluminium panels, the interiors appear to be formed from molten concrete that has melted and oozed its way down through the vertical section. Rough-cast and apparently unrelated to the building's otherwise modular grid, these cave-like interiors expand and contract in section, and contain a number of additional programmatic functions, such as a the performance space that extends from the basement to the first floor, a double-height study space on the second floor, and group lounges on the subsequent upper levels. The principal stair from the main foyer is also set in cast concrete, and has a similarly sinuous form.

In section, the vertiginous crevasse-like spaces are seen to cut across the plan to create dramatic diagonal figures. These clash with the building's orthogonal structure and playfully impose themselves on the corridors, as their rough-cast external faces sit eccentrically, like brooding masses, within the rather orthodox and otherwise

bland linear corridors. Externally, when these curious molten forms meet the skin, curvaceous apertures are formed as diagonal cones meet vertical walls, unbalancing the regularity of the otherwise relentless waffle-slab module.

Externally, this vertical waffle has been articulated with colour, with each reveal being crisply framed with aluminium in blue, green, yellow, orange or red, which has the effect of reducing the monotony of repetition. Internally, this biaxial order is revealed throughout, with each of the study-bedrooms typically relating to nine modules, three wide and three high, with single-occupancy rooms grouped in pairs around a small threshold with space storage and access to a shared bathroom.

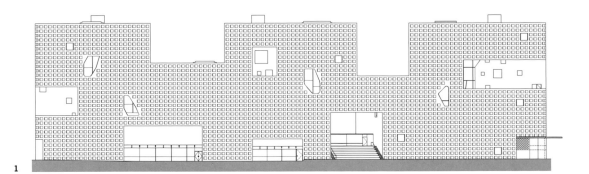

1

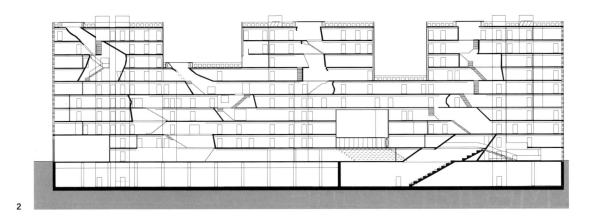

2

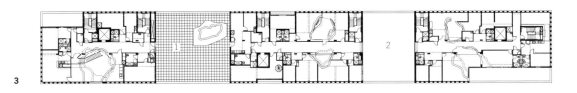

3

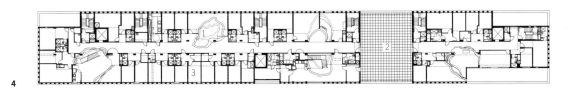

4

5

A

A

6

0   5   10m
15   30ft

Sendai Mediatheque

Toyo Ito

Sendai, Japan; 2001

The Sendai Mediatheque by Toyo Ito is a rare example of a building that is as clear in its final built form as it was when published as a competition-winning strategy. With an enduring conceptual clarity, it is composed of three base elements – 'plate', 'tube' and 'skin' – that collectively accommodate the requirements of a ground-breaking and incredibly complex multi-functional brief. At the time of its inception, the Mediatheque was a new building type that has since been replicated in many other cities around the world. With the architect's underlying intention to destroy the conventional archetypes of civic buildings, the Mediatheque contains a series of complementary, yet highly individual, programmes.

At Sendai the brief proposed a gallery-cum-library-cum-visual media centre; functions that would traditionally be serviced within discrete, individual and, at times, highly formulaic building types. After apparently endless and inconclusive post-competition discussions with user groups and citizens, the architect concluded that the focus of the concept did not need to change – a concept that prioritized flexibility over architectural formalism. While potentially contradictory, Toyo Ito's approach was to establish a highly specific

architectural framework, the so-called hardware, that would have a formal order and logic within itself without prejudicing how each part of the building would eventually be used. The plate/tube/skin strategy is an excellent example of how a strong attitude to formal determinism can paradoxically help unlock and accommodate indeterminate and highly changeable future functions without reverting to a soulless, bland, empty and structurally regularized box. So, with a strong formal proposal at Sendai, the architect addressed head-on the challenge of how to create an appropriate piece of architectural hardware that would be inherently flexible and culturally appealing.

Considered in plan, section and elevation, the three elements are mutually reliant. The plates are expressed as a series of six square slabs, creating recognizably similar, yet separate and distinctive, domains of accommodation; the tapering tubes pierce the plates and act as oversized conduits of spatial, structural and servicing continuity; and the skin that envelops them all reveals the five principal slab edges and the 13 fishnet-like tubes beyond. The four largest tubes situated at the corners of the plates provide the principal means of support and bracing, while of the nine smaller tubes, five are

straight and contain lifts, while the rest are crooked and carry ducts. The tubes conform to the obvious analogies with trees and nature, providing clear and logical means of support and acting as the vehicles for the flow of information, energy and vertical movement. While future cellularization of space would not be desirable, each floor plate is extremely flexible, and through the integration of structure and services is also extremely efficient with little hidden or lost interstitial space. Ito himself likened the space to a liquid and saw the tubes as strands of seaweed drifting through a glazed aquarium.

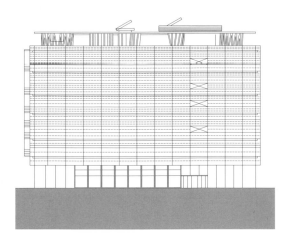

1

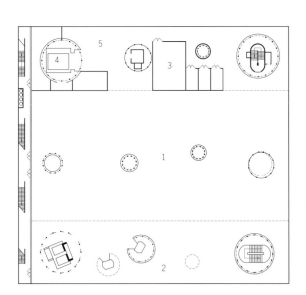

2

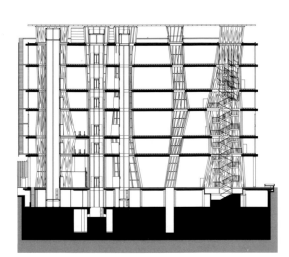

3

4

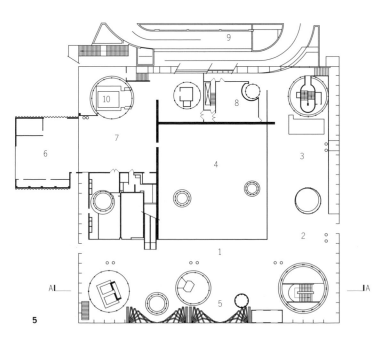

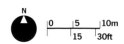

N

0 5 10m
15 30ft

5

America's Cup Building – Veles e Vents

David Chipperfield Architects and b720 Arquitectos

Valencia, Spain; 2006

Good things don't come exclusively to those who wait, as demonstrated to maximum effect by this fine building in Valencia, designed and built in less than a year by the methodical British architect David Chipperfield. Working in collaboration with the Barcelona-based practice b720, the designers had to think quickly, and in many ways the lack of time eliminated any opportunity for unnecessary deliberation. The outcome significantly surpassed the original design brief for a series of VIP lounges and boutiques to pamper the fraternity of the 32nd America's Cup. Instead, by extending the brief to achieve something more significant for the city, Chipperfield and his associates promoted the opportunity to use the building to break down the sort of elitist barriers that often surround sports like sailing. This egalitarian approach soon won support from the America's Cup management company and the city of Valencia consortium, resulting in what is essentially a huge harbourside foyer, with largely free access for all.

Conceived and arranged as a series of stacked and staggered decks, the building is the epitome of simplicity in both plan and detail, and in composition can be read as a summary of two of Le Corbusier's most celebrated and enduring

preoccupations, being part Domino House derivative and part ocean-going liner. With four deep steel decks supported on four cores, the principal objective was to maximize spectator comfort by compressing shaded views between generous overhanging terraces. With 60 per cent of the floor area given over to external viewing decks, the balance between boutique and public realm was suitably adjusted, allowing both ground and first floors to be fully accessible to the public. This not only allowed the so-called V-VIPs to be elevated even higher – which no doubt was a popular outcome – but also improved the experience for anyone who happened to be passing along the broad esplanade that neatly houses two levels of car parking.

The four cores are easily discernible in plan and section, with two glass and two sloping steel enclosures that extend through the building's full height. Between these compositional fixes other enclosures are neatly and simply inserted where required, providing internalized space suitable for sheltered seating, eating and drinking – and, of course, the odd luxury boutique or two.

Despite the limited time on site, with occasional signs of rushed workmanship here and

there, the building maintains a very refined quality, and serves as a fitting pronouncement of the Modernist dictate 'less is more'. An issue that is proudly underlined is the architect's claim that the pavilion was built from just six details with six materials. Fact or fiction? It need not matter as this building is certainly the undisputed winner of the 2006 fast-track race – driven by adrenalin, fit for purpose as it crosses the line, and spectacular in more ways than one.

1 Section A–A	2 Third Floor Plan	3 Second Floor Plan	4 First Floor Plan	5 Ground Floor Plan
	1 Foredeck Restaurant	1 Louis Vuitton Lounge	1 Access Ramp	1 Lobby
	2 Kitchen	2 America's Cup Lounge	2 Spectator Deck	2 Bar
	3 Wellness	3 Consorcio Valencia 2007 Lounge	3 Public Deck	3 Restaurant
	4 Foredeck Restaurant Terrace	4 Louis Vuitton Boutique	4 Louis Vuitton Boutique	4 Kitchen
	5 Reception		5 America's Cup Boutique	5 Back of House
	6 Foredeck Club		6 Bar	6 Storage

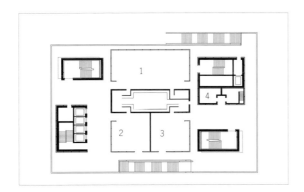

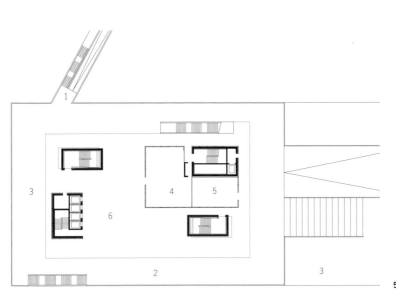

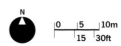

Lloyd's Register of Shipping

Richard Rogers Partnership

London, UK; 2000

The City of London is no stranger to innovative office buildings. Within its uniquely haphazard and largely unplanned medieval grain, it hosts some of the country's most celebrated commercial office buildings, with designs by Richard Seifert, James Stirling, Richard Rogers and Norman Foster. Even Mies van der Rohe produced a design, but sadly this never left the drawing board. Among these, Richard Rogers can be seen to have developed his own distinctly recognizable aesthetic which, deriving from his first significant building in the City, articulates the office type as a vertical organization of discrete functional elements. By separating each element into towers, office floor plates, escape stairs, service risers, scenic lift stacks and sanitary units, the Lloyd's of London building (1986) was one of the first significant office buildings in the world to derive its form from a plug-in notion of prefabrication and machine-age articulation. Like the Beaubourg (the Pompidou Centre), its externalized services left internal volumes free for flexible and changeable use, and brought British High-tech deep into the heart of the City.

Rogers has since adapted this formula to a number of unique sites, with its elemental composition able to adjust to the idiosyncrasies of almost any urban condition. The Lloyd's Register of Shipping is one of a number of Rogers' buildings that has exemplified this technique.

Unlike other showy office buildings, this building yields sensitively to its context, fitting in and adjusting its geometry according to the historic buildings that surround it. Located deep within an existing city block, it is accessed through an intimate courtyard, reached by an historic passageway. From the street, the building gives little away, with Rogers' distinctive lift shafts only visible above the parapets from certain angles. It is not until visitors cross the threshold into the forecourt that the full extent of the building is tangible, rising dramatically over 14 storeys, with two slender towers of accommodation.

In plan, the building comprises three ranges of office accommodation, one of which sits behind a retained façade. Between each range are two atria that support the building's lighting and ventilation strategies. With a slight taper in both office and atria plan, the five-fingered assemblage fans out to fill the site and to resolve the eccentric shape of the plot. At the back of each range are two service cores, containing escape stairs and toilets. To the front, facing the intimate forecourt, two of Rogers' trademark lift and stair towers flank an entrance that leads up to an upper-ground-floor lobby. Identical in their orientation, and avoiding the formal tendency to frame the entrance with symmetrical clusters, the cores contain four fully glazed scenic lifts and a glass and steel stair. When occupied and activated, these elements bring a perpetual dynamism to the façade, following the apparently ceaseless movement of office staff within. In section, the building responds to its sensitive context by stepping up from seven to 11 to 14 storeys.

1 Twelfth Floor Plan	2 Fifth Floor Plan	3 Section A–A	4 Ground Floor Plan	5 Section B–B
	1 Atrium		1 Passage	
	2 Floor Plate		2 Courtyard	
			3 Entrance	
			4 Floor Plate	

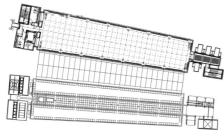

1

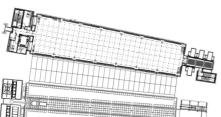

2

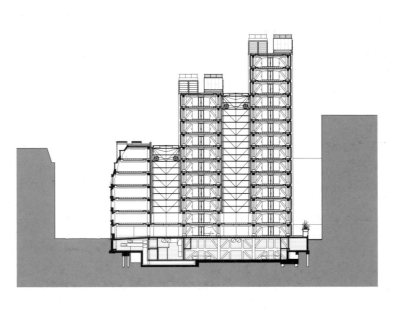

3

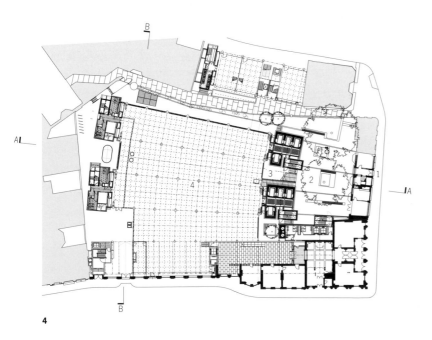

4

5

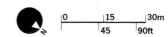

0	15	30m
	45	90ft

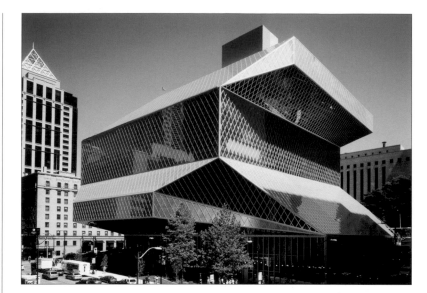

Seattle Library

OMA

Seattle, Washington, USA; 2004

In the heart of downtown Seattle, the distinctive form of OMA's new city library is justified on more than purely visual grounds. Despite the building's accepted need to stand out – both to provide the necessary degree of civic presence and to entice visitors into what is seen by many as an increasingly obsolete building type – the starting point for this distorted form came from OMA's characteristic and graphically led method of functional analysis.

When seeking a clear way to break down the complex brief, a series of colour-coded bar charts was devised, giving an immediate sense of the scale, order and disposition of each of the functions and their interrelationships. When arranged vertically, and ordered in a logical spatial sequence, the bar charts soon became a means to understanding the potential cross-sectional organization of the building. The process also began to identify and distinguish between the building's two modes of space-making: that of the contained and the container.

The brief evolved into five articulated boxes, each devoted to one core library use. These, *the contained*, when separated, staggered and enveloped in a tight shrink-wrapped skin, generated a wide range and variety of interstitial spaces; a dramatic and dynamic series of *containing spaces*, for both specific shared uses, and for circulation and servicing. With this, the building's two modes of planning had two modes of articulation, with the contained spaces being largely orthogonal, rectilinear and (broadly) enclosed – translated from Seattle's square city grid – within a more eccentric and dynamic container, articulated by a series of distinctive diagonal accents generated when two eccentrically displaced orthogonal floor plates were joined, either in plan or in section.

The sort of spatial malleability that this created, which can be seen as a manipulation of Le Corbusier's domino diagram, is both spatially exciting and functionally flexible. In this application it has given the Seattle Library a distinctive identity, and arguably has brought new form to a well-established institutional type. The largest of the building's distinctive diagonals signifies its major public spaces, such as the expansive Living Room that runs virtually the full length of the east elevation – overlooked by the conference suite, the Mixing Chamber (the reference library), and the lowest of four levels of book stacks. By contrast, the building's cellular spaces have the necessary coherence and containment to make them operationally efficient, meeting stringent acoustic and environmental criteria. When combined, these modes of spatial articulation have produced a practical and popular public facility – a building that not only challenges stylistic conventions, with its stretched fish-net cladding, but which also challenges long-standing and conservative institutional and architectural planning conventions. The spaces not only look and feel fresh but, it is hoped, they will also smell fresh, avoiding the accumulation of stuffy sour-smelling air through the appropriate reuse, recovery and recirculation of exhaust air through the building's lofty and loosely connected internal spaces.

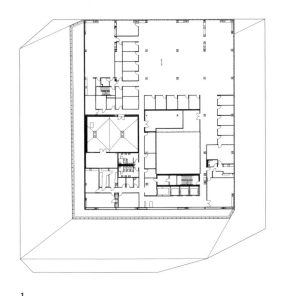

1

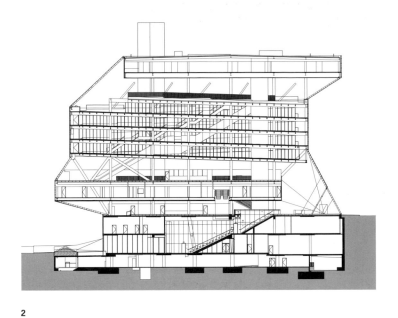

2

1 Eighth Floor Plan

1 Library Administration

2 Section A–A

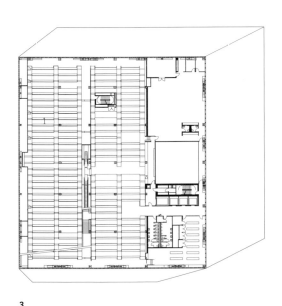

3

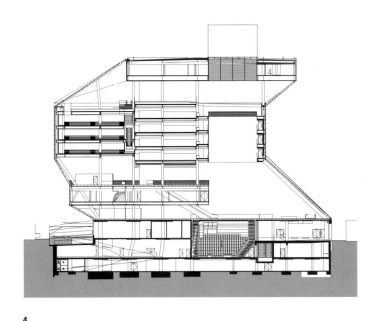

4

3 Fourth Floor Plan

1 Book Spiral

4 Section B–B

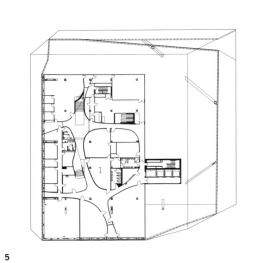

5

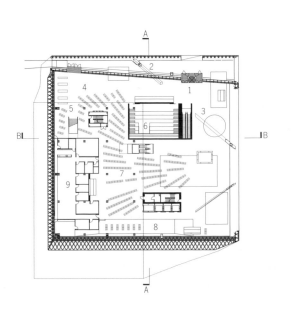

6

5 First Floor Plan

1 Conference and Meeting Rooms

6 Ground Floor Plan

1 Entrance 5th Avenue
2 Arcade
3 Reception
4 Café
5 Shop
6 Auditorium
7 Fiction Stacks
8 Teenage Section
9 Office

0 5 10m
15 30ft

Rosenthal Center for Contemporary Arts

Zaha Hadid Architects

Cincinnati, Ohio, USA; 2003

The architecture of Zaha Hadid is most commonly associated with contorted forms, sharp edges and extensive low-lying spaces. Energized with very specific spatial and organizational attitudes to movement, Hadid's spaces are almost exclusively experienced as horizontal terrains. On this corner site in downtown Cincinnati, however, the four boundary walls of the plot effectively set the building's footprint in stone. Respecting obligations to the requirements of the brief, and to the existing morphology of the city's formal grid, Hadid's trademark spatial virtuosity was on this occasion saved for the building's interiors; the principal planning move here being to celebrate vertical rather than horizontal movement throughout the main spaces. Unlike the many neighbouring commercial properties, where vertical circulation is relegated to discrete hidden corners to maximize the lettable space that they serve, here there is a generosity in plan and section that responds well to the client's request for spatial and formal dynamism. With the main accommodation pulled towards the street elevation to the south, circulation is organized within a full-height top-lit void that is set against a new party wall to the north. In addition, this void wraps under the assembled masses

above, helped on its way by a radiused junction between party wall and foyer floor; the only curve in an otherwise chisel-cut environment.

To help the foyer act as what has been described as 'a fluid continuum of the city', the ground-floor envelope is entirely glazed along its easterly and southern street façades, until it reaches a discrete service and delivery bay in the southwest corner. This service wing extends along the westerly party wall, beyond the line of the northerly party wall, to accommodate the extensive storage and servicing requirements of the front-of-house exhibition and performance spaces. While the inset glazed lobby is relatively mean, considering the scale of the building, it is planned to draw in the visiting public from the street and to reorient them towards the base of the first of six lazy stairs (or stepped ramps). More subtle geometric shifts occur in applied floor patterns that extend out to the public realm, and in the slant of the rhomboid columns, which all serve to amplify the skew of the upper-level geometries.

The galleries above have been articulated as monolithic blocks that vary in shape and size to provide curators with a wide range of environments for their eclectic mix of exhibition media.

This haphazard arrangement of forms is then expressed externally to create the two distinct principal façades: the southerly façade being punctuated with a large area of glazing to attract the attention of passing onlookers, and the easterly façade providing a dense sculptural relief. With the turning of this corner, Hadid exploited the opportunity to create a dramatic composition in relief that is not only distinctive in its own right but, more pertinently, provides a strong corner to the urban block, deriving its form from the dense clustering of spaces within.

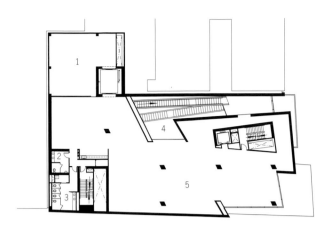

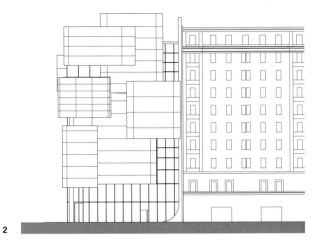

1 Level 6

1 Storage
2 Men's Toilet
3 Women's Toilet
4 Void
5 UnMuseum

2 East Elevation

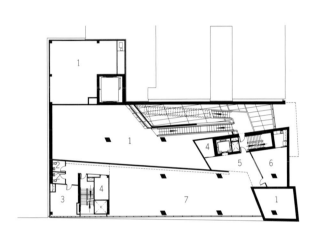

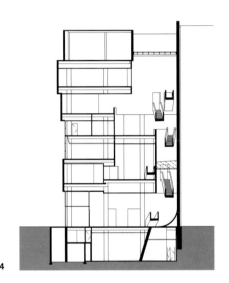

3 Level 3

1 Void
2 Toilet
3 Office
4 Storage
5 Reception
6 Staff Lounge
7 Open Office

4 Section A–A

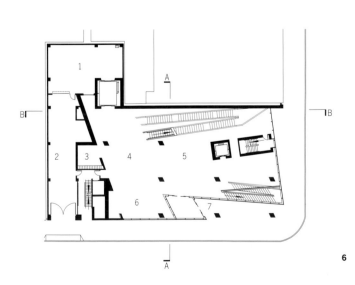

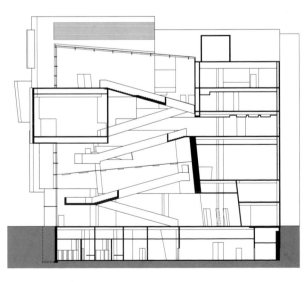

5 Ground Floor Plan

1 Receiving
2 Loading
3 Cloakroom
4 Reception
5 Lobby
6 Shop
7 Entry

6 Section B–B

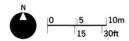

N

0 5 10m
15 30ft

House & Atelier Bow-Wow

Atelier Bow-Wow

Tokyo, Japan; 2006

When considering tight sites – like those that epitomize Tokyo – it is important not to neglect architecture's third dimension. Ingenuity in section, as well as in plan, can often unlock the hidden potential of a site, as was the case with this small live/work premises designed by Atelier Bow-Wow, where spaces for the architect's own work and home life have been arranged one above the other.

Despite the high cost of land in Tokyo, this particular site was relatively cheap due to a number of complicated planning restrictions that limited development. With specific sectional constraints, the external profile of the four-storey volume was heavily governed, resulting in both the north and west façades having to slope in order to maintain light levels to adjacent properties. In response to this, and in order to maximize the volume of permitted development, the architects chose to amplify the building's eccentricity by proposing eight split levels of accommodation that stepped up and around the building's interior. The split levels have been used not only to optimize space within the distorted section (condensing floor levels as head room diminishes), but also to increase the proximity between each floor, allowing a substantial amount of breakout space to be colonized on each

half-landing in between – the benefit being that with each half-landing, three usable floors become more closely linked, each separated from the next by just seven steps.

Accessing via a narrow passageway, visitors enter what is effectively a single volume, with four principal L-shaped floors arranged above and below on the half-level, each linked by a generous intermediate landing. As the least private space, the atelier is the first area to be encountered, spreading across the upper and lower ground floors, and clearly visible from the entrance. Above this is the kitchen and living area, linked to the atelier by a half-landing-cum-gallery, and above these (most private of all) are the bedroom and bathroom, situated below the roof terrace and linked to the living room by a landing-cum-snug.

Throughout the internal volume, the configuration of the stairs and landings has been arranged to give each space its own unique quality, turning and twisting in orientation, morphing in style and changing in scale – with landings varying from 3 square metres (32 square feet) to 10 square metres (107 square feet). The specific nature of the spaces also changes as you rise through the building, as sloping walls converge to

constrict the two upper levels, giving the living accommodation a more traditional domestic scale and attic-like quality, being timber lined and more intimate in character.

To further distinguish one level from the next, each has been given a different orientation, directed by access to specific external views. The composition of walls also changes, with the upper-ground-floor atelier being dual aspect, with large glazed windows facing north and south, and the second-floor living room being triple aspect, extending the glazing further along the eastern façade.

The thermal quality of the continuous vertical space is controlled by a heating and cooling radiator that is integrated into the partition wall. This thermoconditioning system uses well water from 40 metres (130 feet) underground as its energy source.

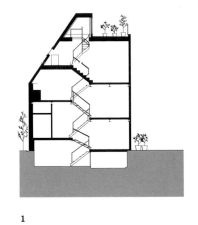

1

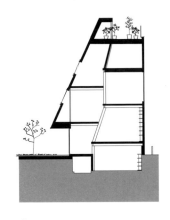

2

3

4

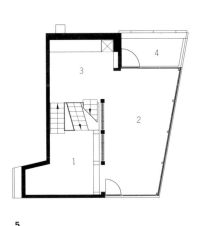

5

3   Roof Plan

1   Roof terrace

4   Second Floor Plan

1   Snug/Half-landing
2   Bedroom
3   Toilet
4   Bathroom

5   First Floor Plan

1   Half-landing
2   Living Room
3   Kitchen
4   Roof Terrace

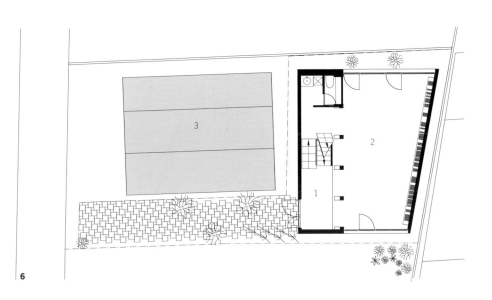

6

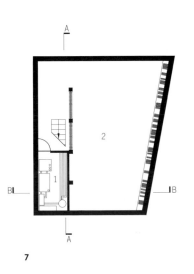

7

6   Ground Floor Plan

1   Hall
2   Studio
3   Neighbouring Property

7   Basement Plan

1   Plant Room
2   Studio

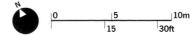

Water Tower House

Jo Crepain

Brasschaat, Belgium; 1996

This distinctive house in Brasschaat demonstrates how to creatively adapt an existing multistorey structure. It also demonstrates how the notion of vertical living can be interpreted, with the functions of this home being separated, one per floor, over seven levels.

Despite having suffered 50 years of neglect, the existing water tower was a distinctive landmark and inspired Jo Crepain and his client to adapt it in this exciting manner. The original tower comprised a cylindrical water reservoir raised 23 metres (75 feet) in the air on a five-stage structure; a beautifully simple and rational building, expressed as a stack of square concrete tables.

At the base of the tower, a two-storey plinth has been added that extends beyond the structure's footprint to contain the principal living spaces. Within this double-height volume are the kitchen, living and dining spaces set beneath an inset mezzanine level that contains a generous, enclosed bathroom suite. Above this, the plan form then reverts to the constraints of the tower, which has been glazed and enlarged to contain a narrow stair to the front.

The spaces in the tower are all set within the four columns of the original structure, and these are clearly articulated and set apart from the new glass skin. On three sides, the glazing takes the form of obscured glass planks, ensuring privacy from the road and neighbouring properties, while to the rear a clear glass wall provides uninterrupted views of the surrounding woodland. The connection with the garden and landscape beyond is further exploited with a generous roof terrace, which sits immediately above the double-height living room and beneath three small balconies, all of which are square in plan.

Rising through the tower, on the narrow stair that sits between the original structure and the new skin, the first level contains the master bedroom, which benefits from the adjacent roof terrace and its proximity to the bathroom suite below. On the next level is an office, and above this, with a degree of privacy from the master bedroom, is the guest room. In both cases the two bedrooms deal with light and privacy in the same manner, by using a circular curtain to provide an extra level of enclosure. With all levels essentially open to one another, this is perhaps the simplest and most practical method. Avoiding the integration of walls and doors, this simple device maintains the spatial coherence of the tower, and the curtain's circular rails resonate with the geometry of the water tank above and a cosy and acoustically soft space is created that recalls the heavy curtains traditionally used inside the door of an unlobbied restaurant or bar. Above all this, the upper two floors provide an appropriate and curious twist, with the top floor of the tower containing a winter garden, and the water tank itself, accessible only through a circular manhole, containing what has been described as a 'place for entertainment'.

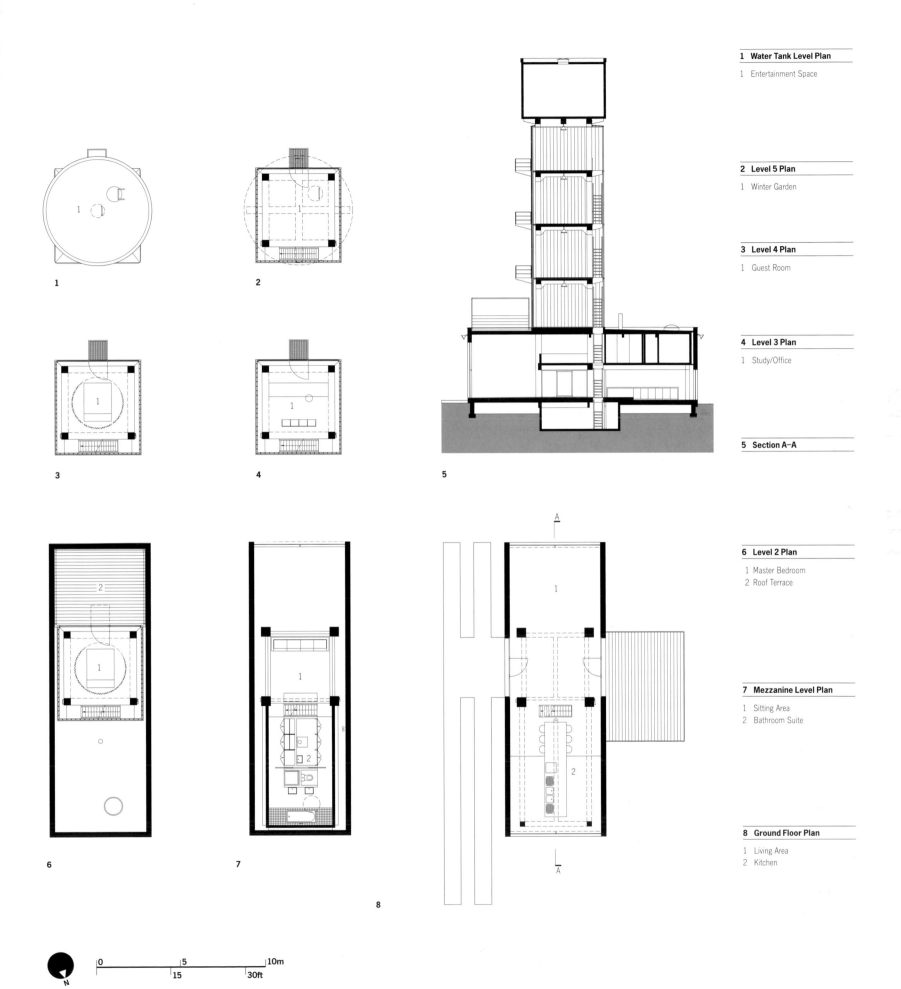

1 Water Tank Level Plan

1 Entertainment Space

2 Level 5 Plan

1 Winter Garden

3 Level 4 Plan

1 Guest Room

4 Level 3 Plan

1 Study/Office

5 Section A–A

6 Level 2 Plan

1 Master Bedroom
2 Roof Terrace

7 Mezzanine Level Plan

1 Sitting Area
2 Bathroom Suite

8 Ground Floor Plan

1 Living Area
2 Kitchen

0   5   10m
15   30ft

N

Air Traffic Control Tower

Zechner & Zechner

Vienna, Austria; 2005

Featured in the 2005 *Architectural Review* Awards for Emerging Architecture, Zechner & Zechner's Vienna Airport Air Traffic Control Tower may seem to be an unusual choice for commendation. It may also seem an oddity within this selection of exemplary stacked planning models. It is, however, a unique and admirable exception to established rules; rules that to date have distanced such structures by placing them physically and notionally remote from any meaningful architectural discourse, traditionally isolated in expansive, placeless and bleak airport landscapes. This structure is noteworthy due to the significant contribution it makes to its immediate local urban condition, set within the recently replanned airport cityscape. As such, this tower should very much be considered a building, rather than a dead-ended vertical stump. With a tripartite composition, with base, middle and top, it contains a number of distinct internal environments, and twists to resolve the skew in geometry between the orthogonal streetscape below and the control rooms above that are aligned with the orientation of the flight paths of the aircraft.

Built to serve the airport's increasing levels of air traffic, the 109 metre (358 foot) tower sits on a prominent site near the airport entrance. Set in its own plaza, the lower eight levels (including two basement storeys) are contained within a sleek glazed cube. Consistent with the scale of the adjacent buildings, this volume provides six levels of offices and conference facilities, together with accommodation for those of the air traffic control team who do not need direct visual contact with the planes. Those who do are accommodated at the top of the tower in one of three control rooms, each exploiting unobstructed views of the runways below and skies above. With faceted windows that help to eliminate distracting reflections, these spaces give the tower a discernible head that turns to face approaching aircraft.

The central trunk of the tower, which is equivalent to 11 storeys of accommodation, contains no habitable space. Instead, it forms a corset-like waistband that helps to resolve the tower's twisted geometry, with a stretched membrane skin that morphs from the square plan form of the base to the ovoid of the control rooms above. It also forms a landmark beacon, acting as a giant back-projection screen, displaying super-sized images of the natural world projected by three high-definition digital projectors.

Pinning each of the three stages together is a concrete core, the tower's principal means of support, which contains two lifts and the main accommodation stair. While the spatial resolution at the lower level is somewhat disappointing with the concrete core being cloaked in an orthogonal arrangement of toilets and stores, within the control rooms above the core this is fully expressed, with a circular corridor serving a radial arrangement of support spaces.

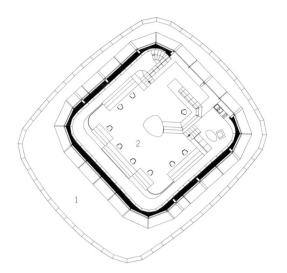

1

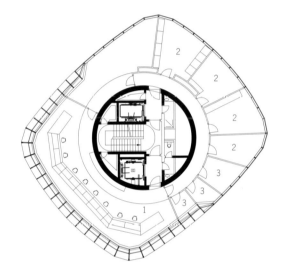

2

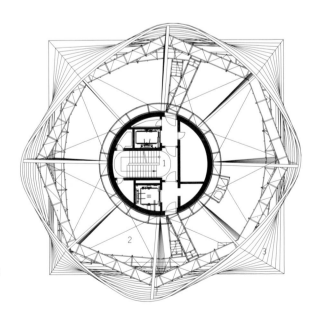

4

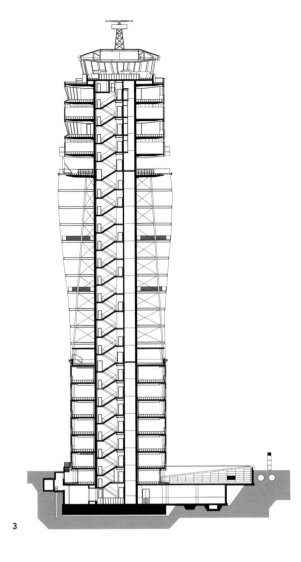

3

5

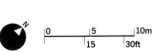

1	**Level 23 Plan**
1	Catwalk
2	Control Booth

2	**Level 19 Plan**
1	Monitor/Office Room
2	Offices
3	Changing Room

3	**Section A–A**

4	**Level 15 Plan**
1	Central Trunk
2	Interior of Membrane Skin
3	Membrane Skin

5	**Level 0 Plan**
1	Main Entrance
2	Lobby, Pilot Information
3	Offices
4	Meeting Room

0 5 10m
15 30ft

Courtyards — Orthogonal

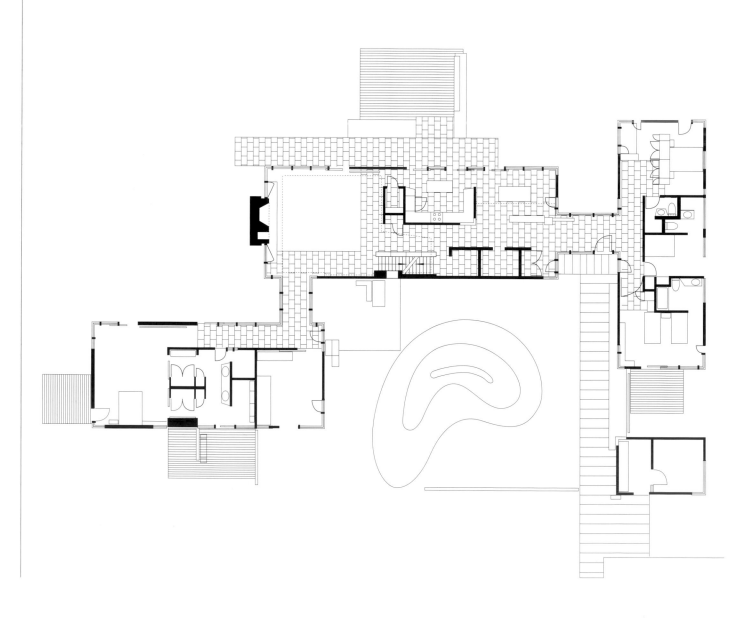

Bauhaus Building, Walter Gropius
Façade and Ground Floor Plan

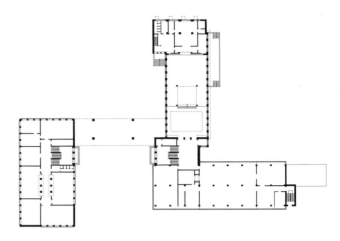

Courtyard arrangements have a rich and varied array of historical precedents. From primitive pre-historic settlements and the evolution of simple agricultural farmyards to more considered architectural ensembles such as monasteries, university quadrangles and cathedral cloisters, something inherently powerful occurs when two, three or four buildings are gathered together in one place. Once assembled, groups of buildings reach a certain critical mass when a shift in emphasis occurs between figure and ground. From this point on, the space between buildings becomes as tangible as the solid edges of the buildings that define it. Once this critical mass is reached and spatial fusion has occurred, courtyard arrangements make for doubly interesting reading when plans,

sections and elevations are scrutinized, allowing us to measure not only internal and external spaces together, but – equally significantly – the interstitial spaces in between.

Throughout the twentieth century, a number of important courtyard buildings were built, with at least five appearing in Richard Weston's *Key Buildings of the Twentieth Century*. **Walter Gropius' Bauhaus Building** in Dessau is one such example, which may not immediately seem a likely precedent in this category. However, in three dimensions the building takes a decisive hold of external space through the pinwheel composition of its plan. In elevation, too, the articulation of the façades gives each aspect its own unique identity. Similarly, Richard Neutra's Kaufmann Desert

House in Palm Springs, California, also demonstrates how apparently incomplete arrangements can succeed in creating well-defined external spaces without conforming to traditional closed-courtyard models. In this case, Neutra achieves this sense of place with a cruciform plan that creates four distinct external areas in an otherwise expansive and essentially undefined landscape, reinforced by a number of horizontal planes such as terraces and a swimming pool that reflects the equally expansive sky. By contrast **Alvar Aalto's Säynätsalo Town Hall** is a return to form as one of the twentieth century's finest courtyard buildings, inspired by its architect's admiration for traditional Italian *cortile*. With four complete ranges of accommodation

Säynätsalo Town Hall, Alvar Aalto
Façade and Ground Floor Plan

producing a well-proportioned and balanced raised courtyard, the southwestern range has been pulled away to create a cross-route which is articulated by the raised volume of the council chamber and two contrasting external stairs; a formal stair in brick and an informal stair with timber retained grass treads.

Finally, when considering internal covered courtyards, Giuseppe Terragni's Casa del Fascio in Como, and Roche and Dinkeloo's Ford Foundation Building in New York present two fine examples, both being singular monolithic forms that contain centralized, enclosed spaces that dominate, orchestrate and allow users to circumnavigate the building's inner realm.

The contemporary examples in this chapter were selected to offer a similar range of courtyard types, from loosely defined assemblages to fully contained configurations, beginning with a modest domestic project, the **Long Island Residence** by **Tod Williams Billie Tsien Architects**, which follows the twentieth-century examples set by Gropius and Neutra. **Villa V** by **3 + 1 Architects** in Tallinn, Estonia, consolidates its internal spaces into a single block in the middle of the plot, which uses a series of sunken, elevated and inclined external courtyards to help anchor it to the landscape.

On a larger scale, two university teaching blocks in Spain have been included which use courtyard configurations to give each self-contained departmental building a greater sense of place. The first is **Lecture Halls III**, a linear array, in Alicante, where **Javier Garcia-Solera Arquitecto** compressed seven linear blocks into a low-lying walled precinct with six narrow sunken courtyards between each suite of classrooms, and the second is **Juan Carlos Sancho Osinaga and Sol Madridejos's Teaching Pavilion** at the Arrixaca Hospital in Murcia, which carves two big courtyards into the side of an otherwise solid stone mass.

In the city, courtyards also help to resolve very deep urban blocks. **de Architekten Cie.'s Whale Housing** uses its sheer size to create a dramatic new landmark as part of a harbourside regeneration project in Amsterdam, with a buckled form, labyrinthine circulation and elevational trickery that allows the building to radically reinterpret the ubiquitous housing block. Finally, at this scale,

Villa V

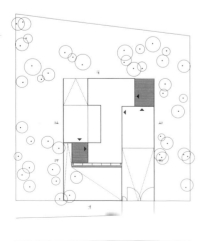

Lecture Halls III

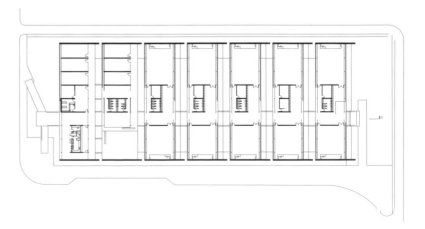

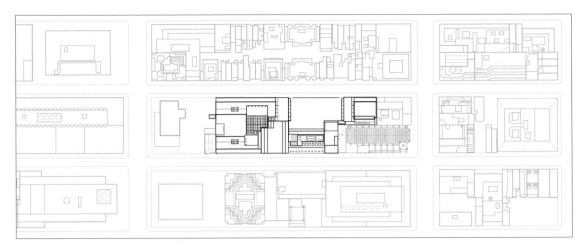

where no context exists and sufficient accommodation is required, **BRT Architekten's Swiss Re Offices** in Munich demonstrate how courtyard configurations can be used to create their own context, creating space for more than 800 employees.

Three internal courtyard schemes are also considered, beginning with an urban response in the heart of Manhattan with **Taniguchi and Associates' MoMA**. This significantly enlarged cultural destination places a generous four-storey patio at the centre of the plot that serves as the principal point of orientation and access to five levels of galleries. Next is **Alberto Campo Baeza's Caja General de Ahorros** which arranges office space around an enormous offset cubic void,

demonstrating how an orthogonal structure can be arranged to bring dynamism to an otherwise static geometry. And, finally, **Axel Schultes and Charlotte Frank's** powerful **Baumschulenweg Crematorium** in Berlin arranges four chapels around a central void which, being occupied by 29 standing figures in the form of columns, helps to create a space in which visitors can find their own place for contemplation.

The chapter concludes with two schemes that return to historical models. The first is **Waro Kishi + K Associates'** delightful **Hu-tong House** in Japan which draws inspiration from the Chinese house traditionally found within the neighbourhoods of Beijing. The second is the **Novy Dvur Monastery** by **John Pawson**, one of a few contemporary

designers given the opportunity to design a new monastery, in this case within the remains of a redundant farmhouse in the Czech Republic.

Novy Dvur Monastery

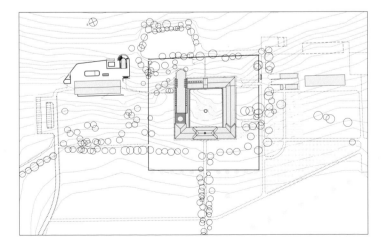

Long Island Residence

Tod Williams Billie Tsien Architects

Long Island, New York, USA; 1999

While not strictly set around a formal orthogonal courtyard, this private house by Tod Williams and Billie Tsien demonstrates how simple rectilinear forms can be positioned to organize a number of related internal and external spaces, using basic building blocks to transform space in a simple and effective manner.

Set within a 1.2 hectare (3 acre) plot, the house has distant ocean views, and is shielded from its neighbours by surrounding pine trees. Designed as a weekend retreat for a professional couple with grown-up children, the house had to provide spaces for entertaining, quiet contemplation and privacy, and hence has been arranged as a series of discrete yet connected components.

Comprising four volumes, the functions of the house have been broken down to include a principal public block for receiving and entertaining guests, two private blocks that contain master and guest bedroom suites, and an isolated storage shed. Through the disposition of these four elements and their relative interconnection, the site has been arranged to frame specific views and to provide each block with its own unique external space without the imposition of garden walls or excessive landscape intervention.

Upon arrival, the storage shed serves to screen the house from the approach, and punctuates the composition in plan. Sharing the same width as the adjacent bedroom wing, an intimate bedroom garden is created to the right of the path, sheltered by a single tree and balanced on the left by a more formal square front lawn.

At the entrance, which is contained within a re-entrant court, a glazed link leads guests either directly into the principal living area on the left or to one of two private bedroom suites on the right. The second bedroom suite is located at the other end of the house, through the living room, giving the hosts and their guests private and common ground.

To complete the hierarchy of the composition, the central pavilion is given formal priority with an attic level of clerestory windows. Internally, a small stair gives access to a reading loft contained within this additional volume, which in turn extends to a small external balcony from where the best views can be enjoyed. The central pavilion is further articulated by a massive New York bluestone masonry chimney, visible internally and externally, which rises above the raised section of roof.

Set apart as discrete elements, each of the three principal blocks of accommodation can be naturally ventilated, and having direct access to their own external terraces they command more space than they individually contain. In tune with its wooded setting, timber is used in the frame, fenestration and finishes.

1 **1 Section A–A**

2   **3**   **4**

2 Section B–B

3 Section C–C

4 Section D–D

5 First Floor Plan
1 Study
2 Roof Garden
3 Void

6 Ground Floor Plan
1 Master Bedroom Suite
2 Living Room
3 Kitchen
4 Guest Bedroom Suites
5 Storage Shed

5

6

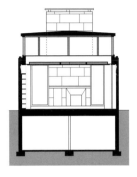
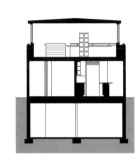
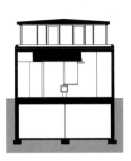
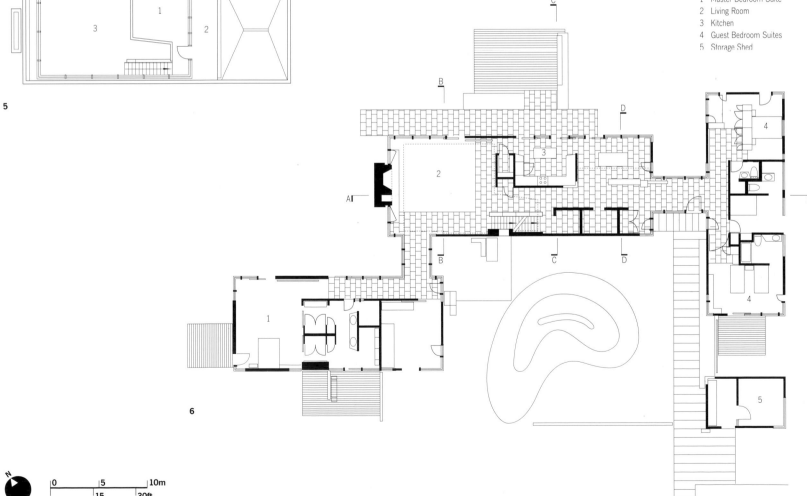

0 5 10m
15 30ft

Villa V

3 + 1 Architects

Tallinn, Estonia; 2000

Although this house does not bear the immediate qualities of a traditional courtyard house, closer scrutiny of the plan reveals how its spaces have been broken down into a series of interconnected orthogonal volumes. The architects have described the building as being set upon a folded landscape, which in plan is seen to form a hard-lined rectangular footprint. Within this footprint the building is articulated by three forms: a partially buried lower ground floor cast in concrete; an upper-level timber box; and a series of inclined external terraces. The essentially horizontal composition, which is exaggerated in the orientation of the timber boarding, contrasts fittingly with the verticality of the surrounding forest in a pleasant suburb of the city of Tallinn in northern Estonia .

The lower ground levels contain the principal living spaces. With large areas of glazing set flush into smooth concrete walls, the central space extends out onto two low-level terraces. These external rooms are accessed via inclined planes, one leading to a double garage, the other to the house's principal entrance. The sunken terraces also serve to open up and frame long views that extend across the plot, through the principal living rooms and out to the forest beyond.

Internally, the living spaces are arranged around a double-height hall in the middle of the plan. From this space the living quarters are arranged as single-storey spaces and include a snug and a large kitchen/dining space. A large sliding glass screen is placed between the hall and the kitchen, offering a degree of spatial flexibility.

The upper-level spaces (those that are contained within the raised timber box) have been divided into two functionally independent apartments: a one-bedroom apartment for the parents, and four bedrooms for the children. Each apartment has its own stair that connects it with the communal spaces below, and the smaller of the two also benefits from its own entrance (accessed via an inclined external ramp) and a gallery that overlooks the central hall.

With exposed concrete as the predominant material, the lower-level spaces have a solid, subterranean feel. This contrasts with the openness of the views that the spaces command, setting up strong spatial tensions between the interior and the exterior.

1 Section A–A

2 Section B–B

3 First Floor Plan

1 Bedroom
2 Living Room
3 Wardrobe
4 Laundry
5 Bathroom

4 Ground Floor Plan

1 Garage
2 Hobby Room
3 Plant Room
4 Living Room
5 Kitchen
6 Dining Room
7 Sauna
8 Storage

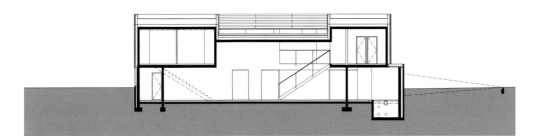

1

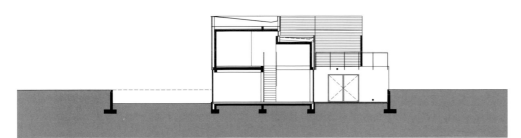

2

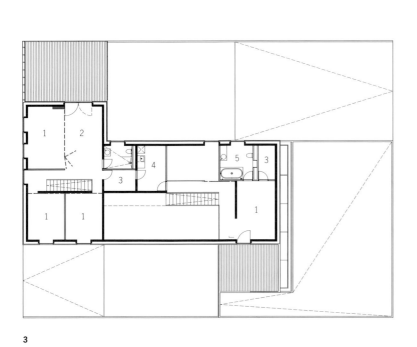

3

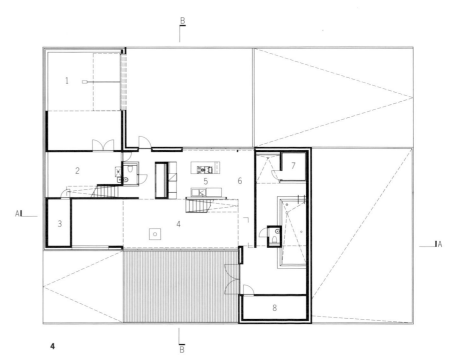

4

Lecture Halls III

Javier Garcia-Solera Arquitecto

Alicante, Spain; 2000

This simple array of teaching spaces, set within a single unified block, is a hybrid plan format, part-terrace and part-multiple courtyard. Built to meet the urgent need for additional teaching space at the University of Alicante, they occupy the site of a partially completed warehouse. Work on the warehouse stopped when it became clear that the site occupied land that might be better used for classrooms, and as a result the architect had to design a new structure that would meet the requirements of the brief while conforming to the setting-out of the existing pile foundations. While a degree of inevitability may have existed, with the foundation layout dictating the serial organization of the new teaching block, and the limited bearing strength restricting the development to a neat single-storey pavilion, the architectural solution that we are presented with represents a clear and highly sophisticated strategy that belies the simplicity of its form. Having been designated for light industrial use, the site was in fact not ideally suited for primary teaching accommodation. Situated at the periphery of the main campus, outside the ring road that defines the people-friendly pedestrianized area, it was surrounded by car parks and set within a relatively hostile environment. It was therefore

essential that this new micro-campus would create its own secure and defined context in order to provide an environment appropriate to teaching and learning.

Considering the layout of the foundations, the brief was reconfigured into seven modules, each identical in plan, but variable in section. Within these modules, two distinct slab and spine wall configurations were proposed that could be supported on the existing 5 x 10 metre (16 x 33 foot) grid. These modules comprised five identical bays, and two more cellular bays set towards the entrance. To help create its own immediate context, each bay is separated from the next by a sunken courtyard and a single-aspect covered porch, both of which extend along the full length of the bays. Each is then linked by a series of light metal bridges that span from raised slab to raised slab. The courtyards bring light, air and nature to the spaces within without compromising privacy or creating space for too much distraction. Within this strategy the narrow gaps cut into the perimeter walls at each end of the courtyard were intended not so much to frame specific views, but to increase the sense of separation from one bay to the next, and to make more explicit the intention

that each space should have its own designated external space by effectively giving each courtyard an orientation towards front and back. The second bay after entering the site by passing the porter's lodge and a small shop contains a more generous courtyard. This space spans the full width of the bay, serves as a focus for the students and teachers, and gives this delightful micro-campus its own heart.

1 Entrance
2 Porter's Lodge
3 Shop
4 Main Courtyard
5 Sunken Courtyard
6 Covered Porch
7 Classroom

1

2

3

4

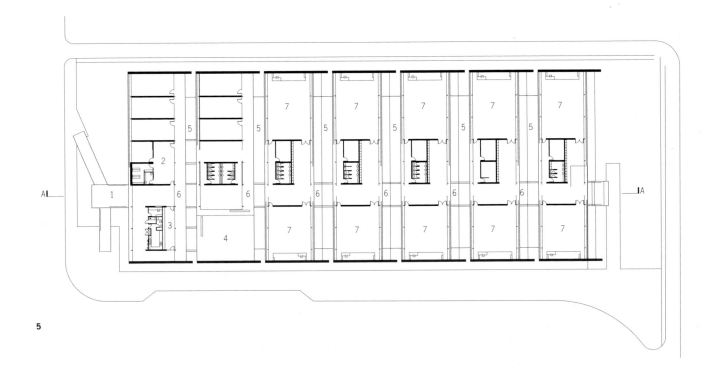

5

N

0 5 10m
15 30ft

Teaching Pavilion

Juan Carlos Sancho Osinaga + Sol Madridejos

Murcia, Spain; 2001

Courtyards are not limited to centrally planned buildings. As this building demonstrates, courtyards can also be placed at the perimeter of plans, served by a circulation spine deeply embedded in the centre. At the Arrixaca Hospital teaching pavilion, this approach has been used to reduce the mass of an otherwise solid, blocky form, and to bring light and air into a relatively deep-plan configuration. The building forms part of a hospital campus in Murcia, southeast Spain, which comprises a number of self-contained and autonomous departmental units, each with their own use and character. Built in isolation, therefore, to house space for teaching, the building takes the form of a solid stone box, crisply cut away along its length to create a sharp step in section. Rectangular in form, with the thin end facing the street, the stepped section drops down to the entrance elevation. The step down leads visitors along the length of the building before inviting them in through the low-lying opening. Internal circulation is also organized along the building's length, contained within a spine that runs along its entire length. This spine connects auditorium, cafeteria and classrooms on the entrance floor with the library on the first floor, and leads on to university

departments along its length. In section, the spine is coincident with the building's distinctive step down, and therefore is able to exploit the quadruple-height split section, to create a dramatic series of galleried hallways. With one side of the building rebated to form a low-lying two-storey range, the back of the building rises to four storeys to contain the principal teaching spaces, and two deep courtyards. Throughout the building, therefore, a complex and varied series of spaces interconnect to provide stark contrast between the lofty four-storey circulation spine, low-lying vestibules and the dramatic open-air courtyards – all contained within a simple stone block

The level of detailed articulation is kept deliberately low throughout the building, with beautifully cut Cehegin stone as the predominant surface finish. Within this, the stone is sharply cut to reveal glazing, which further emphasizes the tense relationship between solid and void, heavy and light, and opaque and transparent surfaces. The extensive use of Cehegin stone also helps to exaggerate the shifting scales of space as each volume, each angle, and each alternation of full and empty space stimulates a heightened awareness of the singularly applied surface material.

As a place for teaching the building enables users to engage with each unique space through the sensitive control of volumes and through the familiarity of the material skin. On a practical level, the teaching spaces have a well-considered balance as they are inward looking – without being dark and gloomy – while the external courtyards provide bright and airy places to spend time between teaching sessions.

1 First Floor Plan

1 Raised Courtyard
2 Classrooms
3 Bridge Link
4 Void

2 Ground Floor Plan

1 Main Entrance
2 Courtyard
3 Lecture Hall
4 Main Auditorium

3 Section A–A

4 Section C–C

5 Section B–B

6 Section D–D

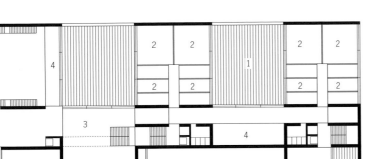

1

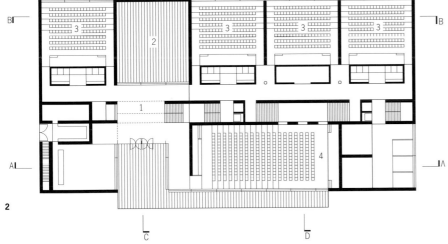

2

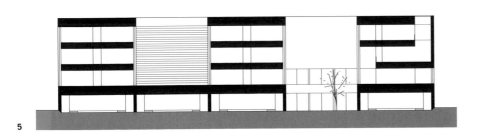

3

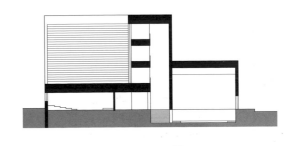

4

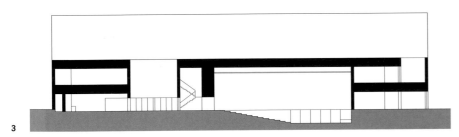

5

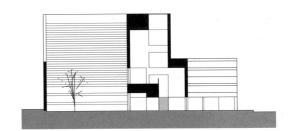

6

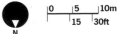

Whale Housing

de Architekten Cie.

Amsterdam, The Netherlands; 2000

Whale by name, whale by nature. This is a hulk of a housing scheme which, despite its mass, is richly layered with sophisticated subtleties.

Organized around a large courtyard, Whale Housing provides a distinctive landmark on a waterside plot in what was formerly the harbour of Borneo Sporenburg. The building's form – which is justified as a means of maximizing sunlight penetration in the courtyard – comprises a rectangular buckled slab with a orthogonal hole in the middle. As it rises and falls around its perimeter length – providing between six and eight levels of housing – its raking lines frame dynamic views into the courtyard and against the sky.

With a mix of uses, including housing units, commercial spaces and an underground car park, the development has sufficient gravity to create a real sense of place. Through its crooked form, the location of each apartment is made unique, accessed via an unorthodox circulation system that adds further twists and turns to the composition.

The circulation is organized within the courtyard, branching out from opposing corners with a series of walkways that appear as deep incisions in the elevations. With duplex and single-storey apartments with internal stairs, these

sheltered streets in the sky are arranged on alternate levels, creating a series of vertical steps in the façade. Further compositional complexity is achieved through each incision extending to a different length along the façade and also through the staggered effect as horizontal slots, windows and recessed spandrel panels meet. To connect one street to the next, in addition to the more conventional stair and lift cores located within the depth of the plan at the corners, a series of precarious steel stairs hang within the courtyard void. These not only provide alternative routes and short cuts, but also serve to enliven and activate the internal elevations when fully animated by people. In contrast to these, therefore, the building's vibrant external façades, which are essentially flush, seem relatively sedate.

A range of different apartment configurations has been included, with most of the units being dual aspect and having views into the courtyard and across the harbour. Inevitably, however, the corner units cannot share this benefit, and therefore feel slightly more remote, losing their connection with the interior.

Materially, the building remains true to its name and is clad in grey metal. This cool and crisp

medium, however, reveals the warmth of timber when cut back to form the elevated walkways. In addition to this, the roof adds further sparkle as the sun and sky are reflected in the shiny standing seam aluminium.

With its twisted form, labyrinthine circulation and elevational trickery, this building is an extremely successful example of how to reinterpret the ubiquitous housing block. It rarely gives the eye time to rest, as it traces the folding perimeter of the courtyard rising and falling along its length. From more distant viewpoints it continues to hold the viewer's interest, sitting conspicuously on the waterside as an extremely intriguing beached whale.

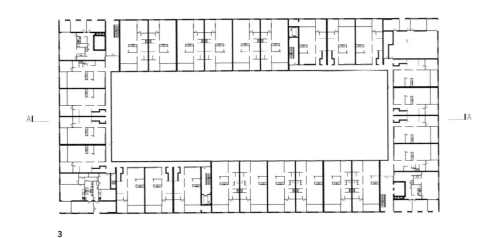

1

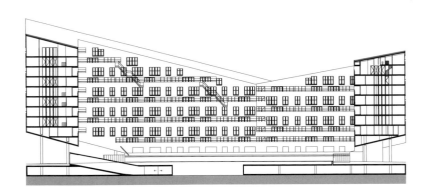

2

3

4

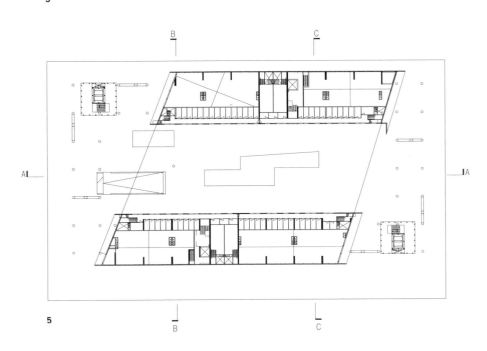

5

Swiss Re Offices

BRT Architekten

Munich, Germany; 2001

When no context exists, and sufficient accommodation is required, why not create your own context as you build? As courtyard buildings have equal obligations to internal and external space, it is possible to simultaneously create both space and place. Such was the opportunity given to BRT when they were asked to design this vast office campus to serve as the German headquarters of the re-insurance superpower, Swiss Re (the client for Foster + Partners' 30 St Mary Axe in London [see pp. 100–101]).

Situated on an industrial estate with no clear identity, the flat, featureless greenfield site had little to offer by way of inspiration beyond the obvious constraints of boundaries and effects of orientation. The architects therefore broke down the brief into a hierarchy that mimicked that which is broadly applicable to an established community, with a series of public external spaces, foyers, main streets, minor alleyways and private internal enclosures. These were then distributed across the site and stacked in section to simulate the sort of apparently accidental juxtapositions that are often encountered in towns and cities.

The scale of the project and the complexity of the many apparently haphazard inter-relationships belie the simplicity of the diagram, which is based on a two-storey glazed ground-level plinth that holds the foyer, meeting rooms and common areas such as the library and dining rooms. Above this, supported on slender stilts, four two-storey hubs (one in each corner) provide access and services to 16 self-contained office suites, with each of the four hubs creating a windmill-like cluster of four two-storey units in a radial configuration.

The entire campus is governed by two principal geometries, superimposed one upon the other, with a rhomboid-shaped perimeter containing orthogonal offices at higher level. The angular shift between the two is then mirrored to establish the orientation of the cruciform circulation links that cross each of the hubs.

The subdivision of over 800 workstations into 16 individual units, each in turn grouped in clusters of four, enables employees to focus on team project work without losing a sense of themselves as individuals or of their place within the wider company structure. While a main corridor connects all working areas, short cuts and alternative routes via bridges and balconies enable individuals to deviate from the principal circuit, promoting the sort of chance encounters that human resources

experts are keen to encourage. External gardens at grade and on the roof of the plinth building offer additional breakout space, both to inhabit and to observe as essential interstitial external space.

Around the perimeter of the campus, a two-storey wall is suspended at high level, coincident with the raised office suites and containing two-level access ways. This hanging screen will eventually be planted and taken over by red and green vines, creating a dramatic landscaped halo to shelter and contain the courtyards and, more significantly perhaps, to act as a point of reference in an otherwise bleak and nondescript industrialized no-man's-land.

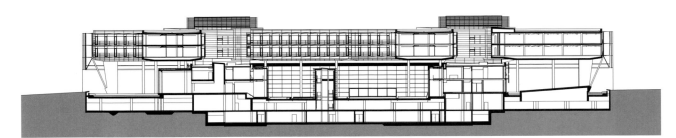

1

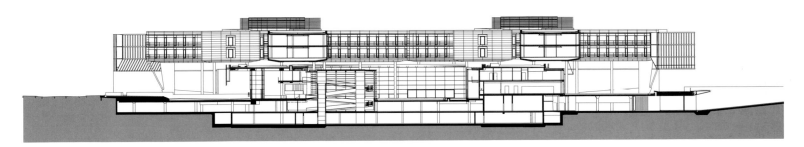

2

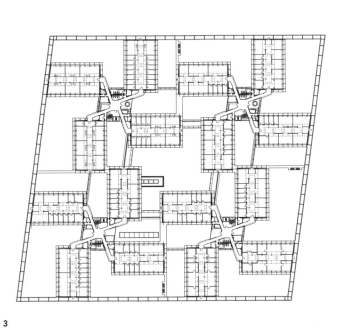

3

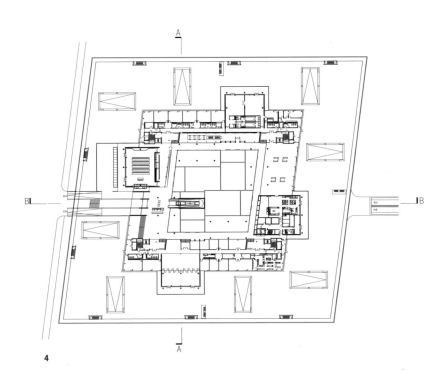

4

MoMA

Taniguchi and Associates

New York, New York, USA; 2005

Over a number of years, New York's famous Museum of Modern Art (MoMA) has colonized an increasing amount of space within Manhattan's dense urban fabric. Beginning in John D. Rockefeller's town house on West 53rd Street in 1932, subsequent adaptations and moves have seen the involvement of architects such as Philip Johnson and Cesar Pelli. In 2005, the institution made a significant leap, extending from beneath the shadow of Pelli's 1984 high-rise condominium to inhabit a large proportion of its urban block. The most recent architect – Tokyo-based Yoshio Taniguchi – saw this as an opportunity to orchestrate a comprehensive expansion programme by creating two new glazed façades on both 53rd and 54th Streets, and restoring a peaceful sculpture garden at the heart of the complex.

While incorporating both the existing Pelli Tower and the 1932 Goodwin/Durell Stone Building, a new entrance concourse has been cut right across the site, west of Pelli's tower. Punctuated by five centrally aligned columns, the low-lying void effectively bridges the plot to connect 53rd and 54th Streets. With a book shop, cloakrooms and ticket desks to the west, visitors are turned east through a double-height atrium that

gives views in to the sculpture garden. From here they rise into the central hall, a four-storey internal patio that serves as the principal point of orientation and access to the galleries that extend throughout the subsequent five levels. The central hall sits in the middle of the building's cross-section to create a dramatic top-lit four-floor cubic void, mimicking but offsetting the sectional proportion of the sculpture garden beyond that runs east–west along 54th Street. Together, these two voids help the complex to find its place within the dense city grain, deeply anchored yet spatially liberated, utilizing large openings, balconies and bridges to establish cross-axial views and routes that contrast with the more calm and largely orthogonally planned internalized galleries.

The nature of the galleries very much extends MoMA's domestic origins, with the majority of the spaces being white-walled, oak-floored, and entered via deep-set doorways. Sensitive detailing of the junctions exists throughout, such as the junction between wall and floor, and wall and doorway, which have been exquisitely resolved with fine metal shadow gaps and integrated air supply slots – suggesting an attention to detail that extends in some respects to the space's domestic character.

The galleries on the fifth floor, however, are significantly bigger, with two large, conjoined exhibition spaces that run parallel to the streets below having more generous floor to ceiling heights that produce a loftier character.

Despite this shift in scale, however, some critics have asked if Taniguchi has been too restrained in his response, with the gallery spaces lacking the drama of the two principal voids. In response to this, perhaps, the architect's prioritization of seamless flows and animated public spaces goes some way in justifying his reduced and defiantly simple approach.

1 Section A–A	2 Section B–B	3 Section C–C	4 Fifth Floor Plan	5 First Floor Plan	6 Ground Floor Plan

4 **Fifth Floor Plan**
1 Gallery

5 **First Floor Plan**
1 Gallery
2 Café
3 Education and Research

6 **Ground Floor Plan**
1 Main Lobby
2 Book Shop
3 Atrium
4 Pelli Tower
5 Restaurant
6 Garden

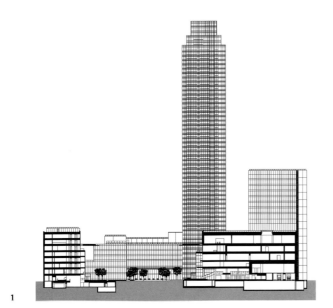

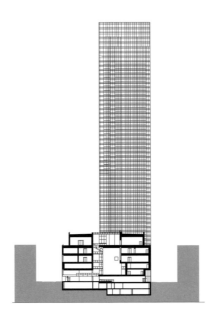

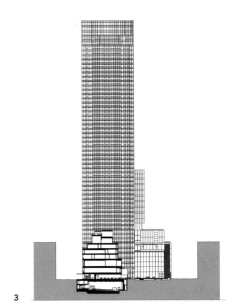

1

2

3

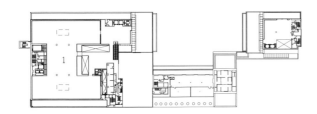

4

5

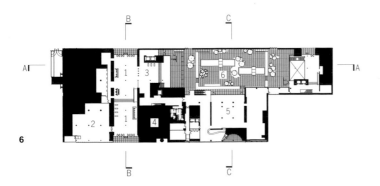

6

N
0 10m
30ft

Caja General de Ahorros

Alberto Campo Baeza

Granada, Spain; 2001

There are clear formal parallels between this building in Spain and the crematorium at Baumschulenweg, Berlin by Axel Schultes and Charlotte Frank [see pp. 144–5]. The two buildings, however, could barely be more different in their purposes. While the crematorium was built as a monument to the cycles of life, providing a dignified setting for individuals to pay their respects to the deceased, this building is a monument to the cycles of economy, celebrating the financial successes of Caja General de Ahorros, a local Spanish state savings bank. This fact, however, while potentially less appealing to issues of the soul, does not diminish the significance of the building, which contains a series of similarly awe-inspiring spaces.

The building is a cuboid form, set out on a 57 metre (187 foot) square plan that is divided into 3 metre (10 foot) modules. On the southeast and southwest façades, the 3 metre (10 foot) module forms continuous 3 metre (10 foot) deep brise-soleil, with an array of concrete fin walls that run at 90 degrees to the façade. To the northeast and northwest, the façade is more conventional with modules ordering the fenestration with glass and travertine set in flush panels. This duality extends inside the building to unbalance the implied symmetry of the square plan, with an eccentrically placed atrium that shifts the perceived centre of the plan towards the northernmost corner along the diagonal axis. This eccentricity is further exaggerated by four massive columns 3 metres (10 feet) in diameter that sit on the diagonal axis, but off-centre in relation to the atrium. And a final shift in balance occurs on the ground floor as a double-height 27 x 27 metre (89 x 89 foot) auditorium extends into the atrium, encasing two column bases.

The overall effect of these eccentricities demonstrates how an orthogonal organization can be arranged to bring dynamism to an otherwise static geometry. The composition is clearly ordered and rational, with not a diagonal line or a curve to be seen, but the spaces are given a twist as the viewer's eye tracks around the perimeter interior. Through the juxtaposition of cubic modules, the space has been radically enlivened.

Internally, two L-shaped ranges of accommodation define the atrium: six modules deep on the southern façades and three deep to the north. Each range presents a different face to the atrium: the southern range is more conventional with full-height glazing in contrast to the northern range which is clad in small panels of alabaster held in a painted steel frame which, while being read as a solid wall, reveals a more ephemeral quality when touched, or when lit from behind. Both ranges stop short of the oversailing roof which, despite its mass, is seen to float above the six storeys of accommodation. This elevated plane is also divided into a cubic module, with a honeycomb of rooflights that project dramatic squares of light, adding a further level of dynamism to this unique cavernous interior.

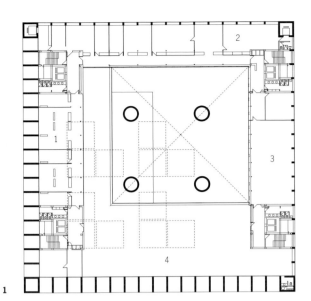

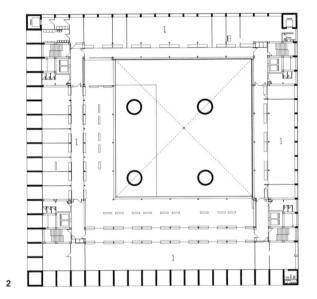

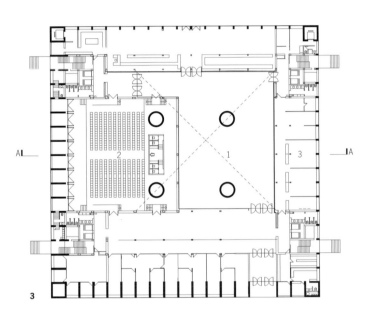

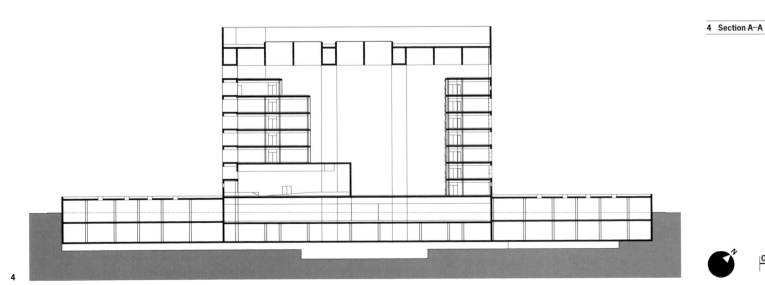

1 Sixth Floor Plan

1 Offices
2 President's Office
3 Meeting Room
4 Interior Terrace

2 Second to Fifth Floor Plan

1 Offices

3 Ground Floor Plan

1 Atrium
2 Auditorium
3 Offices

4 Section A–A

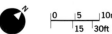

Baumschulenweg Crematorium

Axel Schultes and Charlotte Frank

Berlin, Germany; 2000

The crematorium at Baumschulenweg, Berlin, is a fine example of the courtyard type that could not be excluded from this study, despite the fact that it was completed in 2000. It comprises a highly sophisticated response to a complicated brief, and was both a daunting and exhilarating experience for its architects, Axel Schultes and Charlotte Frank. With no established rituals – in Western civilization at least – the architects had a number of highly emotive issues to resolve, designing a building in which people of all faiths and none could assemble to pay their respects. The spaces they created had to convey a spirit of tenderness and intimacy without overt sentimentality; a sense of occasion without pompous ceremony; and instil a deep sense of awe without inflicting God-fearing terror. They responded with clarity and directness, with a suitably monumental form based around a courtyard that focused on a man-made grove of concrete trees set within a dramatic cubic volume.

The crematorium is arranged as a courtyard building, with the concrete grove at its heart. With its lofty triple-height section, the grove-hall forms the communal core of the building, providing a place for friends and family of the deceased to wait before and after each service. Even when this

space is empty, it is occupied by 29 columns that stand solidly within the space, each of which is crowned with its own halo of light that punches through the flat concrete soffit. With these permanent occupants apparently having found their own place at random within the hall, visitors are also encouraged to find their own place for their own particular moment of contemplation. With 2, 22 or 200 people in this space, the columns remain the dominant occupants, helping to reduce any notion of self-consciousness among the visitors, and bringing a scale and order without enforcing a symmetry axis or route. As standing figures, at once solitary and collective, the grove resonates with a powerful symbolism while remaining suitably non-specific to any religion or form of iconography,

Entering through a portico that frames two small chapels, visitors rise up onto a plinth that contains the vast series of processing spaces for the deceased. With such capacity, the building is able to process hundreds of individual corpses, and with three chapels – two to the front and a larger single chapel at the rear – it is able to hold simultaneous back-to-back services. Despite this mechanical efficiency, however, the building is

certainly not utilitarian. Through the masterful orchestration of material, space and light, the architects have created a building of great significance which, as a piece of architecture, is truly inspirational. As a crematorium, it has a peaceful coherence that is at once awe-inspiring and intimate, providing a place where everyone of every denomination or of no faith can come together to commemorate the lives of loved ones in a suitably dignified setting.

1 Elevation	2 Section A–A	3 Basement Plan	4 Ground Floor Plan	5 First Floor Plan
		1 Cremation	1 Cremation	1 Cremation
		2 Coffin Acceptance Area	2 Condolence Hall	2 Void
		3 Coffin Delivery	3 Small Mourning Hall	3 Administration
		4 Coffin Holding	4 Large Mourning Hall	
			5 Sexton's Office	
			6 Vestry	

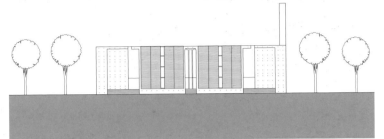

1

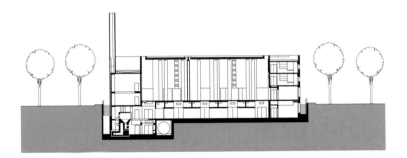

2

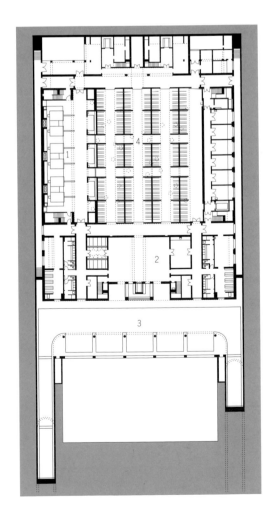

3

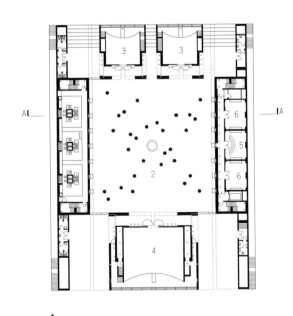

4

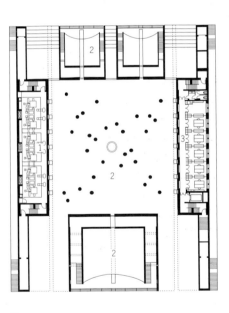

5

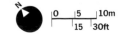

Hu-tong House

Waro Kishi + K Associates/Architects

Western Japan; 2002

The Hu-tong House by Waro Kishi + K Associates draws its inspiration from the traditional Chinese house that until recently established the model of living in the old neighbourhoods of Beijing. As an antidote to the attitude that suggests traditional forms of housing are obsolete (as apparently seems to be the case in China where the authorities are systematically destroying all traces of this rich housing type), Kishi and his client considered the inherent benefits of the traditional courtyard house. The house also blends in qualities from the Hakka house, an adobe version found in the remote mountain regions where the courtyard was more of an inner street than a private garden. On a tight site in a small, historic city in western Japan (the owners have requested that the exact location be withheld), the Hu-tong House gives little away to the street. Instead, it focuses in on itself, with all the spaces leading from a narrow courtyard or street which effectively cuts the site in half.

The accommodation is organized in three volumes, in accordance with the strict planning policy that often limits development footprint to 50 per cent of the plot size. Clearly articulated, each pavilion is defined by a simple monopitch roof, with two volumes facing each other across the central courtyard/street and the third at the rear of the site, set back between two neighbouring properties. Each pavilion serves a specific function, with living and dining in one, sleeping in the other, and a workspace in a two-storey annexe – in this case to provide space for an artist studio.

Despite the planning codes that limit on-site development, virtually every square metre is occupied through the efficient use of external space, with the perimeter of the site being bounded by a 3 metre (10 foot) high wall. The entrance is discreet, set in a narrow slot between overlapping walls. This covered passageway leads visitors into an apparently dead-end entrance space, before turning them 90 degrees on the axis with the principal courtyard/street. With the two monopitch roofs inclined towards this central space, this area forms the heart of the home, provoking movement between living and sleeping spaces. This interrelationship is emphasized through the ordering of the façades. These share the same setting out, with a series of fin walls which, being set at 90 degrees to the axis of the courtyard/street, control views into the interior, functioning as a series of blinkers that only reveal the view as you walk through the space.

Internally, there are no corridors, with all the space being occupied. The monopitch roofs sit above the principal living/sleeping spaces with a low-level service spine running along the full length at the rear, built at the same height as the perimeter wall.

Through the central courtyard/street leads to another dead-end, before turning to the left to reveal the two-storey annex and its own intimate entrance court – a higher building served by an external stair to optimize the internal volume for more purposeful use.

1 First Floor Plan

1 Atelier
2 Japanese Room
3 Loft

2 Section A–A

3 Ground Floor Plan

1 Entrance Passageway
2 Courtyard
3 Lower Deck
4 Bedroom
5 Warehouse

4 Section B–B

5 Section C–C

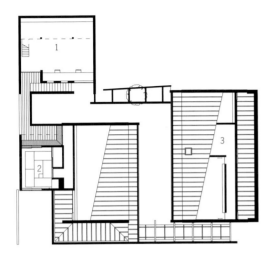

1

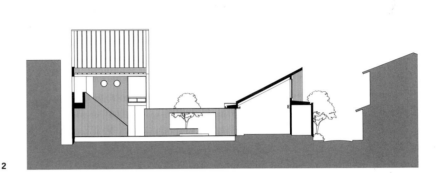

2

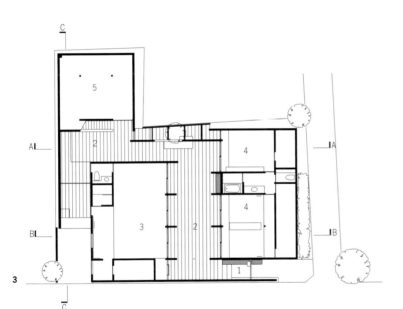

3

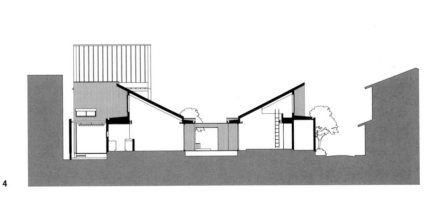

4

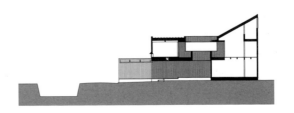

5

Novy Dvur Monastery

John Pawson

Novy Dvur, Czech Republic; 2004

Few architects are given the chance to design a new monastery, but for John Pawson the opportunity seemed almost inevitable. Having spent the formative years of his career applying monastic architectural principles to home and high street, with a number of well-known domestic and prestigious commercial projects, this 'commission of a lifetime' enabled him to bring minimalism full circle, reapplying a commitment to restraint and discipline in the creation of accommodation for a new community of monks.

While there are many visual and aesthetic parallels between Pawson's trademark minimalism and the austerity of Cistercian architecture – where a stripped-down aesthetic helps to elevate the essential and day-to-day acts of sleeping, bathing, dressing and eating – this building gave Pawson the opportunity to work at a deeper level, bringing a specific spatial order to the lives of the 40 or so monks who would make this monastery their lifelong home. So, before the design process began Pawson was invited to stay with the monks in another monastery in Burgundy, where sharing the rhythm of their lives, waking before dawn to attend the first of seven daily offices and taking meals in silence, gave him a profound insight into the

monks' quiet life; a life constructed around simple rituals, repetition, routine and a complete absence of what is not necessary.

Due to the condition of the existing buildings, three new wings were required to complete the cloister, incorporating the original manor house to the west. Following St Bernard's twelfth-century model, the cloister remains the principal ordering device for the entire precinct, linking all spaces and enclosing a steeply sloping site. Running around the inner edge of the new ranges the circulation steps out to pass through the outer edge of the original manor house, further distinguishing new from old. Furthermore, in opposition to the established language of columns and vaults, Pawson chose to create a new reduced form of vault, with a dramatically cantilevered barrel vault apparently floating above a frameless glass screen. While some have questioned this decision – suggesting that cloisters, by their very nature, need the vertical modulation of a regular intercolumniation – Pawson himself saw columns as superfluous in this instance, and instead sought a solution that strengthened the relationship between cloister and courtyard.

While the majority of Pawson's spaces are

housed within relatively discrete and understated forms, set under pitched roofs and behind simple and pared down vernacular elevations, the monastery's composition is articulated with two distinct formal flourishes. The view canyon is the first, located in the east range, framing views to the landscape beyond. The second is the magnificent new chapel, elevated high above the adjacent accommodation and extending beyond the bounds of the courtyard building into a dramatic radiused presbytery. In plan, section and elevation, the chapel distinguishes itself from its backdrop to create a specific and other-worldly environment, carefully lit through top-lit interstitial light-wells, and complete with its own courtyard to provide access for members of the public during offices.

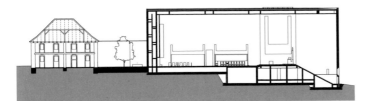

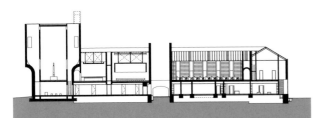

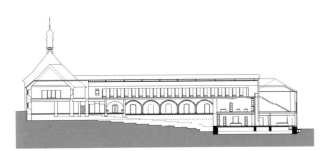

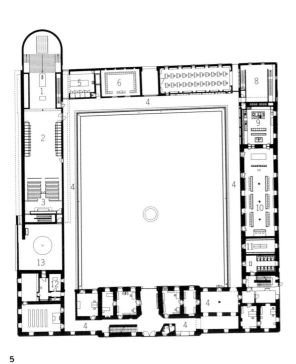

1 Section A–A

2 Section B–B

3 Section C–C

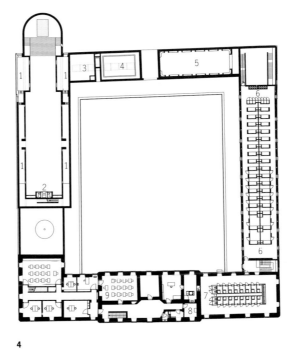

4 First Floor Plan

1 Lightbox
2 Organ
3 Sacristy
4 Chapter
5 Scriptorium
6 Dormitory
7 Washrooms
8 Chapel
9 Novitiate

1

2

3

4

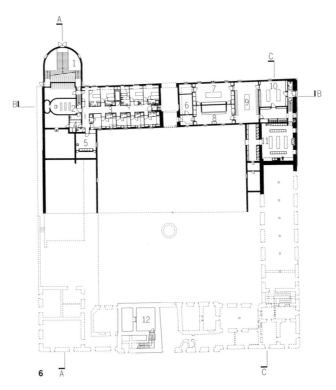

5 Ground Floor Plan

1 Presbytery
2 Monks' Choir
3 Lay People
4 Cloister
5 Sacristy
6 Chapter
7 Scriptorium
8 Cowl Room
9 Kitchen
10 Refectory
11 Lavatorium
12 Chapel
13 Visitors' Courtyard

6 Lower Ground Floor Plan

1 Apse
2 Chapel
3 Infirmary
4 Kitchen
5 Pharmacy
6 Drying Room
7 Laundry
8 Washroom
9 Cloakroom
10 Boot Room
11 Warming Room
12 Wine Cellar

5

6

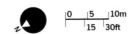

0 | 5 | 10m
15 | 30ft

Courtyards –
Eccentric

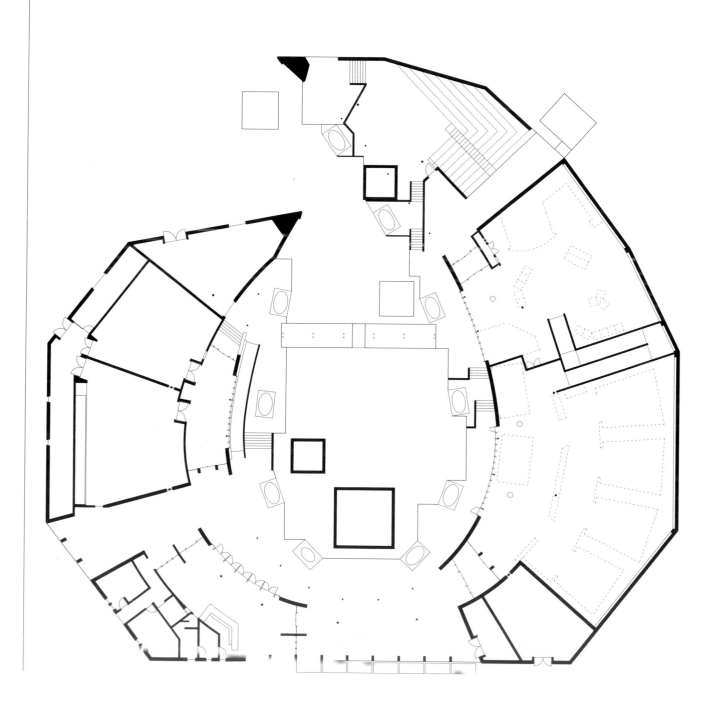

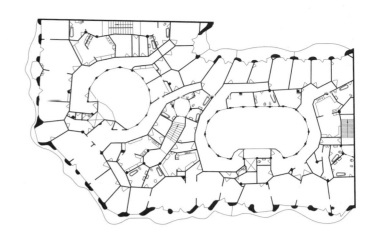

Casa Mila, Antoni Gaudí
Façade and Ground Floor Plan

The category Courtyards — Eccentric relates to projects that use external space in ingenious and powerful ways without necessarily conforming to the characteristics of the more traditional courtyard forms discussed in the previous chapter. Broadly, these were closed systems where circulation and orientation focused on a central orthogonal space, or where the form of the building created orthogonal spaces at the perimeter. This chapter looks at examples where the geometry between the elements is freer in response to site and topography, and where subtle inflections in plan and section produce uniquely shaped spaces.

In *Key Buildings of the Twentieth Century*, Richard Weston drew on a number of examples that also fit into this category. **Antoni Gaudí's Casa Mila** in Barcelona is perhaps the most curious of all, demonstrating the architect's preoccupation with making corners disappear. Externally, the apartment block reduces the prominence of the city's distinctive chamfered grid, while internally two curvaceous light-wells replace the city's traditional rectangular patios with dramatically sculptural communal spaces. In a less dense setting, Alvar Aalto's Tuberculosis Sanatorium in Paimio, Finland, creates a range of specifically shaped external spaces between clearly articulated functional blocks.

As one of the twentieth century's finest courtyard buildings, **Le Corbusier's Monastery of La Tourette** near Lyons, France, is given a unique eccentricity in plan and section through the building's response to the topography of the site and through the insertion of elements within the space, such as the inclined cruciform passageways and cylindrical stair turret. Similarly, **Sverre Fehn's Archbishopric Museum of Hamar** in Norway focuses on elements within a courtyard and celebrates the haphazard eccentricities of the medieval ruins by threading a single linking element through the centre of the plan that unifies and connects exhibits, internally and externally.

When considering contemporary examples, buildings were chosen that presented similar responses to their site, in landscape settings in response to topography and on more constrained urban sites in response to the ad hoc assemblage of incremental city growth.

Monastery of La Tourette, Le Corbusier
Façade and Ground Floor Plan

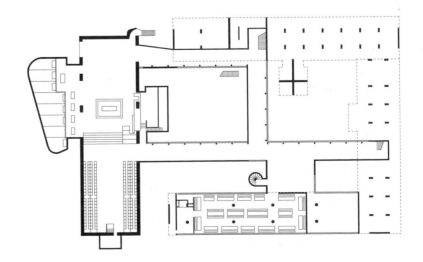

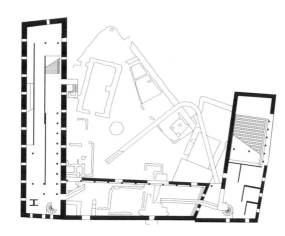

Archbishopric Museum of Hamar, Sverre Fehn
Interior and Ground Floor Plan

At the smallest scale, **Daly, Genik Architects'
Valley Center House** in San Diego, California, is
based around a splayed courtyard that opens up
views across the client's own land. Through the
eccentricity of the taper in plan and the offset
position of the pool, the courtyard has a relaxed
and informal quality, accentuated by an operable
wall that brings a transformative effect to both the
internal and external spaces. On the other side of
the world, on a remote site in Noonamah, northern
Australia, the **Rozak House** by **Troppo Architects**
offers another domestic example of how to anchor
a relatively modest free-form composition to its site.
With domestic functions broken down into three
elements, placed specifically to relate to views
and subtle changes in level, this fan-shaped

configuration creates three informal courts that
provide privacy and shelter in an expansive and
potentially alienating landscape.

On a slightly larger scale, **Tod Williams Billie
Tsien Architects' Mattin Arts Center** at the Johns
Hopkins University in Maryland responds specifically
to the constraints of a tapering and gently sloping
campus site to create an informal new courtyard on
a campus that was previously dominated by neo-
Georgian formality. With two linear ranges that
extend along the full length of the plot, and a shorter
adjoining arm at the top, stairs, ramps and terraces
have been fully integrated, not only to anchor the
building to its site but also to promote the courtyard
as a place that is essential to campus life. A similar
approach was taken by **Morphosis** at the **Diamond**

Ranch High School in Pomona, California, on a
site that was originally considered too steep to build
on. Exploiting the changes in level, the diagram of
the building organizes two groups of playing fields
at the top and bottom of the site, separated by a
linear range of accommodation that was fractured
and pulled apart to create a narrow fissure that
serves as the school's principal high street.

In more urban settings, eccentric courtyard
planning can also exploit residual or complicated
sites. **Zvi Hecker and Rafi Segal's Palmach
Museum of History** in Tel Aviv, Israel, arranges a
series of functions around a much treasured cluster
of trees and rocks, while **OMA's Dutch Embassy** in
Berlin creates an eccentric wrap-around courtyard
in order to rationalize the site and to articulate the

de Young Museum

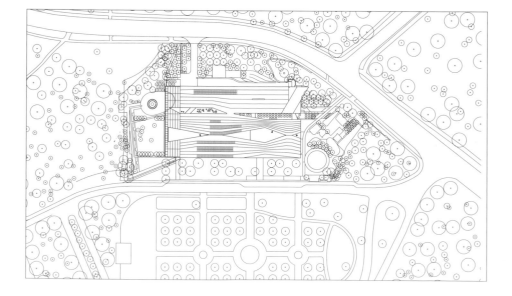

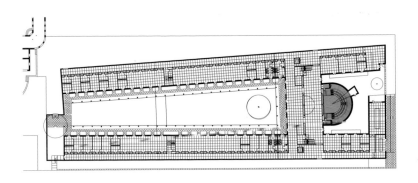

Rectory Building

principal accommodation building as a stand-alone 27 x 27 metre (89 x 89 foot) monolithic cube.

The chapter also includes more sinuous plans, such as **Naito Architect and Associates'** twin courtyard scheme in Shikoku, Japan, for the **Makino Museum of Plants and People**, where the elegantly roofed curved courtyards are seen to nestle within the landscape on a unique hillside setting. In a more urban context, the apparently sculptural effect of **Sauerbruch Hutton's Federal Environmental Agency** in Dessau, Germany, is justified on many more specific levels, subverting the monotony of the highly repetitive brief, weaving its way between a number of existing buildings and contributing to the aspirations of a broader landscape strategy. The building also uses its form

to meet the demands of an extremely detailed functional brief and ambitiously low energy targets, with decisions over plan depth and sectional organization being made in relation to orientation, daylight penetration and overshadowing – all of which have contributed to the architects' success in creating a distinctive building within the context of the city's regeneration strategy and in extending the interpretation of the courtyard type.

The chapter concludes with three projects that articulate apparently orthogonal compositions with expert nip and tuck to create dynamic and unusual internal courtyards. As part of the 2001 housing exposition Bo01 in Malmö, Sweden, **Moore Ruble Yudell Architects' Tango Housing** created an intimate courtyard at the centre of their apartment

block, with eight twisted towers that project into the courtyard to gather casually around the elliptical landscaped garden. In San Francisco, **Herzog & de Meuron and Fong & Chan's** much admired **de Young Museum** continues to demonstrate the architects' masterful ability to create sophisticated and intricate spatial sequences within straightforward, unremarkable structures. And, finally, **Álvaro Siza Vieira** continues to exhibit his exquisite spatial virtuosity through the planning of the elegant and highly refined **Rectory Building** at the University of Alicante in Spain; exhibiting the best of Siza's trademark formal invention, it turns its back on the campus to focus on two beautifully scaled cloistered courtyards.

Makino Museum of Plants and People

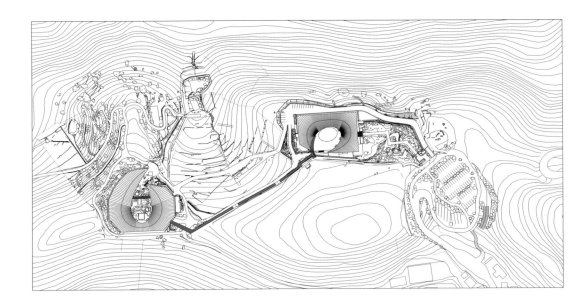

Valley Center House

Daly, Genik Architects

San Diego, California, USA; 1999

Located 550 metres (1800 feet) above sea level, the Valley Center House is located on a dramatic site overlooking the client's 10 hectare (25 acre) citrus and avocado ranch. Set within a dramatic, craggy landscape, it is low-lying and formally simple. Its ingenuity, however, comes through the operable wall that bounds the courtyard, bringing a transforming effect to both the internal and external spaces. Daly, Genik Architects focus on a rigorous investigation into emerging techniques in construction, engineering and component manufacturing, and this house, while simple in form, exploits mechanization to achieve dramatic spatial effects.

Built on an elevated concrete slab that sets the house at the level of the tree tops, the spaces are arranged in two wings of sleeping quarters on either side of a large central living/dining space. Together, the three building elements form a courtyard that contains a swimming pool, providing a sheltered space from where to enjoy extensive views over the groves to the coastline beyond. Through the eccentricity of a slight taper in plan and the offset position of the pool, the courtyard has a relaxed and informal quality; a quality that suits its craggy location without reverting to rocky

motifs, as the grey hues of its skin complement the tone of the granite outcrops.

In response to a direct request from the client, the house utilizes many energy-saving devices, with each zone being separately controlled. It is also built with a fire-resistant construction. When unoccupied, the house presents a closed opaque skin with large panels of corrugated concrete board at the rear and sides. Inside the courtyard this opacity contrasts with perforated metal screens that are more responsive to changing seasons and light. When the house is in use, the operable panels spring into action, changing the nature of the spaces inside and out, and making a theatrical gesture to its changing mode of occupation. Almost entirely glazed, the inner walls are covered with bifolding perforated metal doors and large sun screens. The bedrooms are screened with large vertical panels which concertina to provide blinkered views to the courtyard and define small external spaces in front of each bedroom. In contrast, the living room shelters beneath a large horizontal sun screen that forms a dramatic cantilever. This formal gesture not only provides necessary shelter from the relentless Californian sun, but also emphasizes the hierarchy of the plan,

extending the reach of the principal living space that sits between the sleeping quarters and functions as the communal heart of the home.

The perforated screens respond to climate and to light, allowing all rooms to be naturally ventilated at night as the glazed screens are free to slide behind them. At dawn and dusk they also produce magical lighting effects within the courtyard as internal lights reduce the opacity of the screens, revealing a warm and inviting translucence.

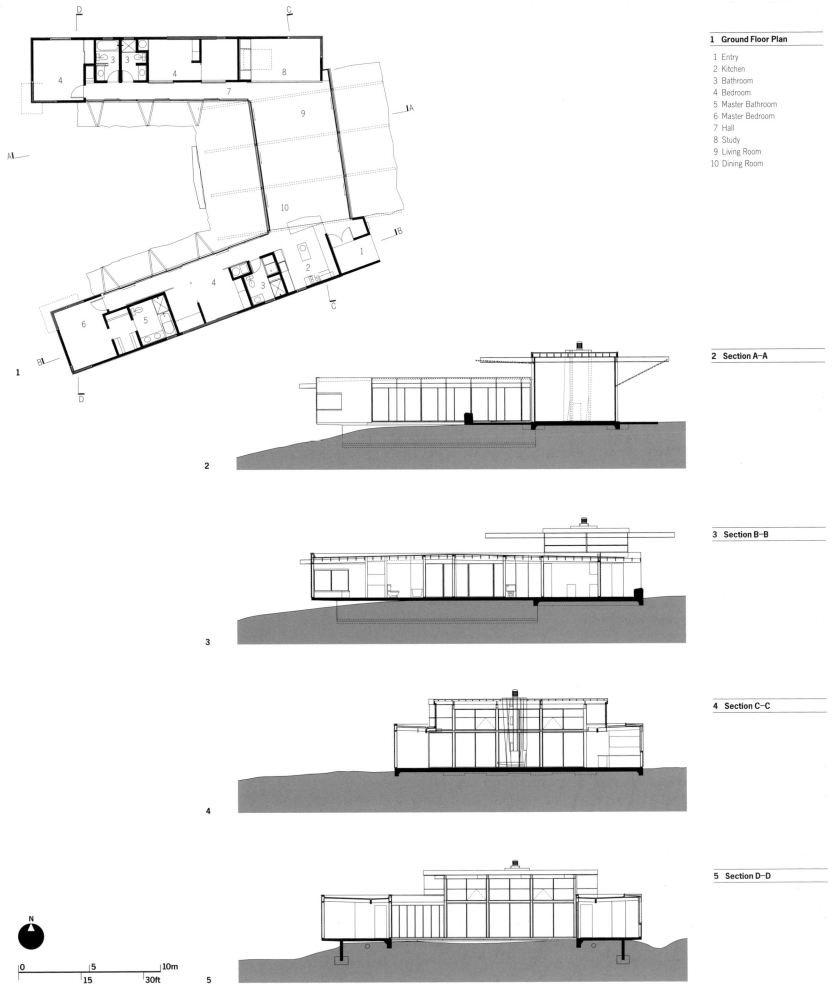

1 Ground Floor Plan

1 Entry
2 Kitchen
3 Bathroom
4 Bedroom
5 Master Bathroom
6 Master Bedroom
7 Hall
8 Study
9 Living Room
10 Dining Room

2 Section A–A

3 Section B–B

4 Section C–C

5 Section D–D

N

0   5   10m
15   30ft

Rozak House

Troppo Architects

Noonamah, Australia; 2001

Troppo Architects is a practice of regionally based architects in Australia who focus on developing regionally responsive buildings. As a network of associated offices in Darwin, Townsville, Adelaide, Perth and Byron Bay, they build on joint venture experience by sharing the intellectual resources of national practitioners, all of whom have the principal aim of making specific spaces for specific places.

Based on their ambition to promote a sense of place, the buildings they design respond to the climate and local setting of each site. Their technique is to deploy a series of adjustable skins that connect inside with out, and their manner embraces the informality of the Australian lifestyle, as they proudly announce that there are 'no bow ties here!'. The Rozak House is a fine example and summary of these ambitions.

When placing this relatively small building within an expansive landscape, the challenge was how to engage with such a vast space that had very few domestically scaled reference points. By experimenting with the disposition of plan, however, they were able to anchor the otherwise free-form composition to its site. The Rozak House is a good example of how the domestic functions of the home can be broken down and specifically placed to relate to views and subtle changes in level. In this instance, the programme has been divided into three equivalent volumes, with two bedroom pavilions and a centralized and shared pavilion for living and dining. While similar in form, and sharing a similar manner of articulation, the three principal volumes twist and turn to take their own specific place within the composition. As the configuration fans out to exploit specific views, and to create subtle thresholds of privacy, the spaces in between the wings create three informal courts. These courts provide more private and sheltered space, setting up dynamic views between each set of internal spaces and elevated verandas.

The wings are planned on similar footprints, within chamfered volumes under split pitched roofs. The bedroom wings are almost exact mirror images of each other, with two bedrooms and a shared bathroom accessed from the tapering veranda. The third wing turns this configuration through 90 degrees, organizing the spaces in series, leading from the kitchen, through the dining room, into the living spaces at the widest end. At this end the spaces are terminated with a spectacular, long view. In the middle, the centre of the composition is punctuated with an observation deck that rises above the roof levels to provide uninterrupted views across the dramatically sparse Northern Territory.

The building is self-sufficient in power and water, with all waste water treated on site. Power is collected through photovoltaic cells, stored on site and converted for use in the house. Water is heated by a solar hot water system using rain water that is stored in 120,000 litre (26,400 gallon) tanks. Waste water is treated in a compost system and all excess water is irrigated.

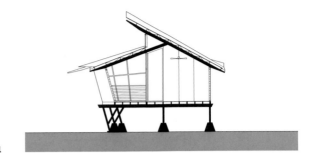

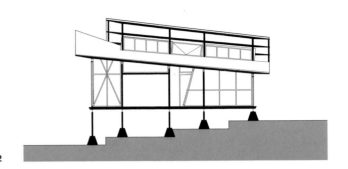

1　Section A–A

2　Section B–B

3　Section C–C

4　Section D–D

1

2

3

4

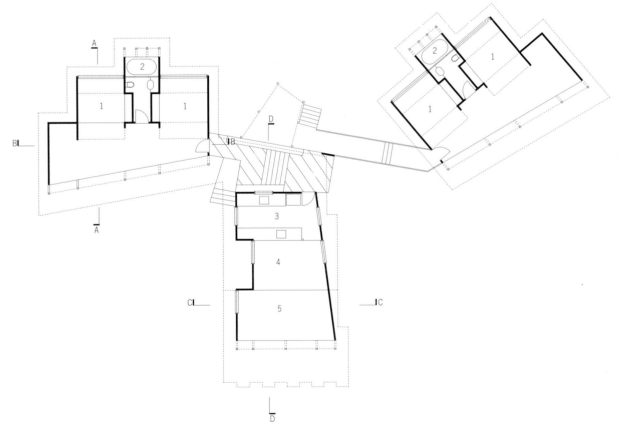

5

5　Ground Floor Plan

1　Bedroom
2　Bathroom
3　Kitchen
4　Dining
5　Living/Viewing

N

0　　2.5　　5m
　7.5　　15ft

Mattin Arts Center

Tod Williams Billie Tsien Architects

Baltimore, Maryland, USA; 2001

This informal courtyard building, designed by New York-based architects Tod Williams and Billie Tsien, responds specifically to the constraints of a tapering and gently sloping campus site in Baltimore, Maryland. It also responds to a certain unwritten ambition of the brief to bring a new vibrancy and diversity to the campus of Johns Hopkins University. With new courses to extend the breadth of the university's curriculum, a series of spaces was envisaged that would increase the formal diversity of the campus. To this end, Williams and Tsien have deployed an ad hoc form of Modernism that respectfully confronts the forced formality of the largely neo-Georgian campus, providing an alternative expression of contemporary campus life.

The arts centre is built to combine the functions of a student union building and a creative arts centre, and accommodation is arranged in three blocks: two linear ranges that extend along the full length of the plot, and a shorter adjoining arm at the top of the site. As the plot slopes down towards the narrow apex, the two longer ranges fall gently with it, enclosing an intimate and eccentrically composed tapering courtyard. At the top of the site, the shorter arm contains a theatre

and café, which combine to serve as the main social focus of the new precinct, overlooking the landscaped space below.

Across the site a datum is established which brings a material order to the intervention. Conforming to the university's widespread use of brick, the lower levels — which contain music rooms, a dance studio and computer suites — extend the use of this material, defining the sunken court and extending up to create a series of low-lying parapet walls to the upper-level terraces. On this upper level, which is landscaped to read as an external terrace, spaces are contained within discrete and isolated pavilions clad in panels of sandblasted glass. These freestanding blocks, which contain art studios that can open directly onto the terraces, are lighter and more refined in their appearance, providing a fitting counterpoint to the solid and weighty permanence of the more massive masonry below.

Integrated ramps and steps — which recall those created by Alvar Aalto — bring additional mass to the podium, and also serve to direct a number of cross-campus routes. With such networks, the new precinct has quickly become fully integrated into the life of the campus, animated by

students and staff at all hours, and it already feels like part of the campus' older bedrock.

As a new intervention in a university that has until recently based its reputation on science and literature, this new arts centre is symbolic in more ways than one, as it not only brings a new vibrancy and diversity to what Johns Hopkins can offer academically, but also to its physical environment; a significant and necessary mechanism to attract students and staff to any contemporary and highly competitive educational institution.

1 West Wing East Elevation

2 Roof Plan

3 East Wing West Elevation

4 West Wing First Floor Plan
1 Black Box Theater
2 Administrative Offices
3 Film/Digital Arts

5 West Wing Ground Floor Plan
1 Black Box Theater
2 Back of House
3 Mechanical
4 Maintenance
5 Meeting Room
6 Dance/Multipurpose

6 East Wing First Floor Plan
1 Art Studio
2 Darkroom

7 East Wing Ground Floor Plan
1 Large Music Rehearsal
2 Small Music Rehearsal
3 Individual Music Practice Rooms
4 Student Offices

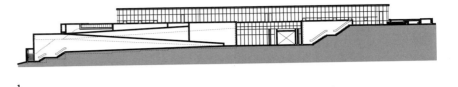

1

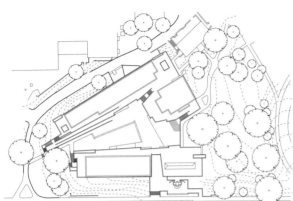

2

3

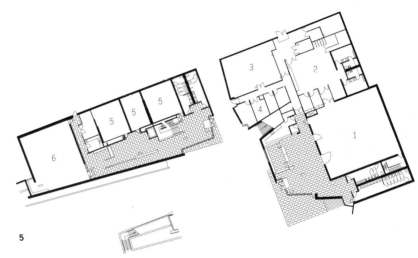

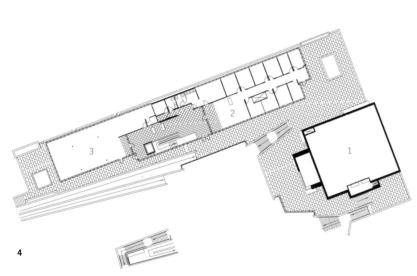

4

5

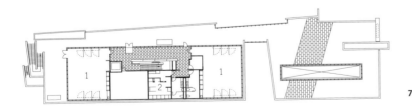

6

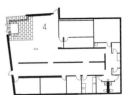

7

N 0 10 20m
30 60ft

Palmach Museum of History

Zvi Hecker with Rafi Segal

Tel Aviv, Israel; 1998

The Palmach Museum of History is situated on the periphery of Tel Aviv University, and is organized around an eccentrically planned courtyard that responds to pre-existing site features. Commissioned by the association that represents veterans of the Palmach – a military unit set up in the 1940s – it includes a theatre, library, museum, classrooms, offices and a memorial room.

The building is in contrast to the other buildings on the university's campus by architects such as Louis Kahn and Mario Botta, which are generally isolated, autonomous and more self-conscious in their manner. The Palmach Museum, on the other hand, is less easy to identify and has a far more ambiguous form: part wall, part landscape and part building. Centred on an eccentrically planned courtyard, the building was built around a preserved cluster of trees and rocks that were protected during construction and retained as a key part of the composition. The building resembles a rocky outcrop, with a series of angular forms that have been pushed together in both plan and section. Its forms also allude to more complicated issues that relate to the conflict experienced by members of the Palmach – the elite striking force of the Haganah, the underground military

organization of the Jewish community.

When considering the plan, the collisions of lines, planes and forms create a complex series of geometries from which three principal forms emerge, each with its own entrance: a linear form that runs along the main street and which contains offices and a reception; and two shard-like forms to the rear, one containing a canteen, the other a two-tiered auditorium. In three dimensions, however, the forms are articulated far more coherently as three inclined slabs, two of which intersect to produce composite triangular volumes. At the intersection of these two forms, the forms disintegrate and the plan yields to the existing trees to create a smaller inset court, overlooked by the canteen and the entrance to the auditorium. The triangular plan forms use the apex spaces for stairs and entrances, with the auditorium neatly fitting within the tapering volume, with the stage at the widest end.

Above ground, the courtyard provides access to all three volumes, with three discrete receptions rather than one singular formal entrance, and is overlooked by two terraces and a first-floor-level bridge link. Raised above street level, this intimate shady space provides peace and tranquillity, and can be accessed from two directions: either directly

via a stair, or more gracefully via a gently inclined ramp that continues the slope of the street.

The entire composition sits above a lower-ground-level exhibition space that traces the footprint of the upper levels. Below ground, however, the three volumes combine to create a continuous circuit around the site (ideal for a narrated exhibition), maintaining essential space at the centre of the site for the roots of the trees.

1 Level 2

1 Administration

2 North Elevation

3 Level 1

1 Administration
2 Gallery

4 Section A–A

5 Level 0

1 Entrance
2 Courtyard
3 Canteen
4 Stage
5 Auditorium
6 Lobby
7 Administration
8 Reception

6 Basement Plan

1 Exhibition Space
2 Memorial Space

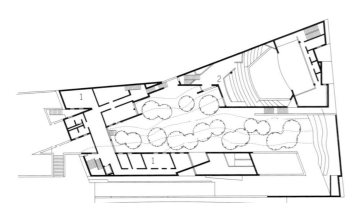

1

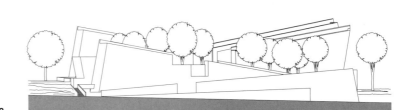

2

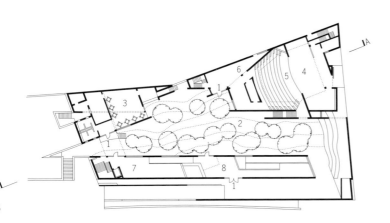

3

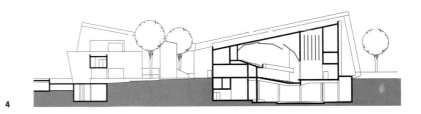

4

5

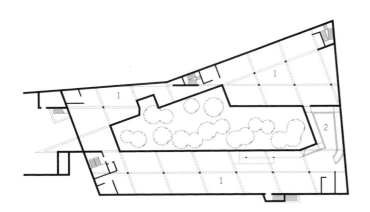

6

0	10m	20m
	30	60ft

N

Dutch Embassy

OMA

Berlin, Germany; 2004

The fact that the Dutch Embassy in Berlin is a courtyard building is very much the result of strict planning regulations; the fact that the courtyard is unorthodox, eccentrically avoiding the ubiquitous centralized atrium type, is very much a result of the approach taken by its distinguished and challenging architect, Rem Koolhaas of OMA.

When considering the design strategy for the new Dutch Embassy in Berlin, in response to chief planner Hans Stimmann's stipulation that any new building on the site would have to occupy all four corners of the plot, the architects chose not to simply replicate the courtyard configuration of the adjoining buildings. Instead, OMA proposed a freestanding cubic monolith, 27 x 27 metres (89 x 89 feet), set away from the existing buildings and enclosed by a slim L-shaped perimeter block. This strategy, while conforming in principle to the planners' conditions, radically altered the site's morphology and gave the building the formal autonomy that you suspect was more a priority of the architect than of the brief.

Dividing the building physically and programmatically, with the cube containing the principal administrative spaces and the perimeter block a series of apartments, the courtyard itself is

essentially a residual space – shapeless perhaps, but nevertheless specific and well proportioned in relation to the dominant presence of the cube. Further articulated by an array of slim bridges and a dramatically cantilevered conference room, the courtyard extends around the rear of the cube and gives the building's southwesterly entrance more than one aspect.

Described as an expressionist labyrinth, the building generates its unique character through the articulation of an intricate route set within the reduced cubic footprint. As a result the courtyard is not experienced in a traditional manner with circulation arranged around its edge. Instead, the architect chose to hollow out the mass of the cube with a continuous 200 metre (656 foot) passageway that extends from the southwesterly corner to the roof terrace above, providing an uninterrupted means of orientation and circulation for all who use it.

The route (or trajectory as OMA prefer to call it), is a continuous linear arrangement of stairs, ramps, corridors and niches that buckle their way around the cubic form. Essentially angular in its geometry, held between both parallel and tapering walls, the trajectory runs clockwise around the

cube, from the ground-floor reception to a second-floor Internet foyer. It then cuts diagonally across, rising from level three to level five through a series of conference and administrative spaces, before running anticlockwise past the ambassador's quarters on level six, a fitness centre on level eight and through the café on level nine, before finally emerging on the roof terrace above. Along its way, as it engages and disengages with the building's external skin, the trajectory projects a series of distorted, stepped and ramped figures in elevation that break the regularity of the cladding grid. The figures also step out in plane to add further depth to the building's essentially flat façades.

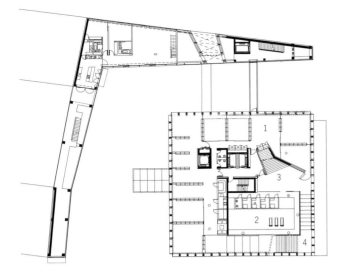

1

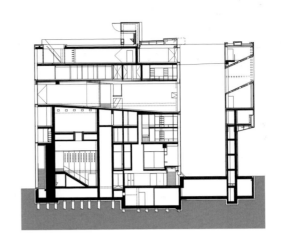

2

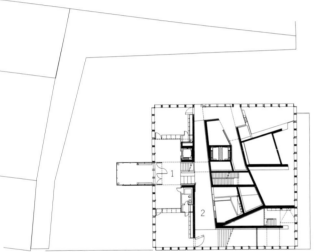

3

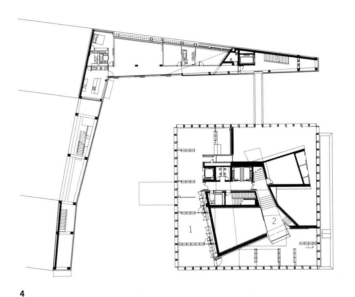

4

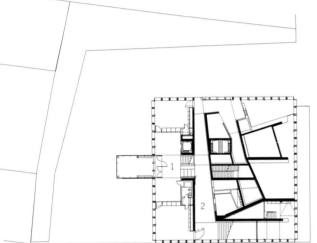

5

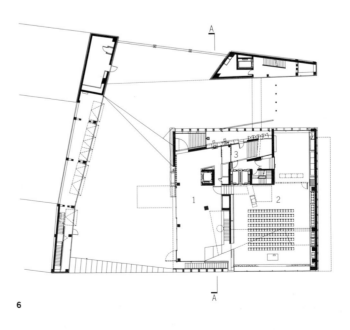

6

N

0 | 5 | 10m
15 | 30ft

Makino Museum of Plants and People

Naito Architect and Associates

Kochi, Japan; 1999

The Makino Museum of Plants and People, designed by Tokyo-based Naito Architect and Associates, was built in memory of Tomitaro Makino, an eminent scholar and the man considered to be the father of Japanese botany. Built to house an extensive library of books and specimens donated by Dr Makino, it also provides research and exhibition spaces that serve to make the material more widely known to the public.

Due to complicated landownership issues, the museum is arranged in two buildings that are linked by a 170 metre (558 foot) corridor. As strange as this seems, this arrangement serves to give each part its own autonomy, with one precinct to the west containing the museum proper (together with its associated research facilities) and the other, to the east, containing an exhibition space and lecture hall. As separated twins, the buildings bear a strong family resemblance while having their own character and identity: the research centre to the west – being the first building reached from the car park – is set within an orthogonal footprint; the exhibition hall to the east – set more remotely into the landscape – is a more expressive form, laid out in an eccentric, tightly coiled, fossil-like crescent. While merging sensitively with the topography of

Mount Godai, each courtyard exploits a different aspect, with the museum opening up to the south and the exhibition hall facing north.

Considering each building in isolation, the museum and research block has by far the most complicated organization, with an extensive basement level that contains storage, offices and book stacks. This area, however, is not a forgotten or gloomy undercroft, but is instead linked to the upper level by a shared central courtyard. Orthogonally arranged at low level, the building shifts at the upper level to focus on an eccentric ovoid courtyard, with the gently curving edges of the light-well mediating between upper and lower realms. In contrast to this slightly ambiguous form, the exhibition and lecture block is far more expressive in its overall configuration, with less of a duality between its inner and outer forms. Resembling a crab in plan, with one pincer longer than the other, the inner court is lower and more intimate. With no internal corridors, the courtyard gives direct and sheltered access to the exhibition spaces that surround it, and at the north of the site the long pincer contains the lecture hall, which extends past the courtyard into the landscape beyond, notionally acknowledging the museum to

the west.

Both blocks are united by the articulation of their sculptural roofscapes, which are clad in zinc and stainless steel, and supported on elegant and fully expressed timber trusses. With low sweeping curves, each roof creates two distinct effects, externally emerging from within the vegetation as smooth and sinuous double-curved forms, and internally having a much higher degree of articulation, as dramatic ridge and truss-chord lines serve to exaggerate the building's curves in both plan and section.

1 Exhibition Hall Elevation   **2** Exhibition Hall Section A–A   **3** Museum Section B–B

4 Exhibition Hall Floor Plan

1 Main Entrance
2 Exhibition Gallery
3 Botanical Illustration Gallery
4 Machine Room
5 Lecture Hall
6 Permanent Gallery
7 Deck
8 Cafeteria/Information
9 Inner Court

5 Museum First Floor Plan

1 Main Entrance
2 Machine Room
3 AV Hall
4 Meeting Room
5 Godaisan Gallery
6 Studio
7 Study Room
8 Japanese Room
9 Deck
10 Shop/Restaurant

6 Museum Ground Floor Plan

1 Office
2 Stack Room
3 Storage
4 Library
5 Machine Room
6 Inner Court
7 Laboratory

1

2

3

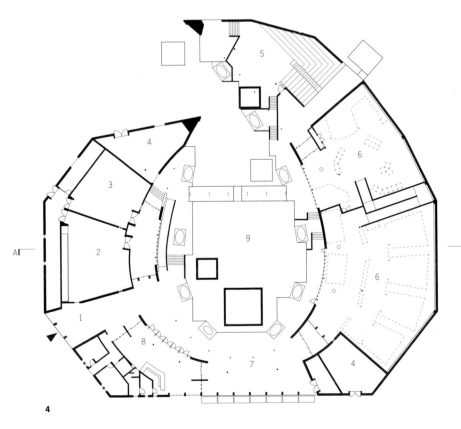

4

N

0 5 10m
15 30ft

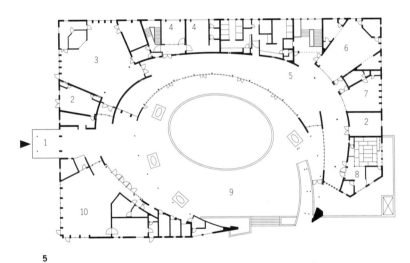

5

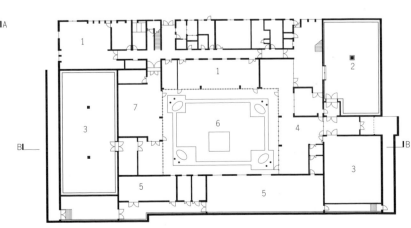

6

Federal Environmental Agency

Sauerbruch Hutton

Dessau, Germany; 2005

The headquarters for the Federal Environmental Agency in Dessau is described by its architects as a symbiosis of technology and nature. With high environmental targets that seek to achieve an operational efficiency 50 per cent higher than current standards, many of the decisions about the building's form and materials were dictated by strict performance criteria. As an example of the courtyard type, therefore, it is distinct from more orthodox arrangements where formal concerns can more reasonably by prioritized. Here, when attempting to meet the demands of a functional brief, as well as extensive accommodation requirements within the context of the site, and in consideration of orientation, daylight penetration and overshadowing, decisions regarding the depth of the plan and the organization of the cross-section were heavily governed. Nevertheless, the architects have succeeded in creating a distinctive building – a significant achievement within the context of the city's regeneration strategy and in extending the interpretation of the courtyard type.

In contrast to orthodox courtyard models, here there are obviously no corners to resolve, as the sinuous form snakes its way across the site. Furthermore, the central void is internalized, in response to its social and environmental obligations, covered by a glazed sawtooth roof and crossed by a series of bridges at each of the three upper levels.

The sinuous organization of the plan not only responds well to the site, as it weaves its way between a number of existing buildings and contributes to the aspirations of a wider landscape master plan, it also helps to subvert the potential for the repetitive nature of the brief – namely the inclusion of office space for 800 workers in 12 square metre (129 square foot) standardized cellular units – to overwhelm the building's collective identity. Arranged over four floors, the plan also exploits the potential for courtyards to create two distinct realms between the interior and exterior. While externally the envelope is smooth and uninterrupted, internally the streamlined elevations are modulated at the upper levels by re-entrant soft spaces situated at the head of each bridge, and at ground level by a number of pronounced 'boulder' rooms that break out into the courtyard. While the soft spaces help to break up the monotony of the centralized corridors, providing important breakout space for incidental interaction, the boulder rooms enclose specific group functions

in a series of larger spaces that cannot be accommodated within the relatively narrow plan depth of the principal linear element.

While enveloped in one continuous roof form, articulated with a fanning knuckle to resolve the cranked geometry, the central courtyard is subdivided as the sinuous tail of accommodation tucks in on itself. In the form of a two-storey inhabited bridge containing more cellular spaces, as the upper two levels span across the void they separate an entrance forum from the main courtyard space. The entrance forum is further articulated by a freestanding boulder containing an auditorium that breaches the full-height glazed entrance wall.

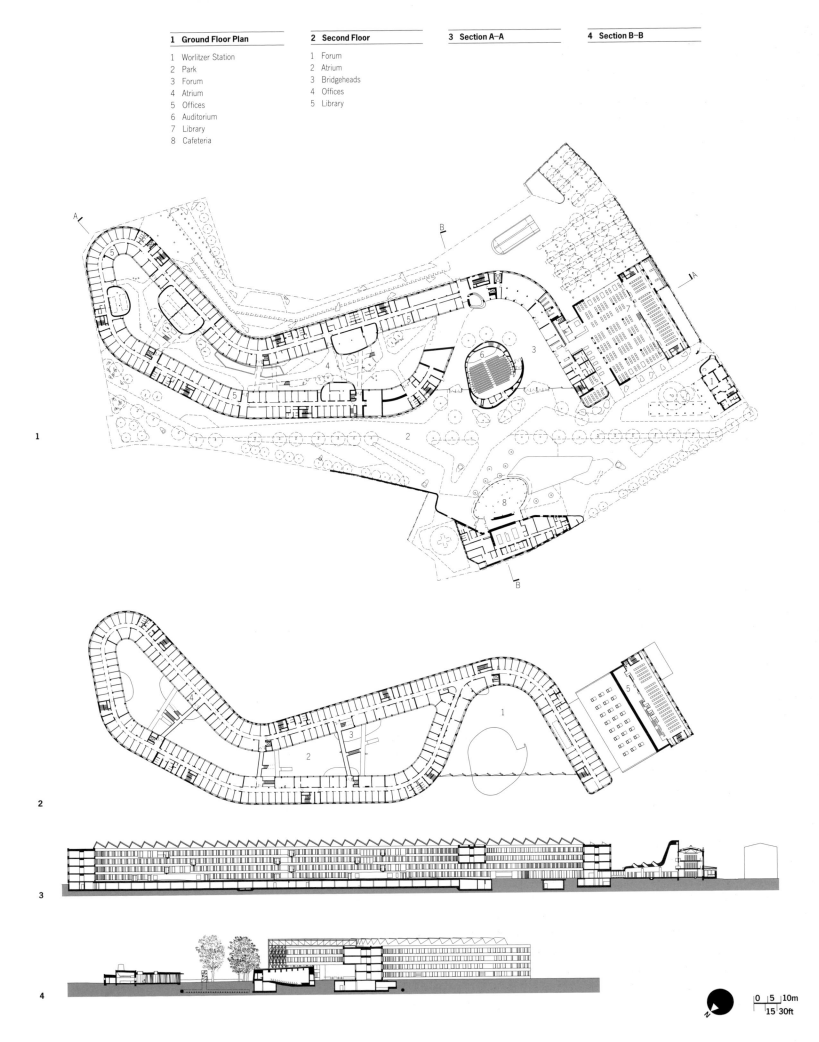

1 Ground Floor Plan

1 Worlitzer Station
2 Park
3 Forum
4 Atrium
5 Offices
6 Auditorium
7 Library
8 Cafeteria

2 Second Floor

1 Forum
2 Atrium
3 Bridgeheads
4 Offices
5 Library

3 Section A–A

4 Section B–B

Tango Housing

Moore Rubel Yudell Architects & Planners

Malmö, Sweden; 2001

This vibrantly coloured and eccentrically planned courtyard housing scheme was designed as part of the 2001 housing exposition in Malmö, Sweden: Bo01. As part of an ambitious plan to build 522 apartments and 37 houses (together with the necessary associated workplaces, schools and amenities), this plot provides 27 apartments in one-, two- and three-bedroom configurations, set around an intimate communal garden.

Inspired by walled towns, the Bo01 expo site was laid out with a protective perimeter wall of four- to five-storey blocks. This plot forms part of the wall, turning its back on the prevailing wind and rain, and stepping down from four storeys on the east to two on the west. Inside the apartments, another shared wall exists, this time in the form of a so-called intelligent wall, which provides all the necessary services and acts as the principal ordering device, separating the orthogonal accommodation at the perimeter from the twisted geometries that face the courtyard. As such, this scheme has a section of two halves, the outer portion forming part of the 'city wall'– relating to the creation of traditional streets and canalside façades – and the inner portion which 'collects' each of the living rooms into eight twisted towers

that project into the courtyard, gathering casually around the elliptical landscaped garden.

The distinction between the two sides is not only manifested in the disposition of the parts but also in the composition of the elevations, with a series of horizontally and vertically ribbed concrete panels giving a haphazard, yet ordered, proportion to the street façades with a subtle rigour that contrasts with large areas of brightly framed glazing that sit within the courtyard, inspired, perhaps, by the colourful façades of traditional Swedish fishing villages.

Internally, apartments share part of the city wall – containing bedrooms and bathrooms, and part of a tower – with kitchens and living areas, each divided and ordered by the 500 mm (19.7 inch) thick intelligent wall. As the spinal cord for each apartment, the intelligent wall contains services and storage, and gives access to Tango's heat, power, Intranet and security systems via in-house laptop, remote computer or cell phone platforms. It even allows residents to reserve the community room or guest apartment.

Each living space shares a garden with its neighbour, exploiting fine views of the Oresund at high level, while providing a more intimate

relationship with the garden on the ground and first floors. The collective dance-like movement of the towers promotes interaction between otherwise separate dwellings with the garden serving as the focus of community life. A small single-storey pavilion completes the courtyard's enclosure to the west, serving as a gatehouse and providing some useful shared utilities. Within the garden itself, small bridges give access to each entrance core, crossing en route an elliptical marsh that processes grey water and provides a subtle privacy buffer to the ground-floor living rooms.

1   **Section A–A**

2   **Section B–B**

3   **Fourth Floor Plan**

1   Living Room
2   Kitchen/Dining Room
3   Bedroom/Study

4   **Second Floor Plan**

1   Living Room with Loft/
    Library above
2   Kitchen/Dining Room
3   Bedroom/Study

5   **Ground Floor Plan**

1   Living Room
2   Kitchen/Dining Room
3   Bedroom/Study

1

2

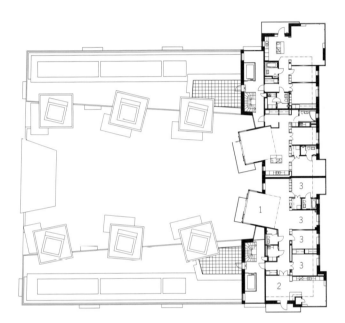

3

4

5

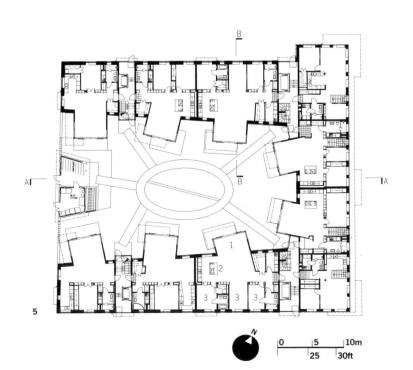

| 0 | 5 | 10m |
| 25 | 30ft | |

de Young Museum

Herzog & de Meuron, Primary Designers/Fong & Chan, Principal Architects

San Francisco, California, USA; 2005

It is no exaggeration to place Herzog & de Meuron at the forefront of the world's architectural elite, consistently producing world-class buildings that operate on many levels. Contextual and iconic, rational and whimsical, tectonically innovative and playfully scenographic, each begins with rigorous analysis of programme, site and material, resulting in buildings – almost without fail – that are spatially and materially unique. The de Young Museum in San Francisco (in collaboration with Fong & Chan) is perhaps the architects' most accomplished to date, and in consideration of the plan as the focus of this brief study, the museum demonstrates Herzog & de Meuron's masterful ability to create sophisticated and intricate spatial sequences within remarkably straightforward unremarkable structures. Few visitors, for example, would be immediately aware of its rectangular plan, or be able to perceive the regular grid hidden within walls and display cases.

The plan was derived in response to the de Young's vast and varied art collection. Described by the architects as 'heterotopical', the museum owns work that dates back to the dawn of human history. In response to its collection and the landscape of the parkland site, early schemes proposed a series of individual pavilions, each housing a different collection and expressing the diverse range of the cultures represented. Rejecting this idea and recognizing the complexities of managing an extensive campus, a strategy was proposed that did precisely the opposite by creating a single unified container and compressing the pavilions – all with their own landscaped borders – into a three-bay mould.

When read as a series of parallel bands, buckled to allow the park's landscape to fill space in between, this interpretation describes an assemblage of conjoined linear spaces. As a conceptual counterpoint, however, the museum can also be understood as an eroded solid; a more appropriate reading, perhaps, when the material qualities of the copper monolith are taken into account. Many more subtleties exist in plan and section, exhibiting expert nip and tuck; such as a gentle inflection along its roof line, the inviting inset entrance courtyards, the gently nodding cantilevered brow, and the graceful twist of its tower which turns to orientate itself to the city grid.

With multiple entrances, one on each of its three parkside façades, the plan works against the formality that dominated the previously axially planned site. Exaggerated by a series of convergent cross-axes that create unorthodox spatial relationships, routes through the landscape deny the convention of frontal planning and, internally, geometries set up highly charged relationships between apparently unrelated parts of the collection.

Throughout this non-hierarchical arrangement the plan is moderated by a number of key topographical fix points, such as the grand stair in Wisley Court, and the two hairpin intersections where acute geometries are resolved. While the architects have not settled on a name for these critical points on plan, they informally oscillate between 'contact' and 'switch'. The electronic analogies suitably encapsulate the highly charged spatial experience that this building provides, leading visitors from the park and across the foyer, through the galleries and across landscaped courtyards, to the final ascent of the tower.

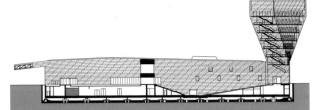

1 Section C–C

2 Section D–D

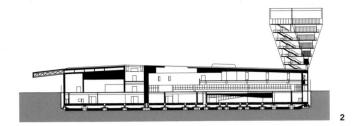

1

2

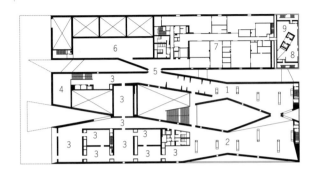

3 Upper Floor Plan

1 Art in Africa
2 Pacific Art Gallery
3 American Art
4 Native Art American
5 Interstitial Gallery
6 Textile Gallery
7 Storage
8 American Art Curatorial
9 American Art Study Center

4 Section B–B

5 Section A–A

3

4

5

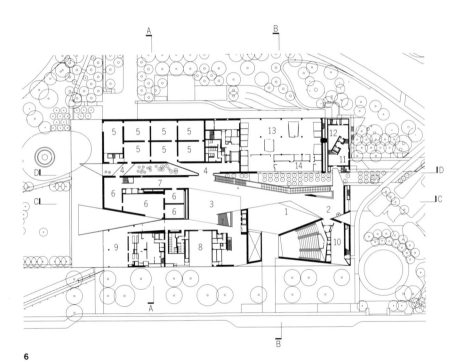

6 Ground Floor Plan

1 Entry Court
2 Reception
3 Wisley Court
4 20th Century Interstitial
5 American Art/20th Century
6 Native Art/American
7 Native Art Interstitial
8 Museum Family Room
9 Café
10 Children's Gallery
11 Tower Lobby
12 Membership/Information Center
13 Offices and Conference Rooms
14 Library

6

7 Lower Floor Plan

1 Entrance from Car Park
2 Information
3 Temporary Exhibition

7

0 15 30m
45 90ft

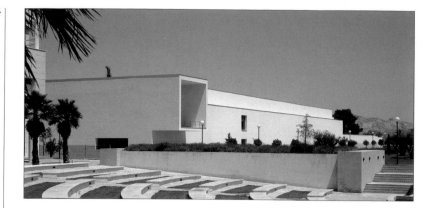

Rectory Building

Álvaro Siza Vieira

Alicante, Spain; 1998

Despite being completed in 1998, Álvaro Siza's design for the rectory building on the University of Alicante campus could not be overlooked as part of any study into eccentric courtyard planning, as it provides an elegant and highly refined spatial solution, and exhibits the best of Siza's trademark formal invention. Built to house office and administration space for the college rector, it typifies the self-centredness of the courtyard type, turning its back on the campus to focus on two beautifully scaled courtyards. Recalling the traditional Hispanic patio type, the building forms an impenetrable fortress, built to protect its occupants from the rigours of the region's harsh climate, with its punishing sunlight and heat.

Adhering to the diminishing proportions of the site's boundary, the low-lying and tapering courtyards provide two distinct environments separated by a cross-axial bar of accommodation that roughly divides the plot into a ratio of 1:3. To the north, the smaller courtyard contains a semicircular auditorium, and access from a foyer within the transverse block. To the south, the larger courtyard forms the principal focus of the precinct, sparingly articulated by a single off-centre tree and divided at high level by a screened bridge that

crosses the space at the point where the building steps from two storeys to one.

The entrance encourages visitors to enjoy the full effect of the courtyard's spatial hierarchy, screening it from view until those entering are turned through 90 degrees to confront the building's principal axis. With a single-storey colonnade that marches relentlessly around the entrance court, this space recalls the bleak, and at times disturbing, ambience of a de Chirico painting with the building's stripped forms casting sharp shadows that trace the sun's menacing trajectory. Despite this, however, through its restrained use of materials and highly refined formal coherence, the space provides a quiet focus within an otherwise nondescript university campus. From the external entrance ante-room, at a pace that is governed by the strict tempo of the colonnade, visitors can either walk under cover to the reception area, or cut across to any one of the offices that have direct access onto the courtyard. On the upper level, a generous cantilevered canopy provides shelter to a column-free cloister that completes its circuit across the screened bridge. The roof of the auditorium also provides an additional upper-level terrace.

Internally, the building's stripped aesthetic continues, and it is clear that Siza is not wary of creating long internal corridors, with both floors served by full-length, windowless, narrow passageways. While these could potentially produce monotonous characterless spaces, Siza's distinctive and well-known use of materials — low-level ceramic tiles, flush skirting boards and highly polished floors — gives these spaces a powerful (if at times rather austere) identity. Throughout the composition, the architect's taut, formal rigour is also evident, with devices such as the semicircular lantern, projecting loggia and double-folded canopies adding to the building's well-mannered eccentricity.

1 Section A–A   **2 Section B–B**   **3 Section C–C**   **4 First Floor Plan**   **5 Ground Floor Plan**

4 First Floor Plan
1 Entrance Court
2 Main Courtyard
3 Footbridge
4 Open Gallery
5 Offices and Meeting Rooms
6 Roof Terrace
7 Roof Terrace above Auditorium
8 Secondary Courtyard

5 Ground Floor Plan
1 Entrance
2 Main Courtyard
3 Auditorium
4 Secondary Courtyard

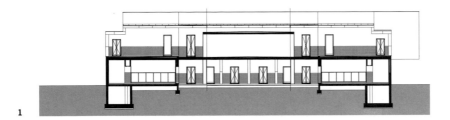

1

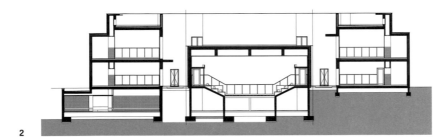

2

3

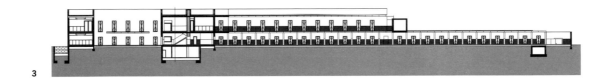

4

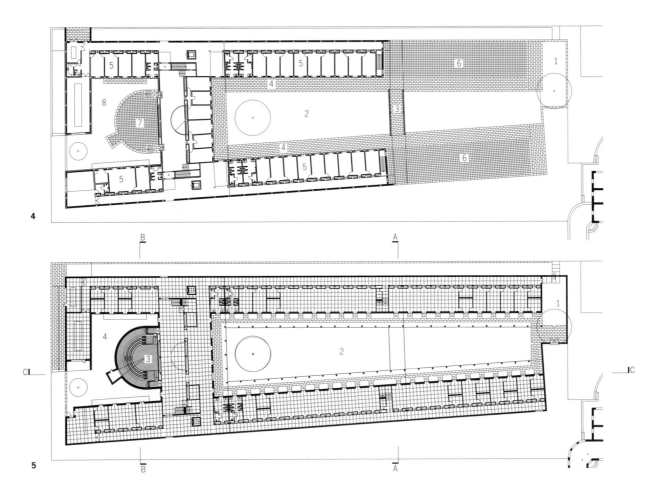

5

Cityscape
Responses

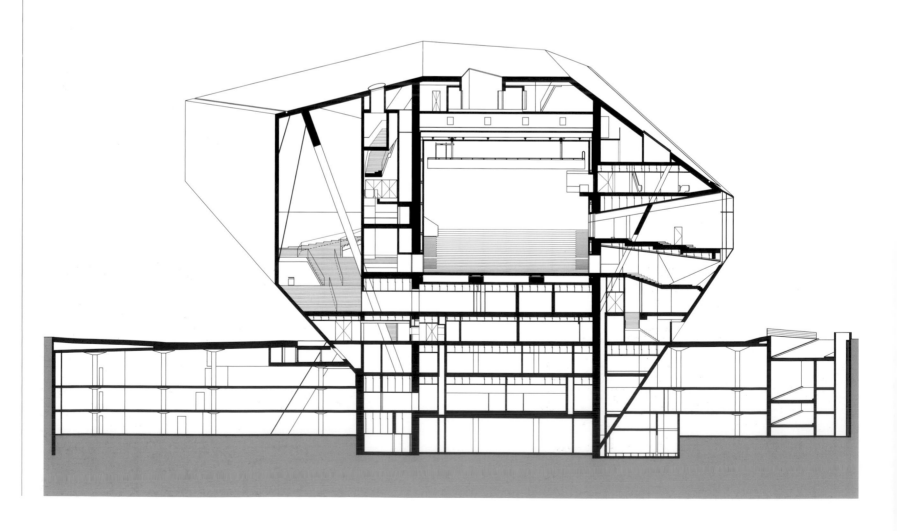

Economist Building,
Alison and Peter Smithson
Façade and Ground Floor Plan

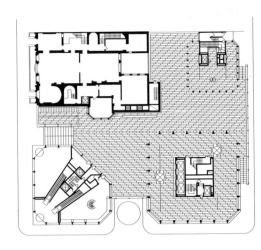

When discussing any of the examples in this chapter, a commentator would be ill-advised to speculate too much about the long-term merits of each building's contribution to the city. Buildings take time to bed in, and only time will tell whether or not any of these buildings will prove to be successfully integrated within their relative contexts. This is said in opposition to a current tendency that rushes to declare any flamboyant new building as iconic when, in reality, image-based observations do little more than produce a new mode of skin-deep criticism that tends to overlook the true merits of the building in question.

So-called iconic buildings are, however, an unavoidable hot topic in today's architectural debate, as many regional capitals compete to make their own mark on the map of cultural tourism, collecting highly conspicuous works by star architects in an attempt to lure more cash-rich people. Within this culture, the emerging imbalance in the emphasis given to the image of 'iconic buildings' seems unavoidable and inevitable, resulting in subtle and often more sophisticated buildings being overlooked. With the benefit of hindsight, a number of significant iconic buildings were rightly identified in Richard Weston's *Key Buildings of the Twentieth Century*, projects that now are emblematic of cities around the world, including Frank Lloyd Wright's Guggenheim Museum in New York, Jørn Utzon's Sydney Opera House, Renzo Piano and Richard Rogers' Pompidou Centre in Paris and, of course, Gehry Partners' Guggenheim Museum in Bilbao, Spain – the latter being the generator of the much sought after 'Bilbao Effect'. With the passage of time, it is of course possible to judge the relative success of each of these buildings, and to say with a certain degree of confidence that all of them are iconic in the fullest sense of the word, as works of architecture and as objects in the city.

There were many other featured buildings in Weston's selection, however, that remain equally significant in terms of their contribution to the cityscape, which despite being less spectacular, have made an equally positive and significant contribution to the world's wider architectural culture. **Alison and Peter Smithson's Economist Building**, for example, built on London's venerable St James's in

Willis Faber & Dumas Headquarters, Foster + Partners
Façade and Site Plan

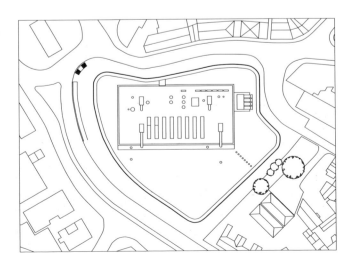

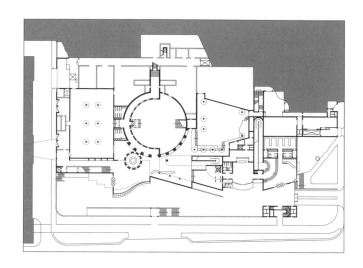

Staatsgalerie, James Stirling and Michael Wilford
Façade and Site Plan

1964, is an exemplary cityscape response that demonstrates how a complex mixed use building can be integrated into an extremely sensitive site. With three towers of differing size, all linked by a two-level basement and raised plaza, the building proposed and continues to propose a radical alternative within its existing context, with each of the three towers responding to its own immediate condition. **Foster + Partners' Willis Faber & Dumas Headquarters** in Ipswich, England, is another exemplary cityscape response, demonstrating the unlikely potential of curtain walling to create a unique and highly specific response. And **James Stirling's and Michael Wilford's Staatsgalerie** in Stuttgart, Germany, continues to endure today as one of the architects'

most celebrated urban projects, defining a unique and powerful cityscape all of its own, as it steps up the site with a public route that ramps, winds and climbs around a new type of urban focus.

In recognition of such a wide range of cityscape responses, therefore, throughout the compilation of this chapter a balance of projects was sought that would range from the extreme to the discreet. The projects, however, are unified by the fact that they can all be seen as responses to the specific qualities of, and obligations to, their urban settings. Responses not only to specific physical qualities of their sites, such as the direct correlation between the plot shape and flat-iron form of **Erick van Egeraat Associated Architects' Mauritskade Apartment Building** in Amsterdam,

but also to subtle, more phenomenal qualities that somehow encapsulate the spirit of the place; qualities that may have begun to suggest and direct the manner in which **Cino Zucchi** integrated **Building D**, housing 16 modern apartments in the heart of the World Heritage city of Venice.

Arranged broadly in an approximate order of scale, other projects include deeply contextual responses in historic settings, such as **Rafael Moneo's** beautifully composed **Town Hall Extension** in Murcia, Spain, which presents a bold new façade that addresses the city's richly adorned cathedral opposite. **Josep Llinás'** tailor-made **Jaume Fuster Library** in Barcelona is seen in contrast to this, presenting not one principal façade, but three deeply contextual and unique elevations that help to anchor

Walsall Art Gallery

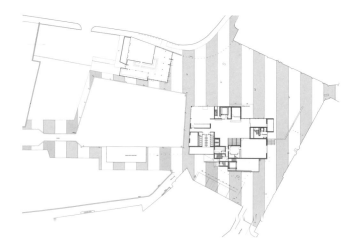

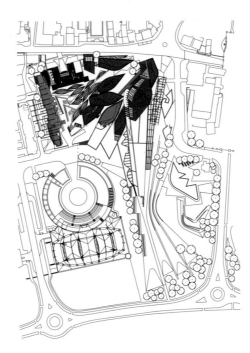

the building into its complicated three-sided site. With fewer contextual constraints, projects such as **David Chipperfield Architects' Des Moines Public Library** in the USA, and **Caruso St John Architects'** exquisitely planned and elevated **Walsall Art Gallery** in England both position abstract forms that can be seen in the round to create dramatic beacons in the wasteland areas of their cities. At the larger end of the cityscape scale, both **Gehry Partners** and **LAB** work with whole city blocks to create radical new forms of urbanism. Gehry Partners' **Walt Disney Concert Hall** has been planted like a flower in the borders of downtown Los Angeles, and **LAB and Bates Smart's Federation Square** provides a bold new focus for Melbourne's citizens, in its proposed

guise as a public square and cultural and entertainment quarter.

The chapter also, somewhat inevitably (but completely unapologetically), includes a number of the most formally arresting projects of recent years – as **OMA's** landed meteorite, the **Casa da Musica** in Portugal, **Foreign Office Architects'** stilted **Yokohama International Port Terminal** in Japan, and **Zaha Hadid Architects'** long-awaited **Phaeno Science Centre** in Wolfsburg, Germany, all of which provide out-of-this-world spatial experiences that provide glimpses into the future of architecture and urbanism. Fittingly, perhaps, the chapter concludes with the last and arguably most accomplished work of the recently deceased Enric Miralles, with **EMBT/RMJM's** controversial but

highly spirited **Scottish Parliament Building** at Holyrood in Edinburgh; a building that through its location and formal expression was to provide a new focus for Scotland's political activity, set against the robust grandeur of historic Edinburgh in a new structure that was conceived to be open, anticlassical and non-hierarchical, with an architectural expression that was de-institutionalized, aggregated and organic.

Federation Square

Mauritskade Apartment Building

Erick van Egeraat Associated Architects

Amsterdam, The Netherlands; 2001

Unique cityscape situations are often formed when building blocks and streets collide to create specific locations and corner conditions. In New York, as Broadway sliced its way across the city's central Manhattan grid, acute angles were created that generated some of the world's most immediately recognizable flat-iron buildings. Similar urban conditions exist in other cities, and Amsterdam, more widely known for its concentric city plan and network of canals, is no exception. Perhaps not as sharp or dramatically figured as D.H. Burnham's seminal original Flatiron (the world's tallest building when it was built in 1902 and one of the first to be supported by a steel skeleton), this contemporary variation on the type by Erick van Egeraat Associated Architects is worthy of note.

On a prominent site in Amsterdam, opposite the Tropenmuseum, this mixed-use building completes the corner of a nineteenth-century city block. With commercial space and an automated car park optimizing the dual-aspect ground floor, the upper four levels are divided into 12 luxury apartments.

Externally, the façades of the building are perhaps the most distinctive feature, not only tying the building into its immediate context with a shift in emphasis from vertical to horizontal as they sweep around the narrow corner, but also in the manner in which each floor overlaps the previous one, creating a series of unequally radiused overhangs. Featuring vertical strips of dark stone, metal spandrel panels and timber window frames, the fenestration appears to shift in pace as it approaches the corner, and a further visual accent is included by varying the angles of the horizontal bands, with the windows on the ground and fourth floors increasing in depth as they approach the corner. When seen in oblique, this has the effect of further pronouncing the building's pointed form, and perspective further distorts the misalignment of levels.

When planning a building of this type, it is clear that achieving an optimum commercial efficiency may be problematic. So in response to this the architect has attempted where possible to optimize efficiency and to maximize exposure to the external walls. By anchoring the internal arrangement to the only right angle in plan, in the southeast corner where the building meets its neighbour, a series of orthogonal spaces that are set back from the opposing external wall has been arranged. This not only reduces the number of triangular spaces within each apartment, but also increases the prominence of this wall as the principal provider of views, with all the living spaces enjoying the best possible aspect.

A single lift and stair help to reduce circulation and service space in order to further optimize the plan, which has been relatively successful, despite the consequential requirement to provide each apartment with its own lobbied entrance hall. As the spatial finale, the prominent prow with its fully glazed triple aspect has been reserved for four of the most exclusive living rooms in the building.

1 Section A–A	2 Section B–B	3 Second Floor Plan	4 Ground Floor Plan
		1 Storage	1 Commercial Unit
		2 Living/Dining	2 Entrance to Apartments
		3 Kitchen	3 Storage
		4 Bathroom	4 Studio Apartment
		5 Loggia	5 Garage
		6 Living Room	

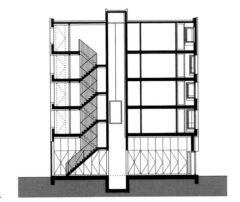

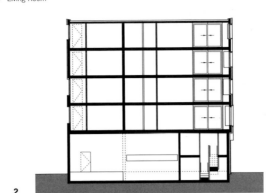

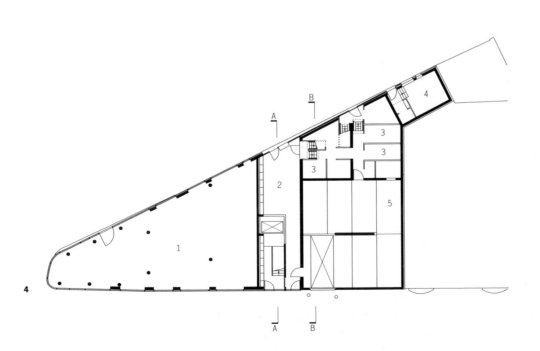

Building D

Cino Zucchi

Venice, Italy; 2001

Significant cityscape responses do not always have to be conspicuous. When a complete physical overhaul is impossible or inappropriate, in historic cities such as Venice, for example, a more delicate mode of operation should be promoted. Building D is a fine example of such an approach, providing much needed social housing in a post-industrial enclave of Venice's Giudecca Island.

Situated on the corner of two canals, the scheme incorporates an existing brick chimney as a relic of the site's previous industrial use. The simple cubic form is then excavated with a triangular court that cuts deep into the centre of the plot, anchored at its corner by the base of the chimney.

Internally, having passed through the sheltered entrance court, 16 apartments are arranged over four storeys. With a variety of one- and two-bedroom configurations, each apartment is accessed from a central hall, containing a lift, a single winding stair, and a single centrally positioned window. With a balustered void connecting levels and bringing light deeper into the plan, the hall is an efficient space with an extremely well-considered composition. The flats extend this careful attitude to planning, with all rooms having an external wall that brings light and air to all

spaces. The views from the apartments have also been extremely well considered and have been used to generate the distinctive elevations that make a significant contribution to the building's immediate cityscape scenario. By experimenting with the proportions of the windows, and the ratio between the size of aperture and frame, the façades reflect what the architect refers to as the impossibility of an historicist replica. While apparently random, the façades incorporate just three window types set into positions that reflect the variety of internal layouts, and maximize views towards the Redentore apse, the canals and the Laguna beyond. More theoretically, perhaps, the architect also alludes to the nature of incremental change in the cityscape, whereby modification and amendment can produce apparently haphazard compositions. Here, then, Zucchi has attempted to compress time and produce a kind of premodified solution in one hit.

The elevations take on a graphic representation of past historical styles, with the white window cornice of Venetian architecture transformed in both proportion and plane. Set within stucco walls, the sills, lintels and base plinth are made from white Trani stone, and to further flatten the image of the façade the perimeter

parapet walls have been extended to hide the traditional roof forms prescribed by local design codes. Only within the inner court, when the façades step down, are copper roof eaves revealed, giving it a less formal domestic character.

In recognition of the sensitivity required when performing micro-surgery in delicate urban conditions, the architect sees this building as a catalyst to address the issue of modernity versus permanence, and of individuality versus the collective artefact of the city.

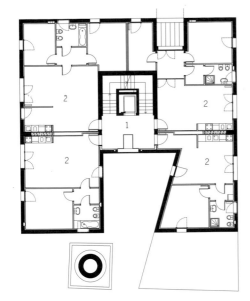

1

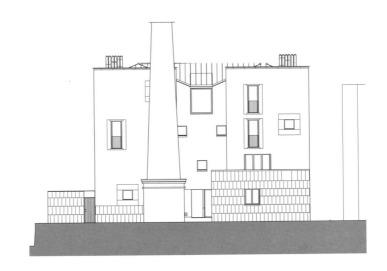

2

1 Third Floor Plan

1 Lobby
2 Apartment

2 South Elevation

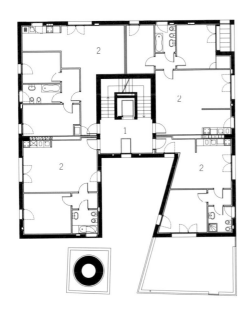

3

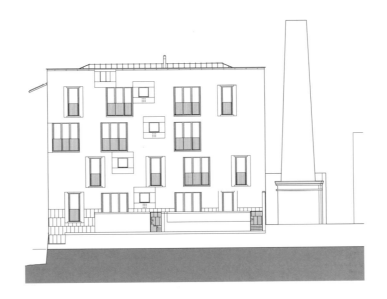

4

3 First Floor Plan

1 Lobby
2 Apartment

4 West Elevation

5

5 Ground Floor Plan

1 Chimney
2 Courtyard
3 Entrance
4 Lobby
5 Apartment

Town Hall Extension

Rafael Moneo

Murcia, Spain; 1999

The extension to the Town Hall in Murcia is one of the finest examples of cityscape intervention in recent years. Unquestionably modern, distinguished from the flamboyant expression of its baroque setting, the building somehow encapsulates the spirit of the area, albeit in a highly reduced and stripped down manner.

Situated at the western end of Plaza Cardenal Belluga, the building is a compact cubic volume, carved to respond formally and compositionally to the dominant presence of the city's richly adorned cathedral. By replaying the Renaissance trick of disjointing façade and plot the building's cranked frontispiece turns gracefully to acknowledge the brooding mass of the cathedral's west front.

A triple aspect produces three distinct elevations, unified by a consistent use of stone (a local Lumaquela stone) and through a sharp attention to detail. Fitting snugly between two parallel streets, the north and south façades are only ever seen in oblique, punctuated to the north by a regular grid of small square windows, while the southern façade is more generously articulated with larger windows, a third-floor loggia and a fourth-floor set-back. By contrast, the principal façade is decidedly frontal in its composition. Set to the east

and addressing the plaza, it is characterized by a distinctive and irregularly trabeated framework of stone pillars and concrete beams. The use of the staggered grid and asymmetrical disposition of openings gives this otherwise rational façade a lyrical demeanour – reflecting in part the baroque notion of movement and emotion. Coincident with the balcony on the adjacent episcopal palace, a double-height balcony and a fully glazed double-height opening break up the façade's proportional order, while quietly accentuating the formal grandeur of the principal reception room on the piano nobile.

Internally, the crank in plan is resolved within a lobby area, in which the curved wall of the auditorium and the oblique angle of the stair and lift core are set against each other. As if to balance this spatial disposition, the lobby is articulated on most levels by a single offset column that is set eccentrically within the space like a well-placed beauty spot.

The building's subtle shift in plan is perhaps most successfully optimized through the location of the entrance, which is to the north in Polo Medina Street. To counter the inclination to enter from the front, the dominance of the principal façade's axial

frontality is further amplified, making it even more impenetrable and almost untouchable, as a low-level curved retaining wall shields a sunken court and deflects approaching visitors to either side.

With church and state facing one another across the Plaza Cardenal Belluga, Moneo's building is a fine example of intervention within the cityscape. Through the manipulation of form, this building successfully communicates and combines the solidity and permanence of civic architecture with the aspirations towards openness and democracy that all local governments should seek to communicate.

1 East Elevation

2 Third Floor Plan

1 Offices
2 Secretary
3 Councillor's Office
4 Terrace/Balcony

3 First Floor Plan

1 Reception Space
2 Offices

4 Mezzanine Floor Plan

1 Offices

5 Ground Floor Plan

1 Entrance Hall
2 Lobby
3 Cashier Office
4 Lecture Hall
5 Offices

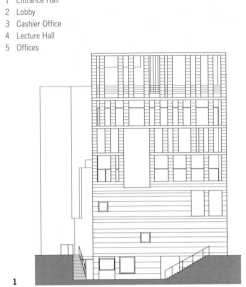

1

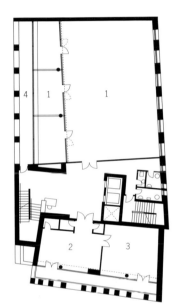

2

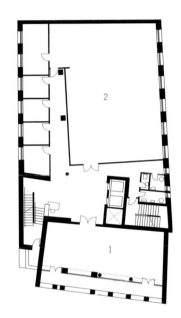

3

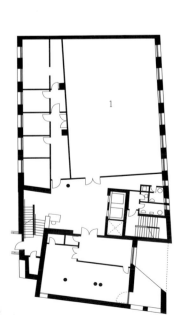

4

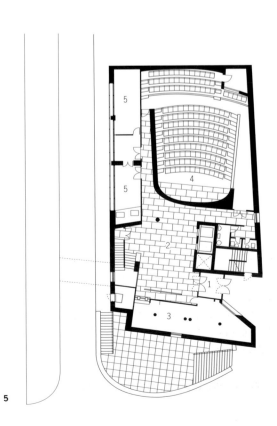

5

0   10   20m
30   60ft

Jaume Fuster Library

Josep Llinás

Barcelona, Spain; 2005

As a study in cityscape planning, the Jaume Fuster Library responds to a very specific urban situation. Unlike the bulk of Barcelona, characterized and regulated by Cerdà's chamfered grid, the neighbourhood of Gràcia has a haphazard and more densely packed grain. On slopes that rise towards Gaudí's Park Guell, the topography takes unsuspecting visitors by surprise when emerging from the Lesseps subway, as the intimacy and peacefulness of Las Ramblas is left behind. Here, a more chaotic view is assembled as the city is compressed against its mountainous boundary; a scenographic backdrop that very much determined the approach taken by the architect, Josep Llinás.

Through an extension of subtle Expressionist tendencies, Llinás' work focuses on what has been described as the permanent renunciation of the finished and rounded architectural object. Through a series of preoccupations that seek to disfigure the prism, undo formalities and make buildings disappear within their context, the rotundity of the object ceases to prevail. Instead, Llinás decomposes and chops, steps and subtracts, envelops and adds to forms in order to deny orthodox frontality, break alignments and amplify contrasting geometries. Despite such apparently

anarchic and formally determined ambitions, however, Llinás also manages to develop buildings that sit peacefully as unified wholes; eccentrically planned – but centred and abstractly disfigured – yet compositionally balanced.

Within its context, the building has an inherent multisidedness based on three formal priorities: to the irregular geometries of Plaça de Lesseps to the south; to the concavity of La Riera de Vallcarca to the west; and to future plans to extend a linear park from the north. By anchoring the building hard against the re-entrant edge of La Riera de Vallcarca, a diamond-shaped plan is derived by mirroring the alignment of existing façades. A strong duality between the narrow street and plaça is then expressed and amplified in section as the building's form is drawn down towards the plaça by a series of low-level canopies that help to diminish its apparent height.

In plan, the main three-storey volume contains principal library spaces, with the auditorium and archive below, reception, media reading room, gallery and café/bar at grade, and two principal reading levels above. While this form is relatively regular, through its adaptation Llinás begins to deny any so-called rotundity, sculpting its prow-like

ends to lose any trace of centralized formality, and giving the form a pronounced emphasis and orientation with a head that turns the southeastern corner to address the two principal public spaces.

When describing the internal environment, Llinás recalls how light and sound were prioritized in order to balance transmission between places of silence and interchange, and between areas with natural and artificial light. Across the two reading floors are a wide variety of environments that range from the orthodox (such as the rectangular galleried reading room) to the expressive (such as the cavernous study bays to the south), and with each nook and cranny individuals are given a wide choice of places to study, offered the opportunity to move from place to place, or to settle in one seat as their own preferred regular place of studious refuge within the city.

1 Section A–A	2 Section B–B	3 Third Floor Plan	4 Second Floor Plan	5 First Floor Plan	6 Ground Floor Plan
		1 Meeting/Study Rooms	1 Book Stacks	1 Book Stacks	1 Covered Entrance
		2 Void	2 Study Areas	2 Study Areas	2 Foyer
			3 City Archives	3 Meeting/Study Rooms	3 Reception
			4 Void		4 Media Reading Room
					5 Café
					6 Gallery
					7 Children's Library
					8 Education

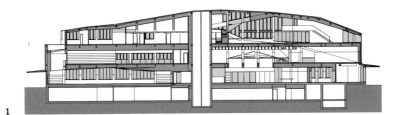

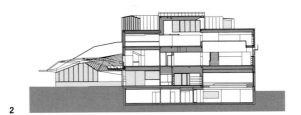

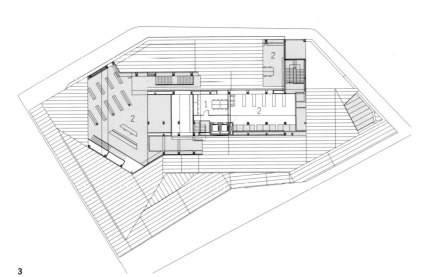

1

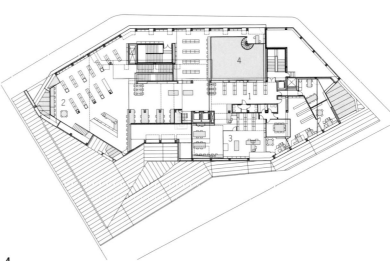

2

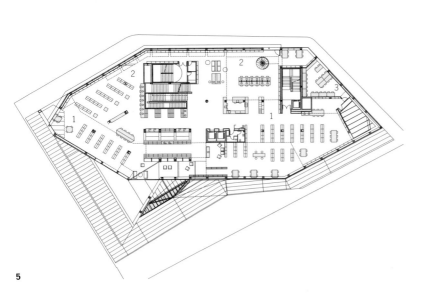

3

4

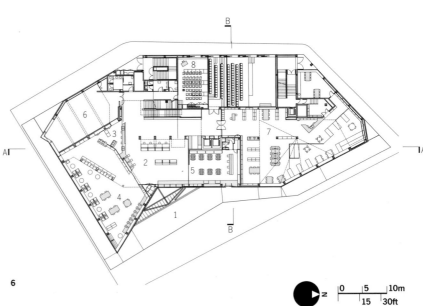

5

6

Des Moines Public Library

David Chipperfield Architects

Des Moines, Iowa, USA; 2006

European architects and urban designers can often be unreasonably dismissive of North American cities. With relatively short histories, and dominated by the prioritization of automobile over pedestrian, 'bleak' and 'vacuous' are descriptive terms that easily spring to mind. Many downtown areas – places which in Europe would be denser and more diversely arranged – are characterized by flat urban voids, neglected, windswept and used predominantly as parking lots. What such vacant plots do allow for, however, is new forms of urban intervention that would rarely be feasible in more tightly meshed cities. With little to respond to – other than four parallel boundaries – they also (only in America, perhaps) allow for the sort of super-sized objectification of buildings where anything and everything (even the most established building types) can be repackaged, rebranded and commodified. For this reason David Chipperfield Architects' library in Des Moines is an interesting case in point as it successfully unifies the increasingly diverse requirements of a modern library – complete with a drive-through lending facility and café-cum-art gallery – within a uniform, seamless architectural package. The building also addresses a number of interesting urban

considerations by reinforcing corners, establishing courtyards and setting up new axial routes.

The lending library is very much an American invention, initiated and supported by individuals such as Benjamin Franklin and Andrew Carnegie. By turning stolid Beaux-Arts repositories into democratic levellers, where the priority was to move as many books through the doors as possible rather than hoard them on shelves, the library type was transformed to welcome the public into a new form of civic institution. The contribution of libraries to the public realm has been increasingly pronounced, making them one of the most regular components of urban regeneration strategies. The one in Des Moines is no exception, conceived as part of an ambitious new city plan pulling away from the city's Jeffersonian grid to create a unique urban counterpoint.

As part of an integrated landscape strategy, the building is both singular in its formal composition and multifaceted, addressing the four (or in this case, five) corners of the plot. With branching arms that extend and buckle to create three re-entrant courtyards, and to accommodate the existing Masonic temple, each façade differs, despite being made of the same copper and glass

frameless screen. As light hits the surface, the building's angular envelope articulates each branch, with principal entrances being subtly integrated where surfaces change direction.

The form of the building not only creates external pockets of space but also draws pedestrians – and drive-by readers – into the site. From east and west on the south side, routes converge and pass through the building in a generous double-height hall. From here, without necessarily having to enter the actual library, casual passers-by are also given access to the café/gallery, toilets and a self-contained suite of meeting/conference spaces.

While the original promise of Zimmer Gunsul's new landscaped park may have failed to live up to the expectations of Chipperfield and his team – who, one suspects, may have preferred to see their building more generously enveloped – the new library has made a significant contribution to the quality of Des Moines' downtown regeneration plans with its undeniably powerful public presence.

1 Section A–A	**2 First Floor Plan**	**3 Ground Floor Plan**
	1 Open Collection	1 Entrance Lobby
	2 Offices	2 Foyer
	3 Special Collection	3 Open Collection
	4 Study Rooms	4 Gateway Gallery
		5 Café Foyer
		6 Meeting Rooms
		7 Book Shop
		8 Office/Back of House

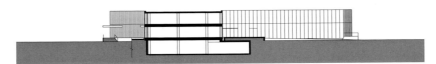

1

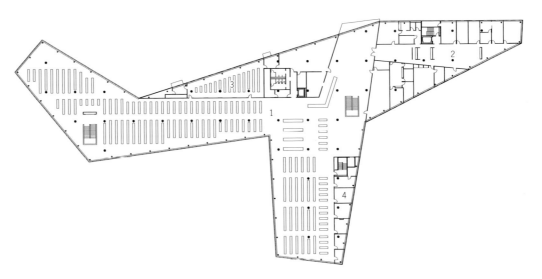

2

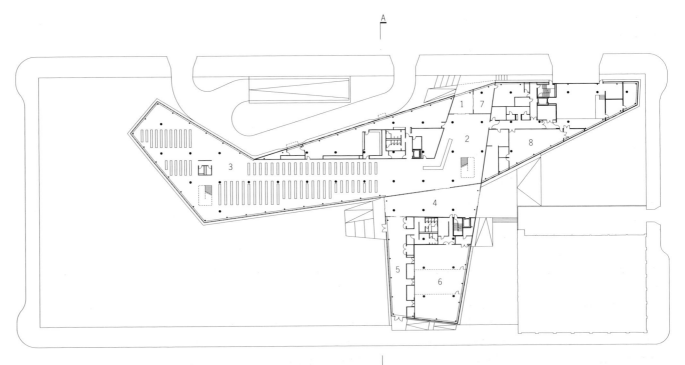

3

Walsall Art Gallery

Caruso St John Architects

Walsall, UK; 2000

Widely accepted as one of the UK's most important recent buildings – remarkably constituting the architects' first significant commission, establishing their now international reputation from virtual obscurity – the architecture of the gallery operates layer upon layer, possessing more subtle characteristics than its apparently bulky external form may immediately suggest. At all scales, from its place in the town down to the junctions between wall and ceiling, window and cladding, handrail and hand, the architects have been precise, considering every detail. It is therefore very difficult to place the building in any single category, and the decision to consider its contribution to the cityscape (or in this instance the townscape), reflects the broad and far-reaching effect of its realization.

The building is planned with accomplished expertise, avoiding the potentially banal and diagrammatic functionalism of separating served and service by providing a more intricate arrangement of varied and interwoven spatial sequences that are served by multiple routes. The gallery is, in fact, two galleries in one, with a suite of temporary exhibition spaces set above a permanent home for its own collection, the Garman Ryan Collection donated by Kathleen Garman. It

also contains extensive education, conference and catering facilities.

As a prominent urban marker within an east end redevelopment plan, the building makes a conspicuous civic contribution to an otherwise unremarkable town centre. Taking the form of a tower placed between the main shopping street and a previously neglected industrial backwater, it is located on the canalside arm overlooking a turning basin. The tower form makes it possible to arrange a wide variety of relatively small floor plans of differing heights, one above the other, each with their own character and function. While some floors are grand, with lofty exposed ceiling structures, others are lower and more intimate, fully lined with timber and plaster.

In response to the scale of the permanent collection – a one-time private collection of small figurative work – the Garman Ryan Rooms maintain the feel of a large house. Placed on first- and second-floor levels, above the foyer that extends from a new public square, and below the clerestory-lit temporary galleries, the permanent collection is planned in a manner more reminiscent of a house than an institutional public art gallery, providing an unusually wide range of interconnected

and domestically scaled rooms, all of which are arranged around a central hall and flanking stair. With windows and doorways that further reference the proportions of domestic architecture, walking through the spaces is like visiting a fine stately home and, in many ways, this is as pleasurable as seeing the works themselves.

The proportion and disposition of openings in the façade have been rigorously resolved. While perfectly aligned with the diminishing grid of the lapped terracotta tiles, the position of each window responds to the internal arrangement of each room, set in considered composition against the size and location of the works hung in each gallery.

1 Second Floor Plan

1 Void
2 Garman Ryan Collection
3 Staff Offices

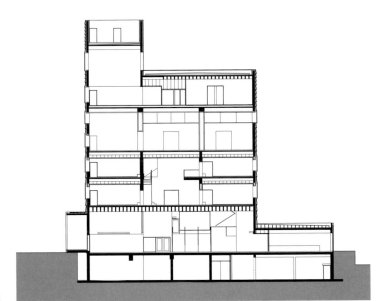

2 Mezzanine Floor Plan

1 Void
2 Temporary Exhibition

3 Section A–A

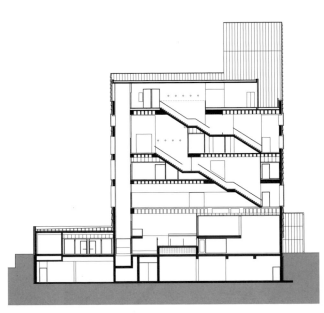

4 Ground Floor Plan

1 Entrance
2 Entrance Hall
3 Café/Book Shop
4 Art Lift
5 Temporary Exhibition
6 Loading Bay

5 Section B–B

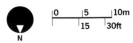

0 5 10m
15 30ft

N

Walt Disney Concert Hall

Gehry Partners, LLP

Los Angeles, California, USA; 2003

A building like this cannot fail to make an impact on its cityscape; and an architect with such a distinctive manner cannot fail to make an impact on his world. Over the past two decades, Frank Gehry has created perhaps the world's most identifiable and transferable built aesthetic – a distinctive, frivolous and billowing style of construction that is not only immediately recognizable (even to the least interested layman), but has also been used to manipulate, organize and adorn a wide range of architectural programmes.

Gehry's buildings always stimulate both the people that encounter them and the debate that surrounds them. But despite their immediately recognizable character as spatial organizations they are far less penetrable, and unlike the clarity of an early Modernist plan, for example, a Gehry plan demands much closer scrutiny. As buildings they are more intuitive in reality than they are in representational form and, very much like the early work of Expressionists such as Hans Scharoun, they somehow predict and respond to the intuition of those who move through their spaces, with directional vistas and eccentric plans creating their own gravitational pull. When translated into two-dimensional drawings, however, despite their often

gestural forms, flows and emphases, each space needs to be carefully unravelled. And, while two Gehry plans may be easily discernible one from the next, trying to make detailed distinctions can be like trying to compare two or more Mandelbrot images.

This building is almost an exception to this rule as, due to the dominant presence of the 2265-seat auditorium, the plan is one of Gehry's clearest.

Within the bounds of a downtown LA city block, the auditorium shifts from the dominant axis to create a strong diagonal emphasis across the site. More than simply distinguishing the building from its cityscape grain, the cross-axis also sets up a tension between the orthogonal plinth below and the flowering super-sized steel petals within, and helps to orchestrate the approach to the plot's northeasterly corner entrance.

Within the auditorium Gehry's baroque sensibility extends to the seats, which are arranged in bow-fronted stalls to either side of the stage, and in three tiers of slim concave balconies and a number of additional stepped rows set behind the stage; even the upholstery extends the organic theme, with a floral abstraction designed by Gehry as a tribute to Walt Disney's widow, Lillian. Long before the audience reach their seats, however, they

will have already taken part in their very own theatrical experience as they effortlessly navigate Gehry's fluid foyers. Entering from the northeast, or more probably from the extensive basement car park, light and form lead the way through foyers with two principal atria that flank the auditorium, east and west.

With a large part of the external podium given to intimate landscaped gardens, with pathways set between deep titanium gorges, Gehry has created not only a stunning series of interiors, but also a new elevated public realm that challenges the conformity of the traditional downtown city block.

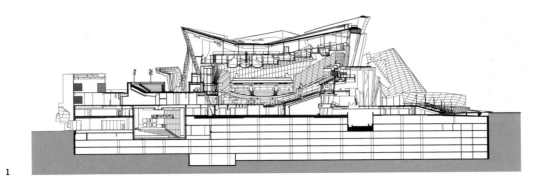

1 Section A–A

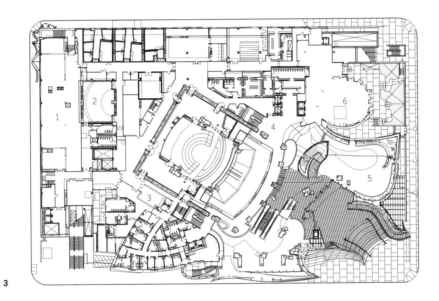

2 Section B–B

**3 Fourth Floor Plan /
Orchestra Level**

1 Offices
2 Choral Hall
3 Dressing Rooms
4 Lobby
5 Pre-concert
6 Founder's Room

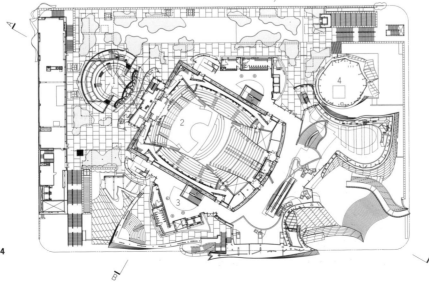

**4 Third Floor Plan /
Garden Level**

1 Open-air Stage
2 Concert Hall
3 East Atrium
4 Founder's Room

Federation Square

LAB architecture studio with Bates Smart, Architects

Melbourne, Australia; 2003

Melbourne's Federation Square could easily be categorized as a piece of urban planning. As a ring-fenced major regeneration project, covering a 3.8 hectare (9.4 acre) city block, built around a large 7500 square metre (80,729 square foot) public piazza large enough to accommodate 20,000 people, and providing thousands of square metres of commercial and cultural space for a range of individual venues, this is clearly much more than a single work of architecture. It is, curiously, at the same time also readable as a single entity completed essentially as a single phase, with a strong visual character and designed with a coherent – albeit complex – design rationale.

From the outset the strategic concept was to create an area that could become the heart of the city, providing a focus for civic activity in a series of spaces that liberated its inhabitants from the constraints of the city's relentless grid. It was also seen as an opportunity to address the barrier effect created by the railway that divides the city from the bank of the Yarra River. By bridging over the tracks with a unified raised terrain, Federation Square creates a new elevated territory with access to the river and improved visual access to the park on the opposite bank.

Reflecting a strong interest by the architects (Donald L. Bates and Peter Davidson) in non-Cartesian urban ordering systems, the resulting urban mix is heterogenous and multilayered, more European than North American, and in sympathy with the hidden laneways and passages of Melbourne's Central Business District. With a wide variety in the scale and nature of spaces, including square, street and alleyway, the complex creates an eccentric urban web; an apparently haphazard attitude to planning that is carried right through to an expression in elevation through the development of the buildings' distinctive fractal façades.

Incorporating sandstone, zinc and glass, the façade system arranges five equally sized triangles into a similar but larger triangular module. The modules are similarly arranged in groups of five to create what is called a 'mega-panel' which generates the organizational component of the façades. By varying the proportion of these components, and changing the configuration of the materials within, many unique and orientation-specific façades could then be composed within a coherent and even grain.

Due to the extensive scale of the site, many varied environments exist both internally and externally. When the scheme is considered in section many cavernous delights are revealed, such as the glazed atrium entrance to the Ian Potter Centre, and throughout the circulation spaces within the National Gallery of Victoria galleries. Despite such delights, however, some critics have raised concerns over the buildings' perceived scale, which is blurred by their fractal façades, and has little that is identifiably human about it. In opposition to this opinion, however, what cannot be denied is that Federation Square is one of the most ambitious recent mega-structure projects, with architectural consideration at all levels from the civic scale right down to the glazing details. Contextual it may not be – but then, at this scale sufficient visual momentum is gathered to make this a very convincing new place.

1 Section A–A   **2 Section B–B**   **3 Second Floor Plan**

1 Piazza
2 Information Centre
3 Cathedral Parvis
4 Offices
5 Cinema
6 North Atrium
7 National Gallery
  of Victoria Galleries
8 South Atrium
9 Yarra Building
10 Pub

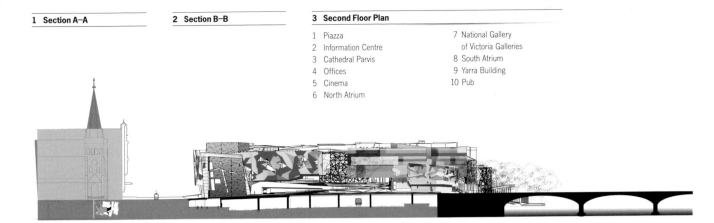

1

2

3

Casa da Musica

OMA

Porto, Portugal; 2005

OMA's Casa da Musica is a baffling building. In the delightful Portuguese city of Porto, the concert hall's bulky and imposing figure – marooned on a bleak travertine piazza, isolated and self-conscious, with little physical or formal connection to its context – has been criticized by many. The architect characteristically makes little attempt to justify its somewhat alien appearance. Others, naturally, have added their own interpretations, with many metaphors emerging, from meteor and UFO to an abandoned television set that has been knocked about a bit. Love it or hate it, however, in terms of Porto's cityscape, this is a significant building, not only in terms of its place in the city, bringing a challenging new scale and character to a region where contemporary architecture is governed by the highly contextual Sizaesque school of thought, but also in how the configuration of circulation and performance spaces serves to connect occupants with their wider civic context.

The building's isolated mood can be justified in relation to how it sets up and prepares visitors for their highly internalized concert-going experience. With such a dominant form, there is no accidental encounter with this building's front door. Instead, having approached the object, journeyed across the bleakness all around and having climbed the broad principal stair, once inside it is immediately clear to all visitors that they have entered an entirely new type of place, an other-worldly experience that continues as they navigate its cavernous and lofty interiors.

Consistent with other recent OMA buildings, such as the Seattle Library [see pp. 114–15] and the Dutch Embassy in Berlin [see pp. 164–5], the organization of circulation and accommodation, if not orthodox, is undeniably clear as a diagram. With two principal performance spaces carved as orthogonal negatives into the distorted concrete solid, the highly charged circulation circuit leads visitors through a range of foyers and hallways that fill the residual space between auditoria and envelope. With the main auditorium effectively cutting the plan in half, the first-floor foyer immediately divides into two routes passing beneath the hall's imposing mass. From beneath this compression each route is then vertically liberated through a series of lofty chambers filled with stairs and terraces that create generous vantage points from where to see and be seen.

Once visitors are through these spaces, and have passed through massive 1000 millimetre (40 inch) thick concrete walls, the heart of the building is revealed within the principal 1300-seat auditorium which, despite the architect's celebrated and inventive sculptural ambitions, conforms to the traditional shoebox format. Where OMA does assert its nonconformist attitude is in the treatment of the walls, with the auditorium lined in gold-lead-adorned plywood, and with the end walls being fully glazed. By connecting the auditorium so directly with external views of the cityscape, the venue finally finds its contextual specificity, with huge corrugated glass panels that not only help to soften the acoustic but also control glare while providing spectacular views.

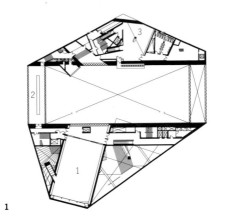

1

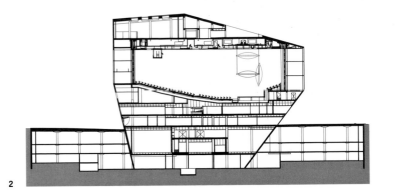

2

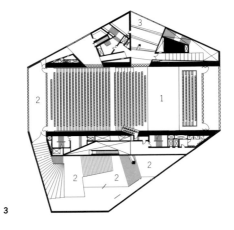

3

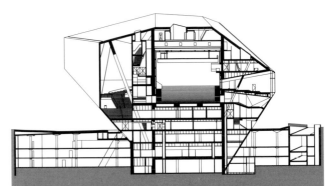

4

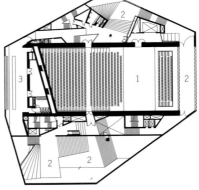

5

6

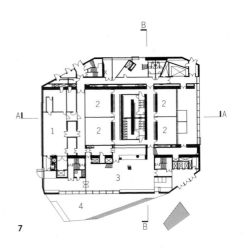

7

1 Level 5

1 Small Auditorium
2 Foyer
3 Education

2 Section A–A

3 Level 4

1 Main Auditorium
2 Foyer
3 Cyber Music Room

4 Section B–B

5 Level 3

1 Main Auditorium
2 Foyer
3 Bar

6 Level 1 (Foyer)

1 Entrance Stair
2 Public Entrance
3 Foyer
4 Tickets
5 Offices

7 Ground Floor Plan

1 Musicians' Entrance
2 Dressing Rooms
3 Private Restaurant
4 Terrace

0 5 10m
15 30ft

Yokohama International Port Terminal

Foreign Office Architects

Yokohama, Japan; 2002

Despite the essential human transactions that occur at transport interchanges, with people meeting, greeting and, on occasion, having to say difficult farewells, very few can be described as first-rate public places, possessing a satisfying and rooted sense of being a place of their own. The placelessness of some of the world's largest airports is often more alienating than welcoming, and as the first port of call for many first-time visitors, some of the best cities in the world have thoroughly disappointing airports and arrivals terminals, with London perhaps being the worst of all. Despite their own national legacy, however, London-based Foreign Office Architects clearly understood the potential to make terminal buildings much more than mere machines for processing passengers, as seen here with their first major international project, in Yokohama, Japan.

Aside from many of the more measurable achievements of this project, FOA's most significant accomplishment was without doubt their 1995 competition-winning strategy to go well beyond the original brief and to make this building – a new domestic and international ferry terminal built atop the Osanbashi pier – much more part of Yokohama's cityscape experience. Much has been

written about the terminal's distinctive self-supporting steel structure that adapted heavy-duty shipbuilding and prefabrication processes. Less, perhaps, has been said about the building's explicit social programme which, by developing the rooftop promenade as a major civic amenity, goes well beyond the brief's complicated organizational obligations to create a new place within the city. Recognizing the relatively low numbers of cruise ships visiting the harbour – with between 50 and 60 ships per year docking for an average of two days each – the architects saw the terminal not simply as a means to an end – in terms of processing passengers – but more as an end in itself, as a major new public space and piece of infrastructure that has the potential to act as a huge foyer to events held within the terminal or beyond, within the harbour itself.

The terminal's superstructure comprises three principal levels with car parking and baggage handling on the lower level, passenger processing on the middle level – with both domestic and international gates – and the decked promenade above. Connected and continuous, the levels are not treated as separate realms, but are instead interwoven as part of the same organizational field,

in a manner that could be seen as the culmination of the influence of the architects' one-time tutor and employer Rem Koolhaas.

Since its completion, there have been criticisms that the terminal is not as well populated as originally envisaged, and that the promenade has been littered with too many hand- and guard-rails. But these comments in many ways miss the point. This is a huge cityscape intervention which is as robust in its social capacity as it is in its material presence. Years, not months, will tell how successful it is as a major new public place.

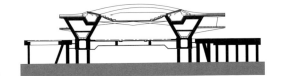

1   Section A–A

2   Section B–B

3   Section C–C

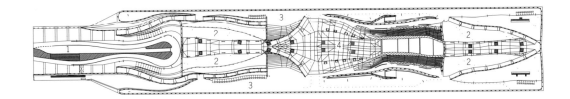

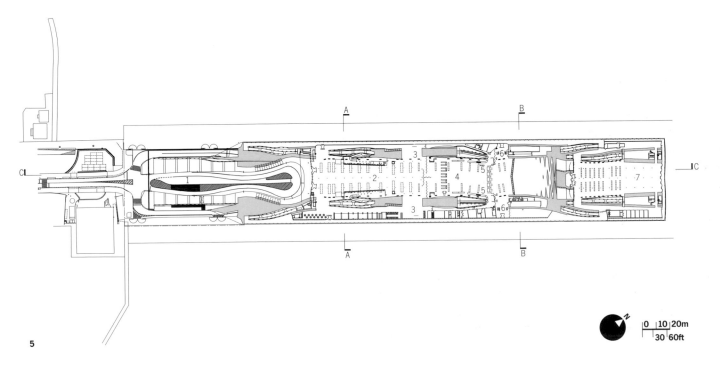

4   Roof Plan

1   Vehicle Arrivals and Drop Off
2   Green Spaces
3   Visitor Deck
4   Open-air Theatre

5   Cruise Terminal at Civic Level Plan

1   Vehicle Arrivals and Drop Off
2   Domestic Terminal Concourse
3   Domestic Gates
4   Customs
5   Plant/Animal Quarantine
6   International Gates
7   Multipurpose Hall

0 | 10 | 20m
30 | 60ft

Phaeno Science Centre

Zaha Hadid Architects

Wolfsburg, Germany; 2005

Since her rise to prominence in 1994 with her unfulfilled competition-winning design for the Cardiff Bay Opera House, Zaha Hadid has in many ways failed to realize her ambitions to create a new form of civic architecture. While a number of buildings have been built which demonstrate her distinctive style, it has been doubted that she would ever complete a building of any great significance. Over the next few years, however, this will all change, with a number of significant cultural buildings in complex urban situations near completion. The Phaeno Science Centre in Wolfsburg is the first to be completed, and represents her most accomplished project to date; it is also one of the world's largest pieces of hand-crafted, fair-faced, in situ concrete, cast from over 27,000 cubic metres (953,500 cubic feet) of self-compacting concrete.

As a civic building, Phaeno's principal success lies in how well it serves to define a new public space and termination to Porschestrasse, the city's main public precinct. For Hadid, Phaeno serves as a critique of the Modern Movement's use of the ground plane, which in her view failed to usefully regenerate land liberated by pilotis. The building's second critique of Modernism focuses on

the limitations of mass production when applied to civic situations, representing Hadid's interest in creating unique civic buildings with one-off responses to specific sites and briefs. The building also serves to apply, unify and extend Hadid's architectural research curriculum of more than 30 years, which in relation to Phaeno includes subject categories like continuous surfaces, carved spaces, excavations, fields and liquid spaces.

While plans, sections and elevations go some way to describe the anatomy of this building it would, of course, be unwise to overlook the important role that digital modelling played in its evolution. While it is unlikely that the form itself derived from computer generation – being a work that exhibits many qualities of Hadid's early hand-drawn perspectives – making the structure work as a single unified entity would have been impossible without AKT's computer-generated complex element analysis, which optimized the structure's integrity and material efficiency.

Raised on ten inhabited concrete cones as a single entity – structurally and spatially seamless, continuous, carved, excavated and liquid – the building comprises three principal terrains: a 15,000 square metre (161,500 square foot) car

park below, a 12,000 square metre (129,200 square foot) exhibition space above, and a public landscape in between. The distorted and eccentric planning of the cones, and the undulating terrain in between provides an experimental landscape in which to open up new approaches to the world of natural science and technology; a place to which hundreds of thousands of people can gravitate to test natural laws, physical truths and ingenious discoveries. The building also serves as the first and final exhibit, expressing the material efficiency of its structure through the thinness of its shell, and responds well to the complexities of the science centre's exhibition, encouraging participants to move through the space like highly charged ions.

1 Section A–A	2 Concourse Plan	3 Concourse Mezzanine Plan	4 Ground Floor Plan	5 Upper Ground Floor Plan
	1 Shop	1 Administration	1 Landscape	1 Shop
	2 Main Entrance	2 Restaurant/Event Space	2 Shop	2 Main Entrance
	3 Group Entrance	3 Exhibition	3 Workshop	3 Group Entrance
	4 Restaurant		4 Main Entrance	4 Toilets
	5 Laboratory/Loading		5 Group Entrance	5 Kitchen/Toilets
	6 Laboratory		6 Bistro	6 Auditorium
	7 Exhibition		7 Auditorium	7 Laboratory/Loading
	8 Bridge to Autostadt Museum		8 Laboratory/Loading	8 Toilets
			9 Event Space	9 Event Space
			10 Coffee Bar	10 Entrance
			11 Ramp to Bridge	11 Staff Room
			12 Access to Parking	

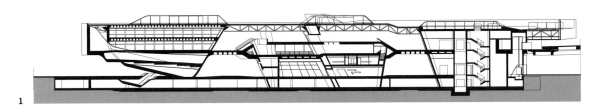

1

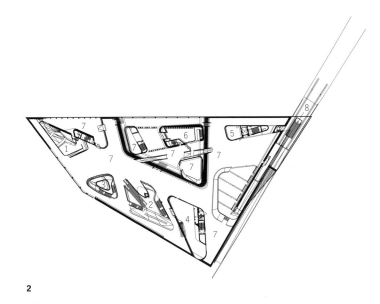

2

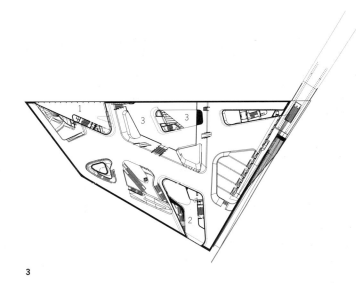

3

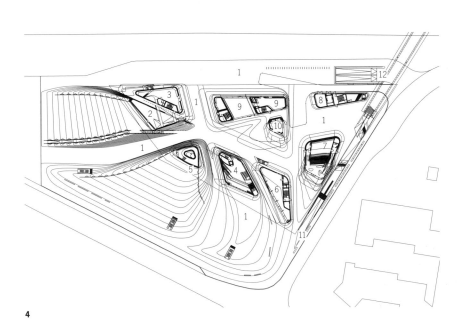

4

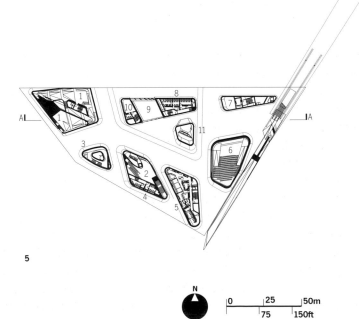

5

N

0   25   50m
75   150ft

Scottish Parliament Building

EMBT/RMJM

Edinburgh, UK; 2005

The Scottish Parliament was one of Enric Miralles' final works, completed five years after his untimely death in July 2000. From the outset the intellectual ambitions of the project were to produce an institution that was open, anticlassical and non-hierarchical, with an architectural expression that was deinstitutionalized, aggregated and organic.

Realized by EMBT in collaboration with local architects RMJM, and despite the absence of Miralles' creative genius, the building was completed largely in accordance with his initial competition-winning vision, and stands today as one of Scotland's most highly acclaimed works of contemporary architecture. Seen by the architect as an intimate gathering in the landscape, the building is exemplary in how it organizes a broad and varied series of spaces within a complicated tumbledown site. Through its amplification of Edinburgh's built and topographical character, it demonstrates how an apparently ad hoc assembly of forms and volumes can bring order and unity to conventionally irreconcilable shifts in scale, density and formal diversity; scenarios that often prevail in today's complicated cityscape conditions.

The choice of site surprised many people, with a number of more prominent and monumental locations being rejected. However, it was this decision, and the idiosyncratic relationship between site and brief, that inspired Miralles' response. Instead of being set within the contrived splendour of the Georgian New Town or high upon one of the city's many prominent hilltop sites, the Parliament nestles quietly within the medieval old town at the foot of the Royal Mile. In formalizing the place where city meets landscape – a place where even the most singularly flamboyant building would have been dominated by the imposing basalt cliffs of Salisbury Crags and the mass of Arthur's Seat – Miralles' building serves as a powerful representation of nature and the man-made, with two distinct aspects: to the west, contained within a series of new and existing blocks that anchor themselves to the ramshackle context; and to the east, in an apparently haphazard arrangement of forms and landscaped terraces that reflect the wild and blustery freedom of the countryside beyond.

During the lengthy briefing process, Miralles' strategy maintained its course, despite significant increases in accommodation that necessarily transformed the formerly loose-knit assemblage into a much more densely packed precinct. Clockwise from the west, the scale and form of the perimeter buildings were increasingly detached from the site's immediate context, with a staggered terrace of members' offices to the west, the rehabilitated four-storey Queensbury house to the north (containing the Dewer Library and offices), and the sculpted entrance and assembly pavilions to the east. Within this cranked quadrangle, a low-lying series of roof forms, gardens and terraces is compressed to form the main concourse; the heart of the nation's new Parliament. Top-lit and articulated by the distinctive hull-like forms, the concourse provides circulation and meeting space for all the building's users, and provides a place where the public can meet their representatives in a relaxed, informal environment.

1 **Section A-A**

1

2 **Section B-B**

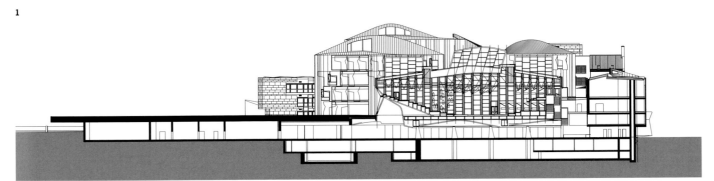

2

3 **Fifth Floor Plan**

4 **Second Floor Plan**

1 Debating Chamber
2 Tower 1
3 Tower 2
4 Tower 3
5 Tower 4

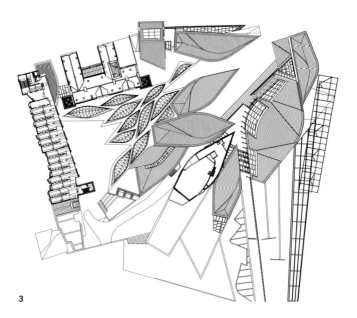

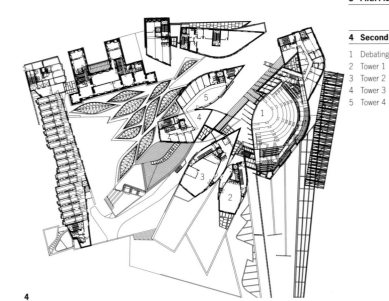

3

4

5 **Ground Floor Plan**

1 Public Entrance
2 Security
3 Exhibition Space
4 Members of Scottish
  Parliament Concourse
5 Tower 1
6 Tower 2
7 Tower 3
8 Tower 4
9 Members of Scottish
  Parliament Offices
10 Queensbury House

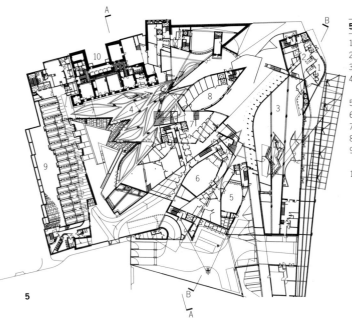

0 10 20m
  30 60ft

5

Infills, Additions and Extensions

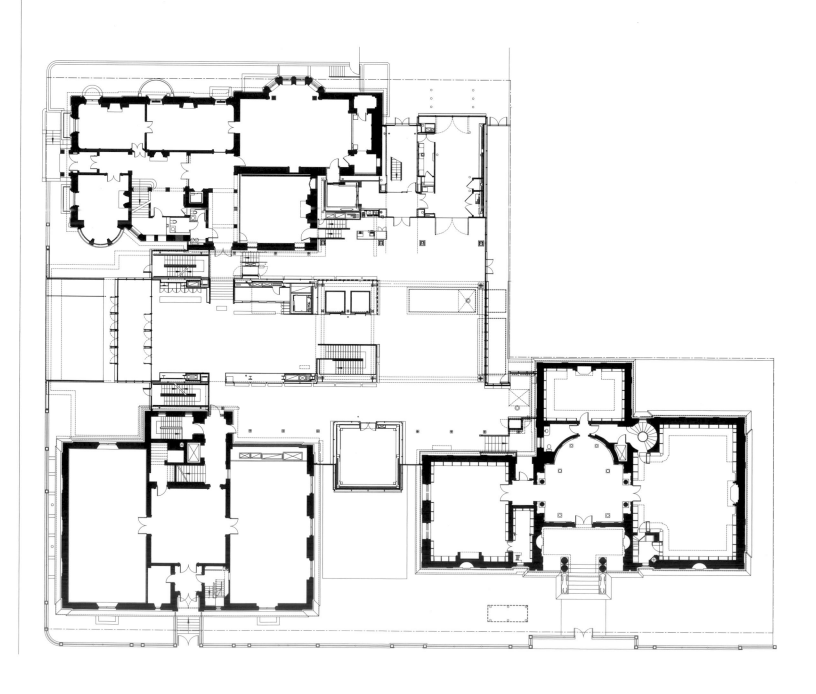

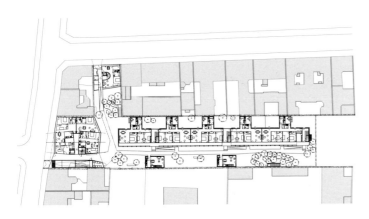

Rue des Suisses Housing

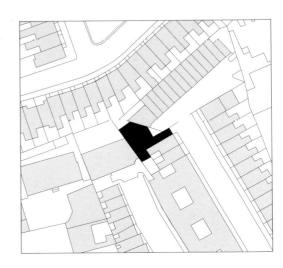

Brick House

As cities continue to evolve, with subsequent generations adding layer after layer, closer investigation also reveals how individual buildings express new uses and changes to their formal configuration. Churches perhaps offer the most obvious isolated examples of incremental growth and layered architectural expression, as tower and nave are extended and added to with aisles, chancel, chapter house and cloister. With alterations that span many hundreds of years, each has its own architectural language from Norman to medieval with round-headed, pointed and perpendicular windows. In contemporary buildings too, new layers and modes of expression continue to be added, and this chapter considers three principal modes with infill and addition. Considering urban space,

infill refers to the treatment of residual plots of land that are reutilized and densified. Additions and extensions, more specifically, consider individual interventions added to existing structures, be they significant historical artefacts or redundant structures that deserve sustainable new uses.

Considering infills first, projects such as **Eva Jiricna Architects' Hotel Josef** in Prague and **Herzog & de Meuron's Rue des Suisses Housing** in Paris, both demonstrate how contemporary buildings can stitch together and repair urban blocks, extending buildings deep into the core of the plots to optimize apparently lost inner realms. On a smaller scale, two virtually invisible properties in London have also been included as examples of a new type of inner-city house. The **Anderson**

House by **Jamie Fobert Architects** digs deep to create a cavernous house on its hemmed-in site, and the **Brick House** by **Caruso St John Architects** inverts proposals for a courtyard configuration to create a unique family home at the end of a typical Georgian terrace in London's Notting Hill.

As hybrid examples of infill and addition, a number of buildings are considered that stitch together existing buildings with adjacent and interstitial plots. With these, it is possible to see how new linkages can be used not only to provide much-needed accommodation, but also to help rationalize and reorientate existing planning arrangements. With institutions such as **Renzo Piano's Morgan Library and Museum** in New York, for example, years of piecemeal growth can result

Hotel Josef

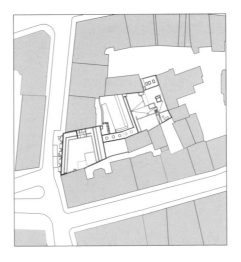

Morgan Library and Museum

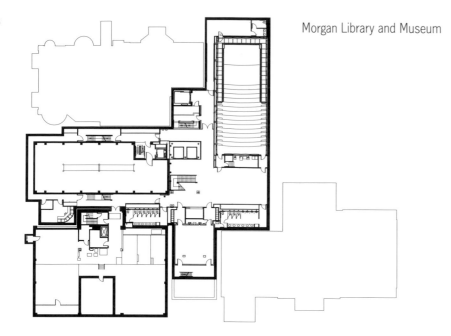

in disjointed relationships between neighbouring buildings, separated and divided by areas of interstitial space that are largely ineffective and unusable. Piano's recent additions, however, have brought a fresh order and efficiency, and have given the library a dramatic new identity. Through burying, linking, extending and infilling, the Morgan now boasts a unified precinct, with a principal entrance that gives access to all areas via a dramatic multipurpose triple-height atrium. A similar approach was taken by **Hopkins Architects** when extending the **Manchester City Art Gallery**. Due to the dominant formalism of the existing neoclassical buildings, in this instance the architects chose to exploit the underlying geometry of the site, which was governed by Charles Barry's symmetrically

planned Royal Manchester Institution. The result is a series of new spaces that reinforce the coherence of three buildings into one unified mass, not only providing additional floor area on a vacant car park site, but also rationalizing the gallery's operation and repairing a significant part of the city's relatively limited urban grid.

Where sites are more eccentric, infills and additions can also respond with an eccentricity of their own, as was the case at the **Crawford Art Gallery** in Cork, Eire. Here a curious and disjointed assemblage of buildings sat either side of an awkward triangular courtyard to which **Erick van Egeraat Associated Architects** added a new infill that served to connect two dead-end circulation spines. Within these, the distinctive curvaceous

brick infill introduces a continuous circulation loop on both levels, provides two new temporary exhibition spaces, and gives the gallery a bold new identity. Staying in Eire with a more orthogonal but equally eccentric plan, **McCullough Mulvin Architects'** extension at the **Model Arts and Niland Gallery** in Sligo also rationalizes and reorders a group of existing buildings, through the addition of a new block of accommodation at the rear of the site, and by infilling a courtyard at the centre of the plan. Even more idiosyncratic examples exist and are discussed, such as **Benson + Forsyth's** richly composed extension and entrance building for the **National Gallery of Ireland Millennium Wing, Francis Soler and Frederic Druot's** ornate veil at the **French Ministry of Culture and**

Crawford Art Gallery

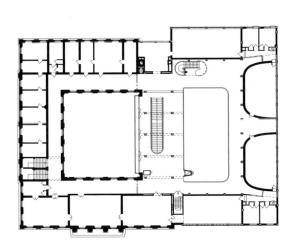

Gothenburg Law Courts Annex, Erik Gunnar Asplund
Façade and Ground Floor Plan

Communication in Paris, and **Peter Cook and Spacelab's Kunsthaus** in Graz, Austria.

The chapter ends with a series of schemes that express the process of infill and addition in courtyard settings. More generally with origins in traditional agricultural buildings, built in configurations centred around a sheltered external space, many courtyard assemblages grow with time. Starting out as single-storey boundary walls with simple lean-to roofs, through changes in use came changes in state as walls became shelters, which in turn developed into enclosed storage, and ultimately habitable, space. With internal and external spaces integrated into singular precincts, courtyards have a holistic coherence that needs to be recognized when further infills or additions are required, and many fine

twentieth-century examples exist, such as the **Gothenburg Law Courts Annex** by **Erik Gunnar Asplund**, which considers symmetry and proportion and circulation, and the more disjointed but nonetheless coherent **Archbishopric Museum of Hamar** by **Sverre Fehn**. This chapter includes three further contemporary examples: the **Lugano University Library** extension by **Michele and Giorgio Tognola**, which reinforces the geometry and order of the existing buildings by introducing a new proportioning system more appropriate to its new use, based on intimate study carrels; and, by contrast, a second example by **Brookes Stacey Randall & IAA**, which adds a new wing to an existing courtyard that sits beyond the boundary of the existing courtyard at the **De Maere Textile**

School in Enschede, the Netherlands, to help update and upgrade the image of its resident institution. Finally, **Hodder Associates'** extension at **St Catherine's College**, Oxford, demonstrates how the architect has successfully added a whole new precinct to Jacobsen's celebrated 1970s campus, drawing out the underlying order from the existing courtyards to create an entirely new group of buildings that bring a long awaited coherence to the wider site context.

St Catherine's College

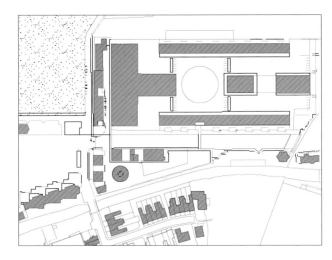

Hotel Josef

Eva Jiricna Architects

Prague, Czech Republic; 2002

Despite having established her reputation creating exquisite spiral staircases and luxurious interiors, the Czech-born London-based architect Eva Jiricna is equally capable when it comes to larger-scale works of urban infill. Working here on her home soil in the Czech capital, Jiricna has built one of only a few new-build urban interventions to have been recently inserted within the historic city centre. Situated in the Jewish Quarter, the Hotel Josef comprises two individual buildings, each located on either side of an intimate courtyard. As urban infills, the otherwise remote buildings are not only connected physically by an enclosed ramp, they are also unified in their character through the architect's distinctive lightness of touch and considered attention to detail. This trademark refinement extends through the new interiors, which include one of Jiricna's delightful stairs, and manifests itself through her subtle unification of ornament and engineering, which is also fully expressed on the façades through a series of delicate fixed screens and retractable blinds.

The principal façade takes its place quietly within the context of the adjacent square; a delightful space that remains dominated by an ornately adorned and spired nineteenth-century

police station. Following the profile of the cornice and step-back attic of its neighbour, Jiricna's new infill is the height of discretion with six floors of bedrooms and a further two levels of sheltered balconies that provide excellent views. With a plain white façade and an even rhythm of shaded windows, the ground-floor entrance is a subtle accent, completely glazed with little ornamentation other than a simple canopy.

In plan, most probably to simplify and satisfy the hotel's operation and security regimes, the two buildings create an enclosed courtyard, with only one entrance being provided through the principal façade. While the desire to create a route through at ground-floor level may have been frustrated by practicalities, the architect has managed, through the manipulation of the façades, to create a distinctive urban inner layer. From the square, the low-lying fully glazed entrance attracts visitors into a luminous and spacious interior which, in turn, leads out into an equally luminous and coherent rear court. With the rear building effectively presenting a second front façade, the hotel's inner realm achieves its coherence through the resemblance shared by both buildings, with white façades articulated by delicate awnings.

Once inside, Jiricna was invited to extend her contemporary aesthetic to the design of the smallest elements, including light fittings, coat hangers and bed linen, in the 110 bedrooms that occupy the eight upper levels. The ground floor is more public, containing the reception and bar at the front, and a large breakfast room to the rear. These spaces have full access to the garden courtyard, and are also linked by the corridor that ramps to resolve the fall across the site, and to leave sufficient space for underground parking.

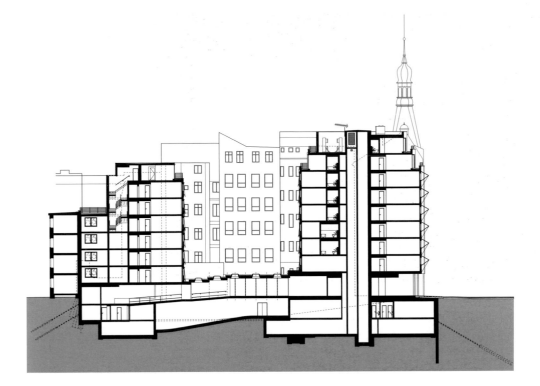

2   Third Floor Plan

1   Bedroom
2   Glazed Bathroom
3   Bathroom
4   Balconies/Terrace
5   Public Lifts

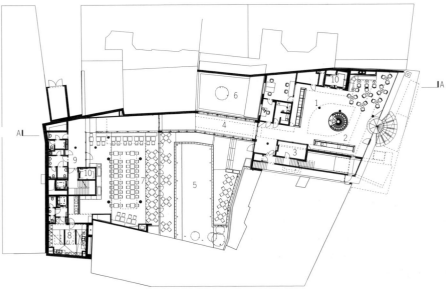

3   Ground Floor Plan

1   Reception
2   Bar
3   Business Centre
4   Glazed Link
5   Winter Garden
6   Light-well
7   Breakfast/Dining Room
8   Kitchen
9   Toilets/Services
10 Public Lifts

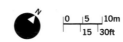

Rue des Suisses Housing

Herzog & de Meuron

Paris, France; 2000

This scheme demonstrates that Herzog & de Meuron are not only architects of iconic stand-alone buildings, they are also extremely well versed in responding to complex and intricate urban situations, here producing a housing scheme that responds to two distinctive as-found urban conditions. It tackles an inner-block site, common to Paris and indeed many other historic European cities, set behind the façades seven or so storeys high, of a typical Parisian street.

The two as-found conditions comprise two street infill plots that together neatly formalize the entrance sequence at the corner of the site, and a low-lying linear terrace pavilion that runs the length of the courtyard. While unified in their architectural manner, the two conditions demanded completely different planning strategies.

Sitting relatively quietly within the streetscapes, the two infill blocks conform to many existing Parisian characteristics. Vertically expressed, and served by a central stair and hallway, both the street and courtyard façades feature shutters. While consistent with other shuttered façades, these represent a new contemporary form with full-height screens sitting between exposed floor slabs. A deflection in plan

further distinguishes them from the norm, with a full-height inflection at the front and rear which draws people through a narrow entrance passageway between street and courtyard.

The pavilion is essentially a single-aspect terrace, as opposed to a back-to-back configuration, that has been pushed tight against the northeasterly boundary to maximize space to the southwest. The terrace recalls the formal relationship of a mews in relation to the urban block, being lower at three storeys, and with no boundary between courtyard and façade. As a result, in order to control privacy and to provide southwesterly shading, the entire façade is made up of sensuously curved timber tambour shutters that recall the sweeping lines of Hector Guimard's designs for the Paris metro.

Served by three communal stairs, there are five self-contained flats on each of the three levels, and while each floor has a slightly different layout, all of the flats benefit from an extensive balcony to the front which is sheltered by the terrace's distinctive screens. While the ground-floor flats have less privacy to the front, these larger units benefit from small private courtyards to the rear as the flats extend within a T-shaped plan. Likewise, the

second-floor flats also have additional external space between adjacent units, as the plans contract within the terrace's linear form.

As a final move, the architects have located two small maisonettes opposite the communal stair entrance. Facing away from the terrace, these tiny houses provide single-bedroom accommodation, and add a further degree of intricacy to the development's interstitial communal space.

While spatially diverse, offering accommodation for single occupants, couples and families alike, this development is unified with a resonant coherence, as materials — concrete, timber and architectural metalwork — are deployed with precision and expertise. Added to this, subtle shifts in planning — indentations, crocked and axial alignments and variations in roof profiles — make each corner of the site unique.

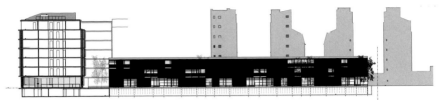

1   Section A–A

1

2   Second Floor Plan

2

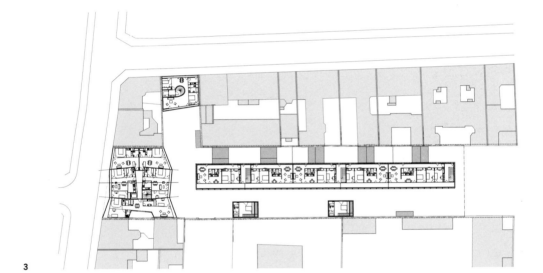

3   First Floor Plan

3

4   Ground Floor Plan

1   Rue des Suisses Block
2   Rue Jonquoy Block
3   Courtyard Block
4   Maisonettes

4

0 5 10m
15 30ft

Anderson House

Jamie Fobert Architects

London, UK; 2002

The Anderson House, designed by the London-based architect Jamie Fobert, presents a new paradigm in urban housing; an innovative model that could be exploited in many historic cities. Within the format of eighteenth-, nineteenth- and twentieth-century town planning, many similar backyard conditions exist where new homes could be delicately inserted into apparently unworkable, inaccessible and contorted sites. Located in the backyard of a central London Georgian block, the planning of this house was an extremely complicated process, generating over 60 party-wall notices within a 7 metre (23 foot) deep site that was hemmed in on all sides and only accessible via a 1 metre (3 foot) wide passageway. Nevertheless, the client had agreed on the site and trusted the architect to make it work, providing a 125 square metre (1345 square foot) home within the volume of the redundant shoe factory that once occupied the site. With no external elevations the house, accessed through a modest single door, gives little away from the street; internally, however, it surprises all who enter, exploiting to maximum effect the vertical depth of the site by creating a series of cavernous top-lit spaces.

Entering from the street through the narrow passageway, visitors are given a glimpse of the sky through a folded rooflight before passing beneath a low-level parapet wall that maintains rights-to-light provision with an adjoining basement flat. From the lowest point of the plan, light articulates the route which runs in two directions: either directly into the lofty living space to the right, or straight ahead via a top-lit stair to the bedrooms above.

The cross-section reveals most about how light is let into the house, showing the disposition of three principal skylights. The first, at the end of the living space, exploits its cathedral-like proportions being more than 5 metres (16 feet) high and is complete with an altar-like bench from which to contemplate the heavens; the second, in the master bedroom, provides an oblique snapshot of the outside world while maintaining the desired degree of containment and privacy; and the third – a three-way light-well at the centre of the plan – brings top light to the kitchen, side light to the living room and both bedrooms, and provides the principal means of ventilation throughout.

While intricate in its planning and surgical in its execution (with all materials having to be brought onto the site through the passageway), Fobert's architecture is robust and solid, demonstrating his trademark use of rippled self-finished in situ concrete, and on-site surprises that produce unique finishes. Set against the crisp white plaster walls and ribbed joinery screens (where the natural cup of the timber is allowed to bow each vertical plank), the limited palette allows the spaces to speak for themselves.

Even if one has visited the Anderson House, scrutiny of the architect's drawings is essential in order to gain a full understanding of its anatomy, as it is a fine example of how an architect's command over plan and section can produce wonderfully creative spatial solutions.

1

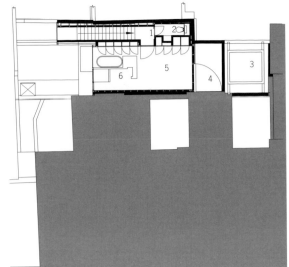

2

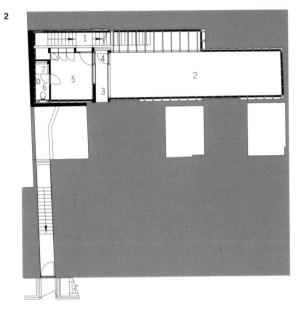

3

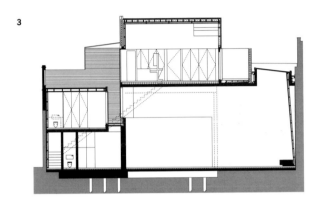

4

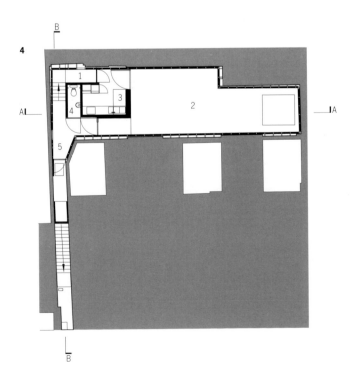

5

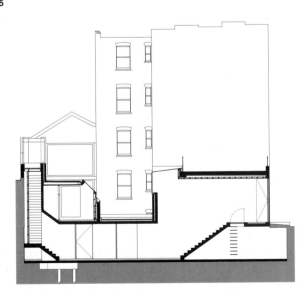

B

A ⌐   ⌐ A

B

N

0		5		10m
	15		30ft	

1 Second Floor Plan

1 Landing
2 Toilet
3 Rooflight
4 Terrace
5 Master Bedroom
6 Bathroom

2 First Floor Plan

1 Half-landing
2 Void
3 Light-well
4 Vent
5 Guest Room
6 WC
7 Shower

3 Section A–A

4 Lower Ground Floor Plan

1 Utility
2 Living Room
3 Kitchen
4 WC
5 Lower Hall

5 Section B–B

Brick House

Caruso St John Architects

London, UK; 2005

Entered via a single passageway, with no external elevations and conforming to no established domestic planning type, the Brick House by Caruso St John Architects shares a number of similarities with Jamie Fobert's Anderson House [see pp. 212–13]. It is, however, much bigger and responds in plan to the site's width rather than its depth on a large, angular plot formerly occupied by a mechanic's workshop.

On a residual end of a terrace plot in the busy district of London's Notting Hill, the house provides a highly internalized home, set on two levels. While the site was sold with consent for a courtyard house, the size and shape of the plot led the architects to pursue a new planning strategy. The courtyard type may have presented a fascinating planning format to work with, but the site was considered too small for a centralized courtyard scheme. Instead the architects pulled the accommodation into the heart of the site and provided minor courts in the three residual corners of the triangular boundary.

With the figure ground inverted from the previously consented scheme, to place voids at the periphery and a solid at the centre the internal spaces remained focused on a single centralized volume at the upper level, crowned by a distinctive concrete roof. Through the resolution of scale, form and geometry, this space has given the home a unique identity and a curiously eccentric sense of being centred, flanked to the south by a separate study and underpinned by more private cellular spaces below.

On entering the house, a gently inclined ramp leads to the top of a narrow top-lit stair, flanked by the principal living space to the right. At the base of the stair, arriving at the centre of the plan, views extend out towards the three courtyards, each accessible from the bedrooms they serve.

In section, the form of the roof is difficult to comprehend due to its eccentric shape and geometry. When seen in relation to the plan, however, it makes more sense, deriving its angular geometries from the tapering plan, as a series of faceted, angular planes rise up from the perimeter walls. In the far corner, a triangular level depression creates a low-level dining space, and at high level light is let in through rooflights that open up the fold lines between adjacent facets.

As its name suggests, the walls are built in fair-faced load-bearing bricks that support the concrete floors and roof. Taking inspiration from the churches of Sigurd Lewerentz, the use of uncut bricks gives the house an unusual material consistency that resonates throughout, extending across the living room floor to the courtyards beyond. With an obsessive and virtually faultless attention to detail, all details are governed by the module of the brick, with full bricks revealed at the end of the walls, and in door reveals and brick-sized socket plates. Throughout the house, the nature and shape of the spaces respond to what the architects call a material basis of form.

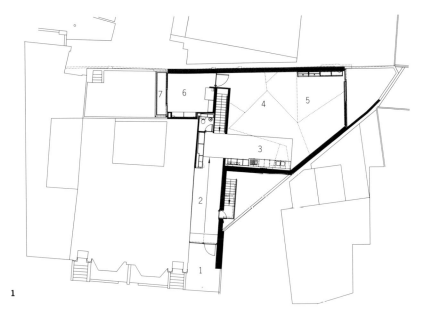

1

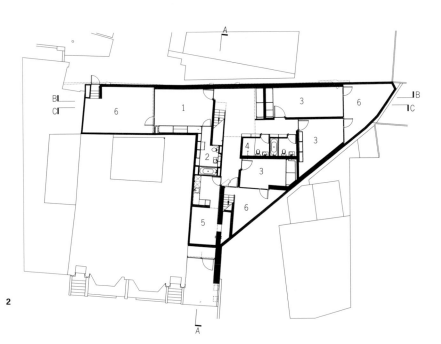

2

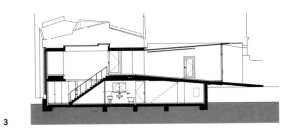

3

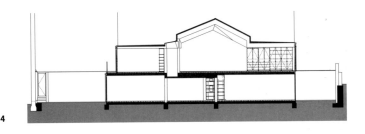

4

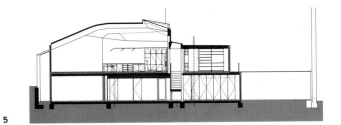

5

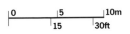

0   5   10m
   15   30ft

N

Morgan Library and Museum

Renzo Piano

New York, New York, USA; 2006

In Manhattan, land is an extremely precious asset. So too, in increasing measure, is the notion of cultural heritage. The city has many cherished institutions, such as the Frick Collection and the Cooper-Hewitt National Design Museum, which have managed to remain small despite the pressure and current tendency to fall foul of the so-called super-size-me mentality. Another similar institution is the Morgan Library and Museum, which has also had to address the dilemma of how to deal with expansion without changing beyond recognition, or at worst having to relocate to an alternative site.

The alternative to moving sites is, of course, to adapt and expand your existing premises. However, if the site is of sufficient historical significance, this brings many more complications of its own. The final option is to employ an expert architect, the sort who is not only sufficiently experienced to provide a state-of-the-art environment suitable for storing precious artefacts, but perhaps more crucially (when technical expertise can always be bought in – at a price), an architect who can do so with finesse and with an appropriate form of architectural expression within an extremely restricted and sensitive downtown site. In this case, the clients did well to select Renzo

Piano, perhaps one of the world's most admired living architects, who continues to approach cultural projects with just the right measure of creative ingenuity and controlled restraint.

Before the expansion, the Morgan Library and Museum was shoehorned into three detached properties situated on the corner of Madison Avenue and 37th Street. With all three properties protected by listing (the original 1906 library, the Morgan's 1850s brownstone house and the 1920s neoclassical annex to the east), the only way to meet the target brief was to remove all extraneous additions and carefully insert new accommodation in between, without losing the identity of the institution's component parts. With over 350,000 rare books, drawings and manuscripts, however, approximately eight storeys of additional space would have been required, and a tower was unlikely to meet the approval of the Landmarks Commission. Excavation was the only option, and now that it is complete, more than half of the Morgan's 13,800 square metres (148,542 square feet) is located below ground.

Piano's planning strategy was to insert three discrete pavilions between the existing buildings, with offices to the north, an entrance pavilion to the

west and a new gallery cube to the south. With these in place, the remaining interstitial space was enclosed by a triple-height glazed atrium, through which visitors would be able to circulate freely between each of the six interconnected volumes. Facing Madison Avenue, the largest of the three new pavilions is seen in section to extend 18 metres (59 feet) below grade, with four levels of basement storage set below the new principal entrance lobby, gallery and reading room above. The basement level also extends further to the north to make space for a large raked auditorium, general storage and essential utilities. From strategy right through to detail, Piano's trademark lightness of touch is evident throughout, making this a fine example of how adaptation and expansion should be done.

1 Second Floor Plan	2 South Elevation	3 Ground Floor Plan	4 Section A-A	5 Lower Ground Floor	6 Section B-B
1 Office		1 Entrance		1 Auditorium	
2 Toilets		2 Rotunda		2 Green Room	
3 Reading Room		3 Cube Gallery		3 Service Elevator	
4 Service Elevator		4 Gallery		4 Glass Elevators	
5 Glass Elevators		5 Lobby		5 Toilets	
		6 Information Desk		6 Public Programme	
		7 Toilets		7 Mechanical Room	
		8 Conference Room			
		9 Shop			
		10 Dining Room			
		11 Service Elevator			
		12 Loading Dock			
		13 Café East			
		14 Glass Elevators			
		15 Piazza			

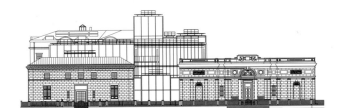

1

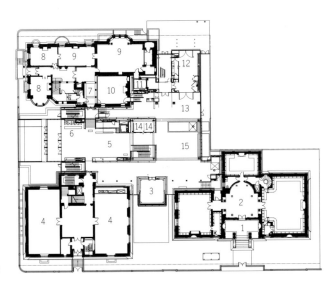

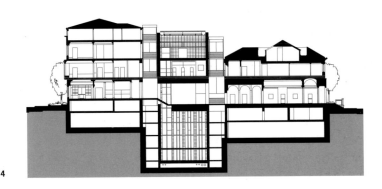

3

4

5

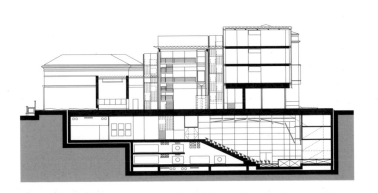

6

Manchester City Art Gallery

Hopkins Architects

Manchester, UK; 2001

Hopkins Architects' extension to the Manchester City Art Gallery did more than simply provide additional floor area on a vacant car park site. By considering circulation through and around the precinct, and orchestrating the integration of the adjacent Athenaeum, the process of infill and addition also helped to rationalize the gallery's operation and to repair a significant part of the city's relatively limited urban grid.

Hopkins' competition-winning strategy was to work with the underlying geometry and massing of the existing buildings. With Charles Barry's imposing Greek Revival Royal Manchester Institution running along Mosley Street and the Athenaeum (later restyled by Barry as an Italian palazzo to accommodate a gentleman's club) set in the southernmost corner, a number of key setting-out lines and levels were established to help shape an appropriate form on the vacant plot. By mirroring the footprint of the Athenaeum around a central axis, an equivalent three-storey block was proposed in the easternmost corner, containing an extensive archive in the basement, three education rooms on the ground floor and two floors of gallery space above. Between this were placed two thin service cores, containing escape stairs, toilets and

service risers, which flanked a central zone for a large art lift, a basement packaging room, a ground-floor loading bay and two further levels of gallery space.

With this strategy helping to establish a coherent and unified mass, the thin slot left between new and old provided a suitable void for a triple-height atrium, with sufficient space for dual lifts and a contemporary reinterpretation of Barry's fine biparting centralized stair located within the institution. Despite the apparent ambitions of this new space, however, seen by many as the new heart of the building, the architects were adamant that the institution's original entrance should be maintained as the principal point of arrival, accessed via the impressive prostyle/hexastyle portico. To achieve this, however, new routes needed to be cut through the existing building to provide direct and semi-direct links from front to back. These routes, together with a new café and local-interest exhibition space, now allow all visitors to roam freely through the extensive ground-floor foyers before rising to the upper-level galleries.

Within the institution, the original suite of galleries was simply restored, with improved lighting and environmental control, and maintaining the

original classical progression with each gallery entered one from the next. Within the new building, this arrangement was reapplied, with a second suite of galleries set out in a similar manner but with an entirely different character.

The building's rigorous organizational order in plan is also reflected in section with the entire first floor being devoted to the permanent collection, with the gallery's Pre-Raphaelite work displayed in the institution, and contemporary work within Hopkins' contemporary new extension. Above this, a series of temporary exhibition spaces have been provided that vastly increase the gallery's capacity to host its own – and national and international – exhibitions.

1 Section A–A

2 Second Floor Plan

1 Decorative Arts
2 Children's Gallery
3 Temporary Exhibition
4 Art Lift

3 Section B–B

4 First Floor Plan

1 Void over Entrance Halll
2 Permanent Collection
3 Bridge
4 Art Lift

5 Ground Floor Plan

1 Entrance Hall
2 Shop
3 Manchester Gallery
4 Café
5 Atrium/Group Arrivals
6 Toilets
7 Seminar Room
8 Education Suite
9 Art Lift
10 Loading Bay
11 Administration

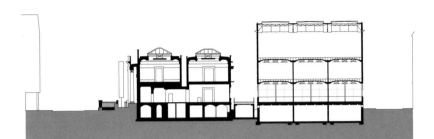

1

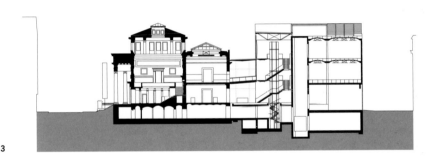

3

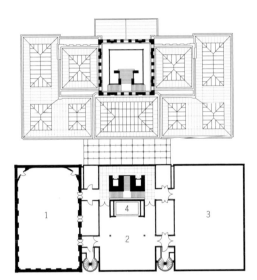

2

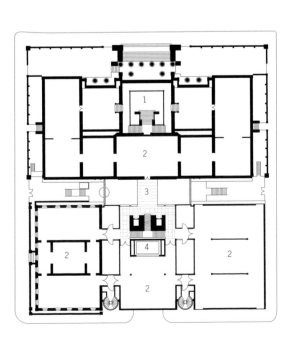

4

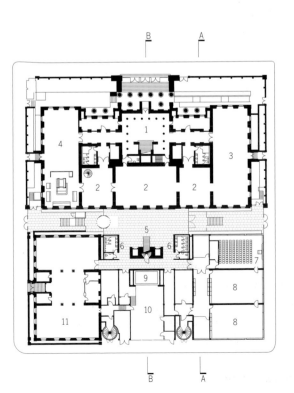

5

Crawford Art Gallery

Erick van Egeraat Associated Architects

Cork, Eire; 2000

Erick van Egeraat's distinctive extension to the Crawford Art Gallery may not, on first impression, seem like an especially contextual example of urban infill/addition. With its dramatic elevated brick screen that bulges out around the corner of Emmet Place and Half Moon Street, the new extension sits in stark contrast to the formal conventions of the original 1724 Custom House (attributed to the architect Sir Edward Lovett Pearce). Closer inspection, however, soon reveals that the addition is built in response to a very specific site and context, and is far more sensitive than its bold form immediately suggests.

The extension was built to unify a curious and disjointed assemblage of buildings that sat on either side of an open triangular courtyard. With one side of the triangle facing the street, the opportunity arose not only to give the gallery a bold new identity but also to rationalize and optimize the existing internal spatial configuration.

Previously organized in two wings, the gallery had suffered from a dead-end circulation route. Now, with a new infill, circulation is made continuous with these spaces serving as a link on both levels, as Erick van Egeraat's new extension provides two new temporary exhibition spaces, one

above the other. Situated behind the new street wall, the ground-floor space is fully glazed, providing a bold and contemporary shop-front gallery. On the first floor the second gallery space is only partially revealed, as the billowing brick skirt lifts its hemline 1 metre (3 feet) or so above first-floor level. Being part roof and part wall, the brick form is seen at high level to roll over the eaves to set up a sectional geometry that repeats and extends with three shallow vaults. Each of these vaults is then separated from one another by vertical clerestory windows that light the upper space, giving it a distinctive internal character that is seen in stark contrast to the more traditional top-lit galleries set within the existing buildings.

On the upper floor, the three tapering shell-like vaults are echoed in plan with a terraced floor that steps down from front to back. This gives the space a directional hierarchy and creates a very specific terrain for curators to experiment with. The stepped terrain terminates with the sculptural form of the brick screen wall which, internally, has been given a smooth white finish, and is itself specifically lit by a vertical lay-light set within its billowing form. Both floors are served by a new stair that sits neatly with a set-back strip of space against the

western edge of the courtyard. Finally, from the street, Erick van Egeraat's playful screen wall completes the gallery's northern elevation by turning the corner against the existing building and embracing its classically proportioned façade. This device not only layers new over old, but also serves to lead visitors around the corner to the newly improved entrance hall.

1 Second Floor Plan

1 Gallery
2 Office

2 Section B–B

3 First Floor Plan

1 Gallery
2 Library
3 Office

4 Section A–A

5 Ground Floor Plan

1 Gallery
2 Sculpture Gallery
3 Auditorium
4 Shop
5 Entrance
6 Office
7 Plant Room
8 Restaurant
9 Kitchen
10 Storage

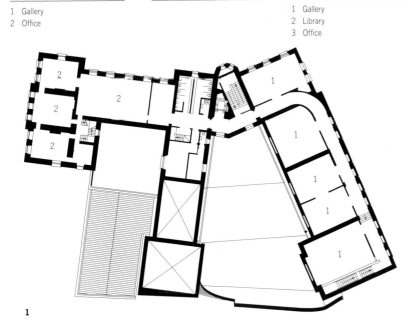

1

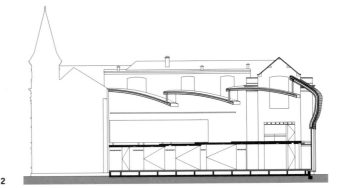

2

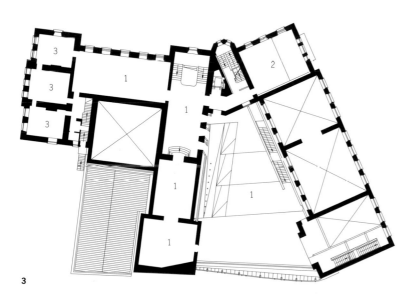

3

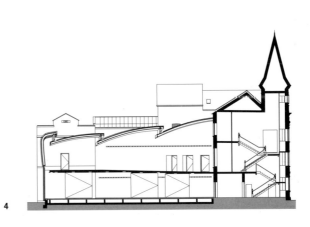

4

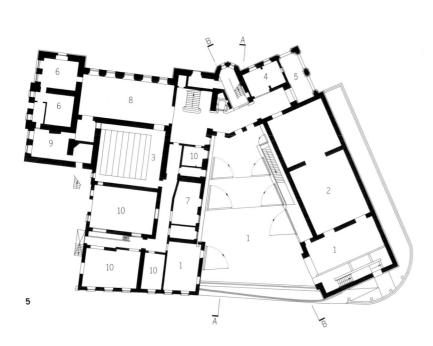

5

0   10   20m
15   30ft

Model Arts and Niland Gallery

McCullough Mulvin Architects

Sligo, Eire; 2000

Dublin-based practice McCullough Mulvin Architects was appointed to refurbish and add additional accommodation for a dual-purpose art gallery and performance venue on the site of Sligo's redundant Model School – one of the many benevolent Victorian institutions that supported the education of children from both Protestant and Catholic denominations. With improved performance facilities required for local art groups, and with the need for additional gallery space to display the city's cherished collection of Jack B. Yeats paintings, the architects set about rationalizing and reordering the existing buildings. This was principally achieved through two key strategic moves: the addition of a new block of accommodation at the rear of the site, and the infilling of a courtyard at the centre of the plan.

The new cedar-clad top-lit gallery block is located on higher ground at the rear of the site, and features a distinctive roofscape, articulated by three angular rooflights that bring a new aesthetic to the precinct. The block also serves to redefine the courtyard, running across the rear of the site and providing the all-important fourth wall. With this, the courtyard very much becomes the hub of the venue, integrating the level change across the

site and creating a bright new focus for the spaces that surround it. Top-lit, with a similar array of four smaller and reoriented rooflights – which run 90 degrees to those on the gallery – the courtyard is not only a space for gathering but also the principal circulation fulcrum, with access to spaces given on all four sides and linking the upper-ground floor café and performance spaces with the first-floor galleries above. Stairs and a lift are neatly integrated behind a series of freestanding screen walls, while the courtyard itself is uniquely characterized by the juxtaposition of the four walls, all of which differ in terms of their material and proportional composition.

The architects have enjoyed expressing new against old, in particular with the remodelling of the existing gallery wing which sits between the new block and the main building. This part of the scheme retains an existing two-storey wall as the base of a new timber and metal attic storey above. The additional height, which extends the line of the courtyard rooflights, has been built up to align with the cornice of the principal range. In a playful juxtaposition between new and old, the slatted timber wall is seen to extend down behind the existing masonry window apertures to create a new

layered elevation.

Through their restrained use of materials, and a simple planning strategy, the architects have successfully breathed new life into a precinct of fine buildings without reverting to pastiche or overt attention-seeking architectural gimmicks. Furthermore, with the new roofscape that gives the venue its subtly different identity, the spaces also comply with the strict Museums and Gallery Commission environmental standards without the need for mechanical air-conditioning.

1 First Floor Plan

1 West Gallery
2 Offices
3 Niland Gallery
4 Atrium
5 Void over Performance
   Space/Film
6 Galleries for Contemporary Art
7 Residential Studio

2 Ground Floor Plan

1 Entrance
2 Café
3 Performance Space/Film
4 Workshop
5 Education Room
6 Retail
7 Galleries for Contemporary Art
8 Security
9 Office
10 Yeats Scholar Viewing Room
11 Paintings/Controlled Store
12 Atrium

3 West Elevation

4 Section A–A

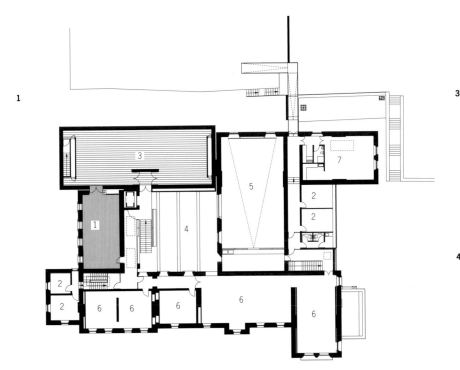

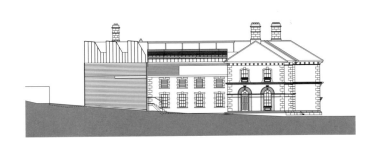

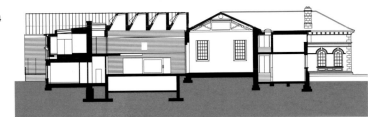

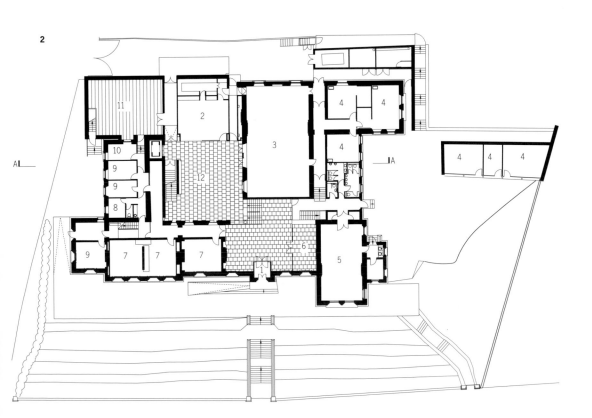

National Gallery of Ireland Millennium Wing

Benson + Forsyth

Dublin, Eire; 2002

Building upon experience gained while extending the Museum of Scotland in Edinburgh, Benson + Forsyth were well equipped to tackle a similar brief in Dublin. The practice was set a daunting task that required them to provide essential new facilities, improve and rationalize circulation and, most significantly, to compose a prominent new principal façade and entrance space.

Situated next to Dublin's Parliament building, the National Gallery's so-called Millennium Wing was the latest addition to a precinct of key civic institutions, including the National Library and the Museum of Natural History. In such company, the stakes were extremely high. As set out in the original brief, the client wanted a new wing that would be 'dignified and expressive of its time and its function' with an interior that was 'legible to visitors and a delight to experience'. And all of this was to take place on the site of a former service road – a relatively narrow plot – further complicated by the requirement to retain a number of existing buildings, including a Georgian house adjacent to the new entrance, and a Regency-style ballroom set deeper within the plot.

Resolving the crank in plan on the wedge-shaped plot gave the architects the opportunity to create a dramatic quadruple-height ravine that runs deep into the site. This space tapers as it extends into the site and was used to form the principal point of arrival, orientation and circulation, connecting new and old. As such, it has become the focus for the gallery, bringing with it a very new and specific identity. Entered through a dimly lit and low cubic antechamber, its spatial effect is significantly exaggerated, not only through the space's height, but also because of the narrowing in plan. From here, visitors pass the book shop to the left, and a new restaurant to the right, and are led by a grand stair situated on an axis with the entrance to the two new levels of galleries above the book shop. At the back of the site the stair also leads to the original galleries, turning visitors through 90 degrees before linking new with old.

As well as being articulated by Benson + Forsyth's trademark and highly mannered stone projections, splays and deep-cut slit windows, the central ravine was made even more dramatic through the positioning of a narrow bridge that cuts across at high level, deliberately set at a sharp angle. Traversing front to back, the bridge not only sets up a strong geometric tension, running as it does against the splay of the ravine as it cuts across the void and passes over the restaurant court. It also alludes to the new wing's hidden gem, as any tour of the galleries should be concluded with a visit to the delightful rooftop observation deck; a fitting culmination that helps to reacquaint visitors with the city and the nation that created and collected the art works on display.

1 Second Floor Plan	2 First Floor Plan	3 Ground Floor Plan	4 Section A–A	5 Section B–B
1 Stair From Level 1	1 Stairs from Clare Street Entrance	1 Clare Street Entrance		
2 Link to Existing Gallery	2 Link to Existing Gallery	2 Orientation Court		
3 Audiovisual Suite	3 20th Century Gallery	3 Reception Desk		
4 Information Desk	4 Café	4 Shop		
5 Temporary Gallery	5 Servery	5 Cloakroom		
	6 Mezzanine in Ballroom	6 Stairs to Galleries		
	7 Toilets	7 Multimedia		
	8 Stairs to Temporary Gallery	8 Restaurant		
		9 Existing Ballroom		
		10 Loading Bay		
		11 Collection Handling		
		12 Retained Georgian House		

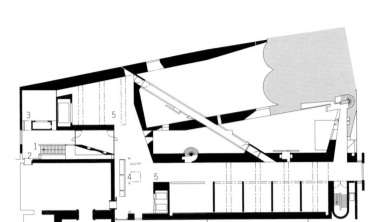

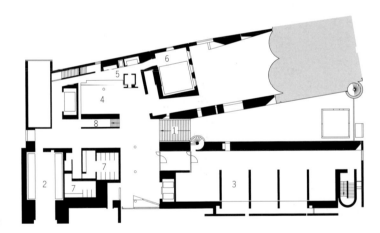

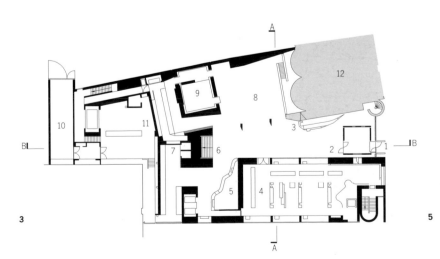

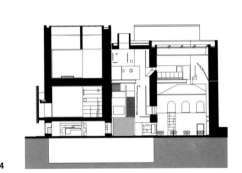

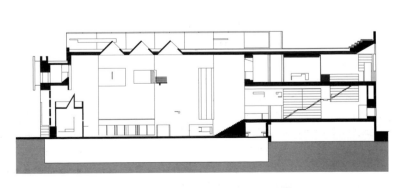

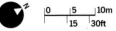

French Ministry of Culture and Communication

Francis Soler, Architect/Frédéric Druot, Interior Designer

Paris, France; 2005

In the past, Francis Soler's work has been criticized for making somewhat of a frivolous display, with schemes that shamelessly apply ornamentation – including chubby cherubs – as part of a larger than life figurative fresco. On first impression, the same criticisms could be levelled at this scheme, as Soler's latest wrap-around strategy applies a more robust but equally theatrical stainless-steel screen around the French Ministry of Culture and Communication.

The application of this screen, however, is justified on more than merely gestural or superficial grounds. Here it relates to an urban intention that seeks to unify a number of buildings from distinct architectural eras. It also reinterprets the established conservation principle of addition, where adding new layers to a building is permitted, extending its history and life story, and giving it a new identity and existence.

The plot forms a complete urban block occupied by two principal buildings: to the north along rue Montesquieu the former Ministry of Finance building, built by Olivier Lahalle in 1960; and to the south a lavish warehouse along rue Saint-Honoré, built in 1919 by Georges Vaudoyer for the Magasin du Louvre department store. To the

west, along the narrow and dark rue des Bons Enfants, a small infill building that completed the block was subsequently demolished as part of Soler's master plan to open the courtyard onto the street and to allow the sun to penetrate deeper into the heart of the plot.

When considering how to unify the buildings, Soler judged each on its own merits, noting that while the Vaudoyer building was not 'interesting enough to be kept as it was', it did have a certain nobility. The Lahalle building, on the other hand, was apparently 'indescribable', having been disfigured by the ravages of recent history. Hence, with two distinct façade options, Soler's intention was to re-establish the site's coherence by effectively smoothing over the façades to allow the buildings to be read at a glance as a homogenous single entity. A lightweight single-layered screen was therefore fixed to the Vaudoyer building, yielding to the existing architectural detail by being cut around cornices and door heads. In contrast, a more solid screen was deployed to envelop Lahalle's building, extending up and over it to include the steeply pitched three-tier mansard roof.

Refreshingly, the architect makes no attempt to justify the application of this screen with lists of

box-ticking merits towards a technical or environmental agenda. Instead, Soler's strategy came from an instinctive response to the site. While such strategies can all too often be translated into thin, cheap and nasty solutions, here this extensive refurbishment project has been executed with sufficient boldness and finesse to make it a convincing and exemplary model of creative reuse. Behind the screen, the fact that the architect has also rehoused approximately 1000 civil servants, created over 450 individual offices, and resolved the apparently endless co-ordination and planning complexities associated with working with existing buildings, goes largely unnoticed.

1 Façade Detail   2 Section A–A   3 Ground Floor Plan

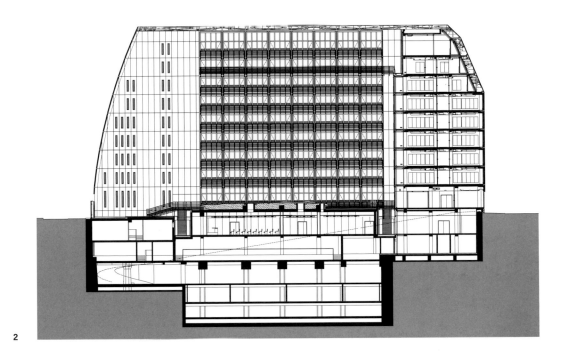

1

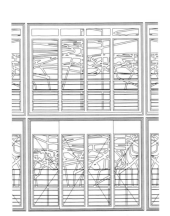

2

3

N

0   5   10m
   15   30ft

Kunsthaus

Peter Cook and Spacelab

Graz, Austria; 2003

Peter Cook describes this building as a 'friendly alien'. With naughty nozzles, a full and curvaceous posterior and a precariously positioned cigar, it is certainly full of character. Resembling nothing that we have seen before, yet seeming strangely and tantalizingly familiar, the new Kunsthaus in Graz was quickly adopted as the city's new cheeky Eurovision mascot, and is without doubt a truly unique creation.

Fulfilling a number of Peter Cook and Archigram's early speculations into inflatable plug-ins and walking cities, the Kunsthaus could be read as an urban myth as it is quite conceivable that this building did, in fact, float down the river before climbing into place. However, as a serious work of architecture our imagination need not work so hard as the Kunsthaus has an extremely accomplished and convincing story to tell. With a brief that took over ten years to evolve, the architects' final response was well worth the wait as the city decided exactly what sort of building it wanted to create, and the architects have been particularly successful in their vision to create a recognizably coherent single form within a highly irregular site. Incorporating a number of existing buildings, they managed to produce a suitably bold response to

one of the most prominent sites within one of Europe's most well-preserved historic cities and, as noted by Peter Blundell Jones in an early review, the Graz Kunsthaus throws into question the popular wisdom that the politest response to historic context is to don [the pastiche] of fancy dress. This building may well be highly made-up, but a pastiche it is not, and the debate about whether or not it is contextual is likely to run for many years to come.

The shape of the new building's bulbous blue body was set in plan by tracing a radiused line that maintained a consistent fire-safety separation distance from the existing buildings. Internally, it contains two levels of gallery space, one fully enclosed and the other partially illuminated by the top-lit nozzles. Bisecting the spaces, and connecting them to the pavement-level foyer and café, are two opposing moving walkways that allow visitors to glide gracefully through the spaces. While more orthodox gallery curators have criticized the spaces for being impractical in terms of displaying art, the dominant character of these galleries demands a more creative attitude to art curation.

From the east, the external composition of the friendly alien is articulated by a fully glazed

viewing gallery that exploits extensive views across Graz's magical baroque roofscapes. As a popular venue for occasional receptions, this element also nods towards the integration of the existing buildings, hovering over the fine and sensitively restored Eisernes Haus with its elaborate cast-iron façades and new rooftop pavilion.

The buildings sit above an extensive new underground car park, and on ground level the public realm extends around the entire city block, with the galleries raised above a fully glazed lobby, and a café and multipurpose room weaving their way between three service cores.

1 Fourth Floor Plan

1 'Needle'

2 Section A–A

3 Second Floor Plan

1 Exhibition Space
2 Information/Library

4 Ground Floor Plan

1 Entrance Foyer
2 Media Lounge
3 Café
4 Multipurpose Room
5 Shop
6 New Media Space

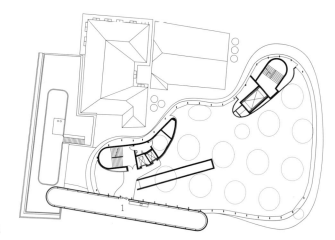

1

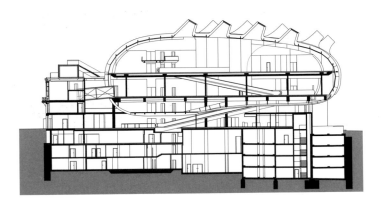

2

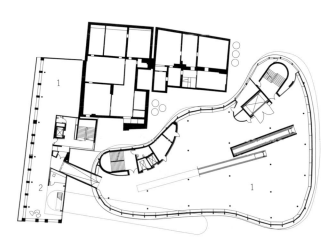

3

4

Lugano University Library

Michele and Giorgio Tognola

Lugano, Switzerland; 2001

It is not always appropriate – or indeed possible – to successfully extend the symmetry of a building when adding more accommodation. Architects often choose to distinguish new from old by shifting the geometry and balance of the original composition. In some circumstances, however, to forcibly ignore the underlying order of an existing structure would be as contrived as symmetry itself, as was the case with this beautifully executed extension at the University of Lugano, Switzerland, which provides a decidedly new face for a fine existing building.

This extension was added not only to provide additional space but also in response to the shifting patterns of development on the university campus. With the original U-shaped building once functioning as a home for the elderly, its entrance was facing away from the centre of the expanding campus. When converted into the main university library, therefore, as part of a master plan that proposed five new buildings, a new wing was built to provide three levels of study carrels and an impressive new formal entry portico.

By reorienting the entire precinct, the new wing becomes the principal façade and consists of two parallel ranges of full-height concrete piers.

With the inner range set within the courtyard and aligned with the end bays of the existing wings to complete the circulation loop, the outer range is set in front of the end walls, extending across their full width. Between the two ranges sits a circulation and service core, containing lifts, toilets and a central stair that supplements the existing winding corner stairs. This new core resolves the building in section, with four new floors instead of two, co-incident with the ground and second floors of the existing wings.

While clearly modern in their expression, the new elevations are well ordered and rigorously governed by the structure's underlying geometry and proportion. They do not, however, conform to the proportions of the existing courtyard fenestration but instead relate more directly to the optimum size of a two-person study carrel, with each bay providing the ideal space for peaceful and focused concentration and shared study. With an extra bay within the courtyard, and four levels rather than two, the proportions clearly express the shift in scale between new and old spaces, and the dramatic increase in the density of new accommodation that has been provided. While the original building contains larger, more formal

spaces – with traditional stacking shelves, meeting rooms and the librarian's office – the new wing is a rational and functional stacked grid. The elevations fully express the repetitive nature of the internal layout, with black aluminium and perimeter glass panels set within a well-mannered square proportion and held between the concrete piers. Concrete is also revealed horizontally to form the soffit of the external portico, and the concrete piers extend beyond the uppermost carrel to align with the pronounced cornice line on the existing wings.

1 Section A–A   2 Section B–B   3 Ground Floor Plan   4 First Floor Plan

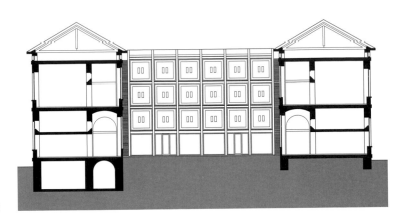

1

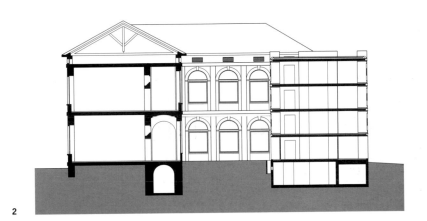

2

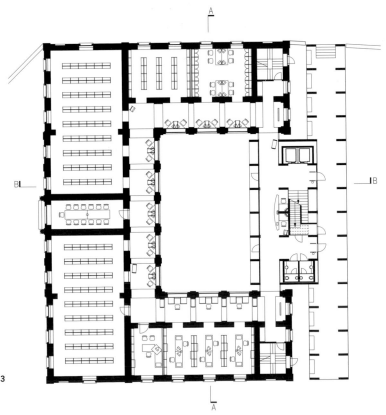

3

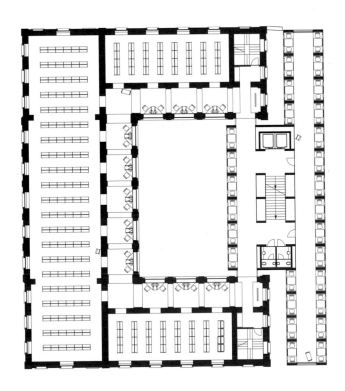

4

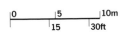

0   5   10m
15   30ft

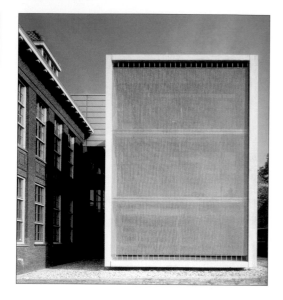

De Maere Textile School

Brookes Stacey Randall & IAA

Enschede, The Netherlands; 2001

When adding to a set of incomplete courtyard buildings, the choice is to work either with or against the precinct's underlying order. In this example, while all of the component parts are united, a new wing has been added that disengages both formally and aesthetically from the character of the existing buildings. The design was by the now disbanded partnership Brookes Stacey Randall (working at the time with the Dutch firm IAA), and the architects were quite deliberate in formulating a strategy that drew a clear distinction between old and new.

The existing buildings that house the De Maere Textile School were built in 1928 and comprise an L-shaped range (in the Arts and Crafts style) and a low-level sawtooth demonstration factory that extends across the almost square plot. The architects not only had to provide new laboratory space – to be located in a new wing – but also had to carefully restore the existing buildings, which were listed as a National Monument. This principally involved clearing out many of the extraneous additions that had cluttered the long-span shed, and recladding it with glass, timber and sheet metal. In contrast to this sensitive refurbishment, the design of the new laboratory wing gave the

architects the opportunity to make more of an impact on the overall composition.

The new wing was built to house the advanced research facilities necessary to bring the school up-to-date with current teaching methods. Space for this was considered to be most appropriately located in a new structure that distinguished itself from the established context, while engaging, where necessary, in a circulation hub. This mediating element – loosely described by the architects as a spatial knot – comprised a three-storey lift and stair housed in a metal-clad tower. With the tower sitting against the gable end of the main existing building and linking all three elements, the new wing was pushed out beyond the line of the principal façade. This move not only helped to articulate the wing as an independent element, essentially being freestanding, but also created space for a calm and simple courtyard to be positioned snugly between old and new.

Extending the horizontal datum generated by the existing eaves level, the new wing had sufficient height for three levels of accommodation, compared to the two that already existed. With shallower floor to ceiling heights, the new wing clearly expresses the three floors on its façade,

making a visual statement about the change in scale and density of the new accommodation with a grid of 54 protruding windows. In plan, the new wing also introduces a geometry that allows it to pull away from the existing building, giving both forms room to breathe. The oblique angle that is created also makes space for an internal triple-height triangular void, from where extensive views are given across the factory roof to the furthest corner of the site, without insensitively impacting on the external continuity of the existing building's essentially orthogonal plan.

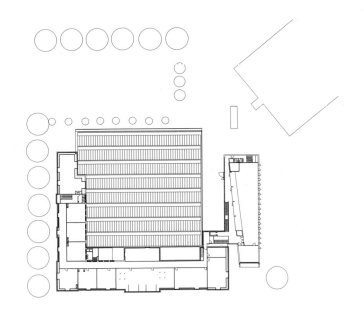

1

2

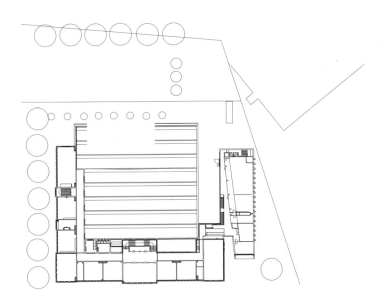

3

4

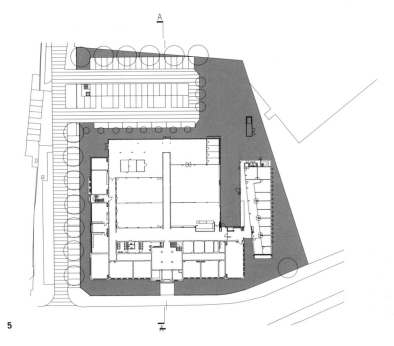

5

6

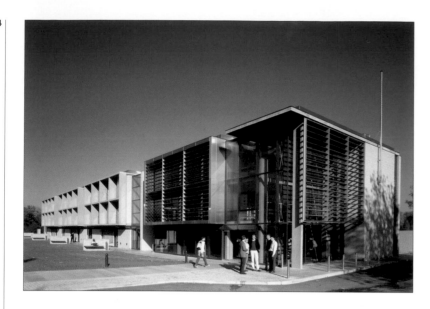

St Catherine's College

Hodder Associates

Oxford, UK; 2000

St Catherine's College, Oxford, is one of the UK's finest post-war buildings. Designed by Arne Jacobsen, and completed in 1964, it has long served as an exemplary model of orthogonal courtyard planning. Despite remaining largely unaltered since, considered by many to be an untouchable architectural set piece, it now also serves as a fine example of addition and infill, with Stephen Hodder's recent additions.

Jacobsen's scheme comprised two long ranges of study/bedrooms (running north–south and arranged around 16 staircases), a lecture hall and library (as freestanding pavilions), and a T-shaped block to the north containing common rooms, offices and the college refectory. With a number of discrete pavilions at the periphery, the unified ensemble broke the mould of British collegiate architecture. As isolated objects placed in space, the strategy did not conform to the closed courtyard model of entering through an arched gateway and being organized around a cloister. Instead, St Catherine's was governed by a rigorous grid laid over a Modernist tabula rasa and the notion of a spatial continuum that extended beyond the limits of its boundary walls. On a relatively remote site, Jacobsen's 'ideal platform' found its

place in the order of the grid, extending from building to landscape to control views, access and thresholds, and bringing harmony and alignment to the building's exquisite concrete frame. Because it was so thoroughly well resolved, many felt that Jacobsen's work was complete, with Reyner Banham noting that the very nature of its design had rendered the college impossible to extend. However, in 1994, the inevitable challenge was set when Stephen Hodder of Hodder Associates was appointed to add significant new accommodation.

Hodder's two-part brief was to add a further ten staircases, the majority of which provide access to eight rooms. The second phase also included a new porters' lodge and a suite of four seminar rooms. Phase one comprised staircases 17–19 which, being located to the north, took their biaxial alignment from the oblique angle of the Holywell Stream. His second phase, staircases 20–26, completed the new north quadrangle by adding north and east ranges, and locating a new porters' lodge in a more prominent position.

With the centre of gravity shifted, the extension of Jacobsen's long lawn is a key strategic move, not only linking new with old but also providing a dominant feature in space that may

otherwise have been dominated by car parking. With the lawn as the principal place-making device, Hodder's new quadrangle adheres to many of Jacobsen's governing rules, identical in height and controlled by a similarly rigorous planning grid. Freestanding walls have also been incorporated, along with two new open corners to the north. Articulated by rotated staircases at each end of the north range, the open corners remind us of Jacobsen's reinterpretation of the closed courtyard, here creating a punt house quadrangle to the west and extending wider views out to the east.

Internally, Hodder reconsidered planning layouts with a new configuration, arranging rooms around fully expressed glazed stair-wells. With no centralized staircases, space is released mid-plan for double-height light-wells to the shower rooms, and at ground level rooms step in to create a modest inset cloister.

1 Section A–A	2 East Block First Floor Plan	3 East Block Ground Floor Plan	4 North Block First Floor Plan	5 North Block Ground Floor Plan
	1 Bedroom	1 Bedroom	1 Bedroom	1 Bedroom
	2 Seminar Room	2 Porters' Lodge	2 Kitchen	2 Kitchen
		3 Kitchen		3 Cleaner's Room/Linen
		4 Cleaner's Room/Linen		
		5 Living Space		

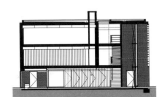

1

2

3

4

5

N 0 5 10m 15 30ft

Further Reading

Index

General Histories

Fletcher, Banister, *A History of Architecture* (Oxford: Architectural Press, 20th edn, 1996)

Frampton, Kenneth, *Modern Architecture: A Critical History* (London: Thames & Hudson, 1980)

On Types

Abel, Chris, *Skyhigh* (London: Royal Academy of Arts, 2003)

Buisson, Ethel and Billard, Thomas, *The Presence of the Case Study Houses* (Basel, Berlin, Boston: Birkhäuser, 2004)

Burnett, John, *A Social History of Housing 1815–1985* (London: Methuen, 1986)

The House Book (London: Phaidon Press, 2001)

Melhuish, Clare and d'Avoine, Pierre, *Housey Housey: A Pattern Book of Ideal Homes* (London: Black Dog Publishing, 2005)

Muthesius, Stefan, *The English Terraced House* (New Haven, CT: Yale University Press, 1982)

Ngo, Dung, *World House Now: Contemporary Architectural Directions* (London: Thames & Hudson, 2003)

Richardson, Phyllis, *XS: Big Ideas, Small Buildings* (London: Thames & Hudson, 2001)

Smith, Courtenay & Topham, Sean, *Xtreme Houses* (New York: Prestel, 2002)

Smith, Elizabeth A. T., *Blueprints for Modern Living: History and Legacy of the Case Study Houses* (Cambridge, MA: The MIT Press, 1989)

Yantai, Shen and Wang, Changqing, *Life in Huttongs: Through Intricate Alleyways in Beijing* (Beijing: Foreign Languages Press, 1997)

On the Analysis of Space

Ching, Francis D. K., *Architecture: Form, Space & Order* (New York: Van Nostrand Reinhold, 1979)

Clark, Roger H. and Pause, Michael, *Precedents in Architecture* (New York: Van Nostrand Reinhold, 1996)

Unwin, Simon, *Analysing Architecture* (London: Routledge, 2003)

On the Theories of Space

Alexander, Christopher, with Ishikawa, S., Silverstein, M., Jacobson, M., Fiksdahl-King, I., Angel, S., *A Pattern Language* (New York: Oxford University Press, 1977)

Dodds, George and Tavernor, Robert, *Body and Building: Essays on the Changing Relation of Body and Architecture* (Cambridge, MA: The MIT Press, 2002)

Forty, Adrian, *Words and Buildings: A Vocabulary of Modern Architecture* (London: Thames & Hudson, 2000)

Herzberger, Herman, *Lessons for Students in Architecture* (Rotterdam: Uitgeverij 010 Publishers, 1991)

Herzberger, Herman, *Space and the Architect: Lessons for Students in Architecture 2* (Rotterdam: Uitgeverij 010 Publishers, 2000)

Inoue, Mitsuo, *Space in Japanese Architecture* (Tokyo: Weatherhill, 1985)

King, Anthony D., *Spaces of Global Cultures: Architecture Urbanism Identity* (London: Routledge, 2004)

Lawson, Bryan, *The Language of Space* (Oxford: The Architectural Press, 2001)

Leatherbarrow, David and Mostafavi, Mohsen, *Surface Architecture*, (Cambridge, MA: The MIT Press, 2002)

Norberg Shultz, Christian, *Genius Loci: Towards a Phenomenology of Architecture* (Rizzoli, 1980)

Penz, Francois, Radick, Gregory and Howell, Robert, *Space in Science, Art and Society* (Cambridge: Cambridge University Press, 2004)

Rooney, Nuala, *At Home with Density* (Hong Kong: Hong Kong University Press, 2003)

St John Wilson, Colin, *Architectural Reflections* (Oxford: Butterworth Architecture, 1992)

Van der Laan, Dom, *Architectonic Space* (Leiden: E. J. Brill, 1983)

Van de Ven, Cornelis, *Space in Architecture* (Assen/Maastricht: Van Gorcum, 1987)

von Meiss, Pierre, *Elements of Architecture: From Form to Place* (London: Taylor & Francis, 1990)

Zelevansky, Lynn, *Beyond Geometry* (Cambridge, MA: The MIT Press, 2004)

Zevi, Bruno, *Architecture As Space* (New York: Da Capo, 1957, 1974, 1993)

Picture Credits

Laurence King Publishing Ltd have paid DACS' visual creators for the use of their artistic works.

About the CD

The attached CD-ROM can be read on both Windows and Macintosh computers. All the material on the CD-ROM is copyright protected and is for private use only. All drawings in the book and on the CD-ROM were specially created for this publication and are based on the architects' original designs. Drawings of works by Ateliers Jean Nouvel are ©ADAGP, Paris and DACS, London 2008.

Drawings are by Gregory Gibbon and Advanced Illustration.

The CD-ROM includes files for all the plans, sections and elevations featured in the case studies of the book. The drawings for each building are contained in a numbered folder as listed below. They are supplied in two versions: the files with the suffix '.eps' are vector Illustrator EPS files but can be opened using other graphics programs such as Photoshop; all the files with the suffix '.dwg' are generic CAD format files and can be opened in a variety of CAD programs.

The generic '.dwg' file format does not support 'solid fill' utilized by many architectural CAD programs. All the information is embedded within the file and can be reinstated within supporting CAD programs. Select the polygon required and change the 'Attributes' to 'Solid'; the colour information should automatically be retrieved. To reinstate the 'Walls'; select all objects within the 'Walls' layer/class and amend their 'Attributes' to 'Solid'.

The numbered folders correspond to the following buildings:

1. Ixtapa House, LCM/Fernando Romero
2. Poli House, Pezo von Ellrichshausen Architects
3. T House, Sou Fujimoto
4. Seifert House, BAU/KULTUR, Michael Shamiyeh
5. Element House, Sami Rintala
6. Eden Project Biomes, Grimshaw
7. City Hall, Foster + Partners
8. Lewis Glucksman Gallery, O'Donnell + Tuomey
9. Sami Parliament, Stein Halvorsen and Christian Sundby
10. Mercedes-Benz Museum, UNStudio
11. Bibliotheca Alexandrina, Snøhetta
12. Jægersborg Water Tower, Dorte Mandrup Arkitekter Aps
13. Imai Daycare Centre, Shigeru Ban
14. ESO Hotel and Information Centre, Auer + Weber Architekten
15. The Peñalolén Campus, José Cruz Ovalle Architects Associates
16. Agosta House, Patkau Architects
17. St Andrew's Beach House, Sean Godsell Architects
18. Peregrine Winery, Architecture Workshop
19. Rowing Club, VJAArchitects
20. Art Pavilion, Rene van Zuuk
21. St Henry's Ecumenical Art Chapel, Sanaksenaho Architects
22. Care Centre, Sou Fujimoto
23. Social Housing, Edouard François
24. Echigo-Matsunoyama Museum of Natural Science, Takaharu + Yui Tezuka

25. Dutch Embassy, Dick van Gameren and Bjarne Mastenbroek
26. Lucky Drops House, Yasuhiro Yamashita (Atelier Tekuto) with Masahiro Ikeda (Masahiro Ikeda Co., Ltd)
27. Amtmandsstien, CASA Arkitekter
28. Sound Wall Homes, VHP s+a+l
29. Exhibition Houses, Architectural Office Marlies Rohmer, Amsterdam NL
30. EOS Housing, Anders Wilhelmson
31. Bastion Island Waterside Homes, DOK architecten
32. Helsinki Terrace, Marja-Ritta Norri
33. Two houses on Borneo Sporenburg, MVRDV
34. 1028 Natoma Street, Stanley Saitowitz/Natoma Architects
35. BedZED, Bill Dunster Architects
36. 30 St Mary Axe, Foster + Partners
37. Torre Agbar, Ateliers Jean Nouvel
38. Torre Cube, Carme Pinós
39. Simmons Hall, Steven Holl Architects
40. Sendai Mediatheque, Toyo Ito
41. America's Cup Building – Veles e Vents, David Chipperfield Architects and b720 Arquitectos
42. Lloyd's Register of Shipping, Richard Rogers Partnership
43. Seattle Library, OMA
44. Rosenthal Center for Contemporary Arts, Zaha Hadid Architects
45. House & Atelier Bow-Wow, Atelier Bow-Wow
46. Water Tower House, Jo Crepain
47. Air Traffic Control Tower, Zechner & Zechner
48. Long Island Residence, Tod Williams Billie Tsien Architects
49. Villa V, 3 + 1 Architects
50. Lecture Halls III, Javier Garcia-Solera Arquitecto
51. Teaching Pavilion, Juan Carlos Sancho Osinaga + Sol Madridejos
52. Whale Housing, de Architekten Cie.
53. Swiss Re Offices, BRT Architekten
54. MoMA, Taniguchi and Associates
55. Caja General de Ahorros, Alberto Campo Baeza
56. Baumschulenweg Crematorium, Axel Schultes and Charlotte Frank
57. Hu-tong House, Waro Kishi + K Associates/Architects
58. Novy Dvur Monastery, John Pawson
59. Valley Center House, Daly, Genik Architects
60. Rozak House, Troppo Architects
61. Mattin Arts Center, Tod Williams Billie Tsien Architects
62. Diamond Ranch High School, Morphosis
63. Palmach Museum of History, Zvi Hecker with Rafi Segal
64. Dutch Embassy, OMA
65. Makino Museum of Plants and People, Naito Architect and Associates
66. Federal Environmental Agency, Sauerbruch Hutton
67. Tango Housing, Moore Rubel Yudell Architects & Planners
68. de Young Museum, Herzog & de Meuron/Fong & Chan
69. Rectory Building, Álvaro Siza Vieira
70. Mauritskade Apartment Building, Erick van Egeraat Associated Architects

71. Building D, Cino Zucchi
72. Town Hall Extension, Rafael Moneo
73. Jaume Fuster Library, Josep Llinás
74. Des Moines Public Library, David Chipperfield Architects
75. Walsall Art Gallery, Caruso St John Architects
76. Walt Disney Concert Hall, Gehry Partners, LLP
77. Federation Square, LAB architecture studio with Bates Smart, Architects
78. Casa da Musica, OMA
79. Yokohama International Port, Foreign Office Architects Terminal
80. Phaeno Science Centre, Zaha Hadid Architects
81. Scottish Parliament Building, EMBT/RMJM
82. Hotel Josef, Eva Jiricna Architects
83. Rue des Suisses Housing, Herzog & de Meuron
84. Anderson House, Jamie Fobert Architects
85. Brick House, Caruso St John Architects
86. Morgan Library and Museum, Renzo Piano
87. Manchester City Art Gallery, Hopkins Architects
88. Crawford Art Gallery, Erick van Egeraat Associated Architects
89. Model Arts and Niland Gallery, McCullough Mulvin Architects
90. National Gallery of Ireland, Benson + Forsyth Millennium Wing
91. French Ministry of Culture and Communication, Francis Soler and Frédéric Druot
92. Kunsthaus, Peter Cook and Spacelab
93. Lugano University Library, Michele and Giorgio Tognola
94. De Maere Textile School, Brookes Stacey Randall & IAA
95. St Catherine's College, Hodder Associates

Author's acknowledgements

A writer's first book should rightly be dedicated to his or her parents; in this case the steadfast Stuart and Raye Gregory. Beyond this, mention should also be made of the bedazzling Louise Rogers, whose impact on my life very nearly led to the demise of this text.